Create
FrontPage® 2000
Web Pages

LISA D. WAGNER
STEVE CALLIHAN

A Division of Prima Publishing

For my mother, Elaine, for always understanding—or trying to, anyway.
—LDW

 A Division of Prima Publishing

Prima Publishing, colophon, and In a Weekend are registered trademarks and PRIMA TECH is a trademark of Prima Communications, Inc., Rocklin, California 95765.

Publisher: Stacy L. Hiquet

Associate Publisher: Nancy Stevenson

Managing Editor: Dan J. Foster

Senior Acquisitions Editor: Deborah F. Abshier

Senior Editor: Kelli R. Crump

Project Editor: Diana Trabel

Technical Reviewer: Warren Estep

Interior Layout: Scribe Tribe

Cover Design: Prima Design Team

Indexer: Ty Koontz

Microsoft, FrontPage, Liquid Motion, Windows, MSN, and Outlook are trademarks or registered trademarks of Microsoft Corporation. Netscape is a registered trademark of Netscape Communications Corporation. AOL is a registered trademark of America Online, Inc.

Important: If you have problems installing or running Microsoft FrontPage, go to Microsoft's Web site at **www.microsoft.com** or call the Microsoft FrontPage support line at (425) 635-7088. Prima Publishing cannot provide software support.

Prima Publishing and the authors have attempted throughout this book to distinguish proprietary trademarks from descriptive terms by following the capitalization style used by the manufacturer.

Information contained in this book has been obtained by Prima Publishing from sources believed to be reliable. However, because of the possibility of human or mechanical error by our sources, Prima Publishing, or others, the Publisher does not guarantee the accuracy, adequacy, or completeness of any information and is not responsible for any errors or omissions or the results obtained from the use of such information. Readers should be particularly aware of the fact that the Internet is an ever-changing entity. Some facts may have changed since this book went to press.

ISBN: 0-7615-1929-7

Library of Congress Catalog Card Number: 98-68248

Printed in the United States of America

99 00 01 02 03 DD 10 9 8 7 6 5 4 3 2 1

CONTENTS

Contents   v

ACKNOWLEDGMENTS

An author is nothing without a strong support team, and the people at Prima Tech are among the best. Many thanks to Senior Acquisitions Editor Debbie Abshier for making sure that I never get any sleep and never lack work; to Project Editor Diana Trabel, who can turn even the worst manuscript into a work of art; and to Warren Estep for his ever-present attention to detail! A special thanks to my co-author Steve Callihan for adding not only a lot of text, but a much-welcomed alternative insight. You do great work, dude. I feel I owe an apology to my cats, who have been ignored even more than usual during this project. It's OK, boys, mamma still loves you. As always, a warm and radiant "*Aho*!" to my companions at THE EXPERIENCE. Doodle, I love you. Remember, life is short—stay awake!

ABOUT THE AUTHORS

Lisa D. Wagner is the founder of Jasper Ink, an independent writing, consulting, and Web design firm in Indianapolis, Indiana. Lisa has more than ten years' experience in the computer and publishing industries. She has authored and contributed to several computer books, most recently to PRIMA TECH's *Outlook 2000 Fast & Easy* and *Microsoft Money 99 Fast & Easy*. A graduate of Butler University, Lisa is also an active singer, actor, and theater producer. She is past president of Women in the Arts, Inc., and an active participant in THE EXPERIENCE (www.theexperience.org), a non-profit organization promoting the celebration of diversity and empowering individuals to change the world heart by heart. Lisa welcomes your questions and comments via e-mail at **lisa@jasperink.com** and invites you to visit her company's Web site, **www.jasperink.com**.

Steve Callihan is a freelance and technical writer from Seattle. He is the author of PRIMA TECH's *Create Your First Web Page In a Weekend, Revised Edition; Learn HTML In a Weekend, Revised Edition;* and *Create Web Animations with Microsoft Liquid Motion In a Weekend.* He has also written several computer-related articles for *Internet World* and other publications. When not writing books, he works as a technical writer on hardware and software documentation and user guides. Steve can be contacted at **fp2000@callihan.com**, if you have any questions or comments. For links to many different Web publishing resources and tools, as well as links to where you can find out more about his other Web publishing books, visit his Web site at **www.callihan.com**.

INTRODUCTION

When I was a kid, I used to think about how very, very old I would be in the year 2000. Now that it's almost here, I don't feel so old. Back then, the Internet was in its infancy, known only to government officials and university scholars working on top-secret national security projects, and the World Wide Web didn't even exist!

Today, it's hard to find anyone who hasn't heard of the Internet. Millions of people all over the planet are online, and the numbers grow exponentially every year. Thanks to companies like Microsoft and products like FrontPage 2000, anyone with a computer and a phone line can not only surf the Web, but also build a nice cozy Web site of their own. What's more, the Internet closes the gap between small companies and big corporations. A Web-savvy business owner can make millions of dollars online—even in a modest, home office environment.

What This Book Is About

Create FrontPage 2000 Web Pages In a Weekend is a hands-on, easy-to-read guide to building a Web site you can be proud of. In seven structured sections beginning on Friday night and ending Sunday evening, you'll create your own collection of attractive, professional-looking Web pages, enhance them with exciting features like dynamic tables of contents and animated graphics, and get your new site all set up to publish in your own little corner of cyberspace. Along the way, you'll get tips and shortcuts to make your project go smoothly from beginning to end.

Who Should Read This Book?

Let's make an agreement right now. If you pick up this book, I'm going to assume you're ready to get down to business. You don't need a fifty-page lecture on how to use a mouse, and you understand the difference between the keyboard and the monitor. You've had some experience using other Windows applications—Word, perhaps, or maybe WordPerfect. You know why you want to build a Web site; you just need some guidance in getting it done. This book includes step-by-step directions and clear explanations written in a friendly, comfortable style.

Microsoft FrontPage 2000 levels the Web design playing field, giving people with even limited computer skills the ability to create Web sites like a pro. With the help of this book and a weekend of your time, you can too.

How This Book Is Organized

You can easily complete the seven sessions in this book over the course of one weekend. Each session will take about three or four hours to complete. Unless you're already experienced in HTML and Web design, I recommend you follow them in order so you don't miss any important information along the way. Here's a general itinerary for your weekend adventure:

Friday Evening: Laying the Foundation. In this session, you'll learn the basics of planning a Web site, get familiar with the FrontPage interface, and then jump right into creating your first page. By the end of the evening, you'll have your initial page set up and ready to build on the next day.

Saturday Morning: Adding Flair and Function. After breakfast, you'll learn how to add new pages to your Web site. You'll also learn how to give your pages some personality using colors, fonts, backgrounds and themes, tables, navigation bars, and more.

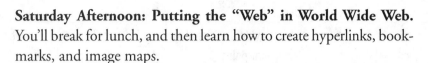

Saturday Afternoon: Putting the "Web" in World Wide Web. You'll break for lunch, and then learn how to create hyperlinks, bookmarks, and image maps.

Saturday Evening Bonus Session: Adding Tables and Frames to Your Pages. If you thought fancy features like frames and forms were beyond your abilities, you'll be singing a different tune as you drift off to sleep Saturday night. In this session, you'll add a frame layout to your Web site, and then design online forms you can use to get feedback and input from your visitors.

Sunday Morning: Putting the Power of Components to Work. FrontPage includes many automated components you can insert into your Webpages, including hit counters, hover buttons, include pages, timestamps, search forms, and more. In this session, you'll learn how to implement them quickly and easily.

Sunday Afternoon: Finalizing Your Pages. To complete your project, you'll clean up and polish your pages, finish your to-do list, and compile some reports that will help keep your Web site fresh and updated in the future.

Sunday Evening Bonus Session: Creating Web Art Special Effects. As a special bonus session, you'll find tips and techniques for creating and enhancing your own personalized Web art using Image Composer 1.5 or PhotoDraw 2000.

In the appendixes, you'll learn everything you need to know about selecting your Internet services and publishing your Web site online. You'll also find coverage of advanced features and additional techniques, such as adding audio and video to your Web site, making your Web site easy to locate, and securing your site with passwords. Finally, you get a glimpse of what's included on the CD-ROM that comes with this book, and a no-nonsense glossary that explains terms and concepts that might be new to you.

Special Features of This Book

Throughout this book, you'll find special text formats and icons to help you work faster, avoid problems, and learn more on your own.

NOTE Notes provide additional information or enhance a discussion in the text by emphasizing a particular point.

TIP Tips offer helpful hints, suggestions, or alternate methods for a procedure.

CAUTION Cautions warn you about mistakes and pitfalls that inexperienced users often encounter.

BUZZ WORD *Buzzwords* are new terms. The new terms are identified in italics in the text and then defined in the Buzzwords section. You'll also find these words in the glossary.

FIND IT ON **THE WEB** This graphic appears next to paragraphs that contain a Web address that may be helpful to the discussion.

FIND IT ON **THE CD** This graphic appears next to paragraphs that relate to material included on the *Create FrontPage 2000 Web Pages In a Weekend* CD-ROM.

Are You Ready?

It's Friday night. Your significant other is out with the gang, the kids are having a sleepover at the neighbor's, and you're itching to get started. Stock up the fridge with some healthy snacks, make a fresh pot of coffee, then settle down at the keyboard and brace yourself: the fun is about to begin!

Laying the Foundation

- ✿ Planning Your Site
- ✿ Working in FrontPage 2000
- ✿ Understanding FrontPage Views
- ✿ Creating a Quick and Simple Web Page
- ✿ Inserting a Graphic

When the Internet first became popular in the early 1990s, publishing Web sites was a daunting task best left to the experts. Today, however, advances in technology have simplified Web site design. Just about anyone with a computer and a modem can create and publish great-looking Web sites with advanced features. This usually requires very little effort or training.

Microsoft FrontPage 2000 takes simplicity even farther, making Web site design almost as easy as using a word processor. So, if you've wanted to build your own Web site, but were afraid you didn't know enough, relax! By the time you finish this book, you'll have created a site to be proud of. Your site will have links, graphics, buttons, and all those other features you've seen and admired out there on the Internet—and you'll wonder why you didn't do it sooner.

Getting Ready

Like any well-planned project, it's best to have everything on-hand that you will need to work on the project. Then you won't have to interrupt what you're doing later to find it.

Gathering What You'll Need

Although you might not know *exactly* how you want your Web site to look, you've probably given at least some thought to what you want. Maybe you have some great panoramic photos from your vacation you want to post. If your site is business-related, you may want to include information about your company and what it offers. So, before you even fire up the computer, get your hunting and gathering out of the way:

- ✿ Get a notepad and a pen to jot down notes.

- ✿ Collect or create any documents or graphics you think you want to use. You can always change or add more later.

● ●

If you want to use photos or other art (your logo, for example), make sure you have them in digital form, such as on a Photo CD or stored as a graphic file on your computer. If you don't have a way to do this yourself, ask your friends. Scanners and digital cameras are becoming more popular and affordable every day, so the odds are good that someone you know can help you. If not, check with your local photo processing company or quick printer. Many businesses offer photo conversion services at reasonable prices.

If you're going to use files already stored on your computer, know where they are located, and that they're as complete and finished as possible. (You can edit them later if needed.)

● ●

Make sure your computer is ready to handle your project:

- ✿ Is the FrontPage 2000 software installed and working?

- ✿ Is the modem working properly?

- ✿ Have you already set up an account with an *ISP* (Internet Service Provider) and Web site provider? If not, Appendix A, "Publishing Your FrontPage 2000 Web Pages," will help you get connected.

- ✿ Is your Web browser up-to-date? (More on this in a moment.)

Do You Need to Update Your Browser?

FrontPage 2000 takes full advantage of the latest and greatest features available in today's Web technology. As a Web site developer (which you are about to become), it's always a good idea to keep your Web browsing software up-to-date. Every browser will read and display Web pages, colors, and text formatting slightly differently. Some older versions do not support newer technology that you might want to use on your site. In fact, if you can afford the hard disk space, you might want to keep more than one browser on your computer, including versions of both Microsoft Internet Explorer and Netscape Navigator. The more browsers you can view your site from as you work, the better feel you will get for how your pages will look.

■■■

TIP

To check your browser's version number, select Help, About from the FrontPage menu bar.

■■■

You can download both current and older versions of the two most popular browsers at the following Web sites:

FIND IT ON ▶
THE WEB

Microsoft Internet Explorer: **www.microsoft.com/ie**

Netscape Navigator: **www.netscape.com**

● ●

NOTE

For this book, I used Windows 98 and Internet Explorer 5.0 as my primary browser. FrontPage 2000 runs just as well on Windows 95, and if you are using Netscape Navigator as your browser, that's fine too.

● ●

● ●

NOTE

The *Create FrontPage 2000 Web Pages In a Weekend* CD that accompanies this book includes several tools and utilities to make Web site design and management more efficient and effortless. For example, the tool called MozillaTracker is a small log analysis tool that tracks which browsers and operating systems Web page visitors have. You can install this tool to learn how visitors are accessing your site. You can then adjust your future design strategies around that information. See Appendix F, "What's on the CD-ROM?" for more information.

● ●

Planning Your Site

Before you actually dig in to creating your own Web pages, you should spend a little time thinking about what you want your site to look like. You

PLAN AHEAD

Figure 1.1

There's a lot to be said for planning.

don't have to plan each page right now, but some initial planning will save you time (see Figure 1.1). Here are a few suggestions and considerations:

✿ Surf the Internet for ideas and examples. When you find a page or site design you like, add it to your Favorites folder or *bookmark* it. I'll show you later how to imitate the style of a Web site you like.

▼ ▼

You can "save" the location of a Web page in FrontPage or your browser with a ***bookmark*** so that you can easily return to the page without typing in the URL again. Microsoft Internet Explorer calls bookmarks *favorites*; Netscape Navigator simply calls them bookmarks. (I've included steps for adding bookmarks at the end of this section.)

▲ ▲

◆ ◆

Be mindful of international copyright laws. Using materials created by someone else without their permission is against the law. You can download free clip art and images from a number of Web sites that you can use without violating any laws. You'll find links to some of these sites later in this book.

◆ ◆

- If you have a collection of hyperlinks related to your content that you want to share with others, bookmark or make a note of them as well. You'll insert the links on a separate page later.

- Think about the purpose of your site and your intended audience. Are they likely to be computer-savvy people or regular Joes? The more technically oriented your viewers, the more sophisticated your site should be. If you're just posting a personal home page, you can keep your design simple.

- Some sites use *frames* to organize the site and make it easier for users to navigate, like the one shown in Figure 1.2. Some users, however, find frames more trouble than they're worth (or their browser doesn't support frames) and might not spend very much time exploring your

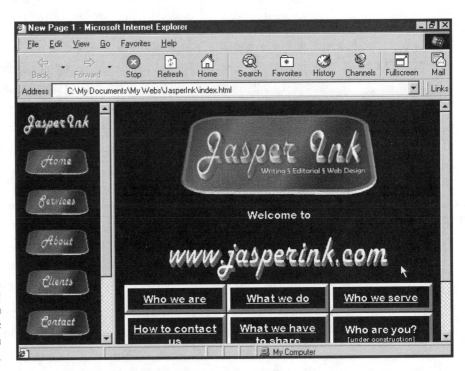

Figure 1.2

You can pack more punch with a frame-based layout.

site. Will your site use frames? (You can also simulate frames using FrontPage's Shared Borders feature, simplifying your Web structure.)

▼ ▼

A *frame*-based Web site displays multiple Web pages at the same time in separate frame windows within a Web page.

▲ ▲

- ✿ Keep in mind that the larger your site and the more pages and graphics you include, the more storage space you'll need, which may cost you more money.

- ✿ What do you want to know about the people who visit your site? Will you need to create forms so they can give you feedback or sign your guest book?

- ✿ If you're selling a product or products, do you want your customers to be able to order directly from the Web site using a credit card?

● ●

NOTE   Conducting business over the Internet requires some complex security procedures and equipment setup that is beyond the scope of this book. If you need to add these features to your Web site, consult your ISP's technical support department for help. Most of them provide design and implementation services—usually for an extra fee. If you're interested in learning more about Internet commerce, check out PrimaTech's *Web Advertising and Marketing, 2nd Edition.*

● ●

- ✿ You should have an overall theme or topic for your site, even if the site is just a personal one. Don't try to include too many different topics—you'll just confuse the reader and lose his or her interest quickly. Remember that you can always build another site.

- ✿ Don't bite off more than you can chew. Start with a reasonably simple design. As you learn more about Web site design and management, you can change and enhance your site with more advanced features and functions. It's easy to commit to a large project when you first

REMEMBER YOUR PLACE WITH BOOKMARKS

You can bookmark your favorite Web sites so you can find them again quickly. To bookmark a site in Internet Explorer:

1. With your browser open to the page you want to save, select Favorites, Add to Favorites. The Add Favorites dialog box opens.

• •

NOTE Depending on your browser version, you may be prompted here to subscribe to the page. If so, say no.

• •

2. If you want to give the bookmark a more descriptive name, enter it in the Name edit box.

3. Click OK to close the dialog box.

To bookmark a site in Netscape Navigator:

1. Click the Bookmarks button.

2. Select Add Bookmark from the menu that appears.

get started. It's also easy to get discouraged if the project drags on too long. The techniques you'll learn this weekend are easily manageable in a few hours' work.

✿ Sketch out by hand some basic ideas for your layout. Sometimes putting a few things down on paper can help stimulate other ideas as you go along.

Working in FrontPage 2000

One of the best things about FrontPage 2000 is that it's easy to use, even for novices. The interface is similar to the other Microsoft Office 2000 applications, such as Word or Excel. You'll recognize buttons like Open, Bold, and Print on the toolbars, as well as the familiar File, Edit, and Help

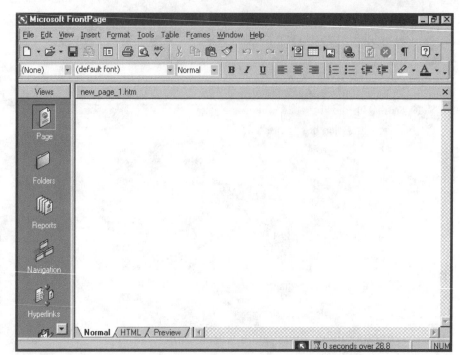

Figure 1.3

The FrontPage 2000 interface looks and works like the other Microsoft Office 2000 applications, so it's easy to learn.

menus, among others (see Figure 1.3). Take a quick look at FrontPage itself and get to know its basic features.

Starting FrontPage

When you're ready to begin, fire up the computer, get comfortable in your chair, and start FrontPage. Like most Office applications, it all begins at the Start button. To open FrontPage, follow these steps:

1. Click the Windows Start button. The Start menu appears.

2. Click Programs, then select Microsoft FrontPage from the submenu. FrontPage 2000 opens and displays a blank document called new_page_1.htm in Normal view, ready for editing (see Figure 1.4).

Getting Familiar with FrontPage

When you look at the FrontPage 2000 interface the first time, you're likely to see some things that look familiar. For example, FrontPage's Standard

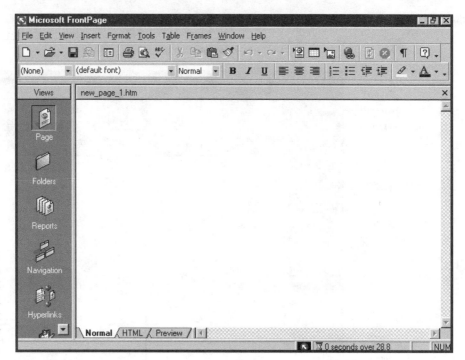

and Formatting toolbars are similar to those you've seen in Word and other Office applications (see Figure 1.5). The Views bar on the left looks similar to Outlook's Shortcut bar. The View tabs at the bottom work like worksheet tabs in Excel.

You'll learn more about the specific tools and features of FrontPage later. For now, just familiarize yourself with the layout of the screen.

Understanding FrontPage Views

One nice feature of FrontPage 2000 is that it gives you quick access to a variety of views, reports, and other information related to your site. Using different views, you can quickly move from editing a page to checking the status of your task list, to listing all of the files and folders in your site.

Page View

You'll use Page view when you're creating and editing Web pages. Within Page view, you have three different ways to see the page you're working on:

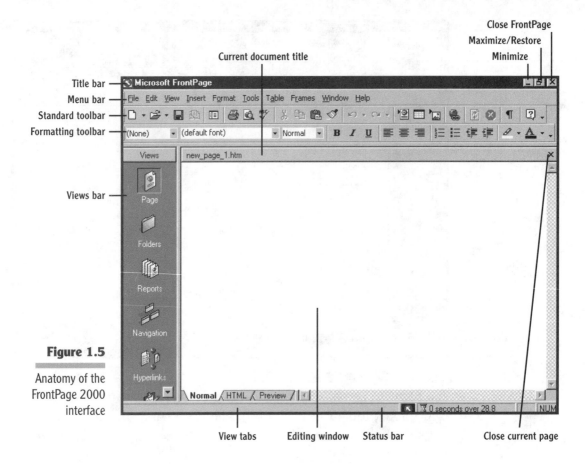

Close FrontPage
Maximize/Restore
Minimize

Current document title

Title bar
Menu bar
Standard toolbar
Formatting toolbar

Views bar

Figure 1.5

Anatomy of the
FrontPage 2000
interface

View tabs   Editing window   Status bar   Close current page

- **Normal.** The Normal view is your main working view. It looks and acts much like Word's Normal view (see Figure 1.6). In Normal view, you can enter and edit text, apply formatting, insert graphics and links, and more.

- **HTML.** Web pages are based on a programming language called *HTML (Hypertext Markup Language)*. You don't have to know anything about HTML to create Web pages. FrontPage automatically generates the HTML code in the background while you work in Normal view. If you want to take a peek at this mysterious language— or you want to edit the code yourself (not recommended for beginners)—click the HTML tab. You'll see something similar to what's shown in Figure 1.7.

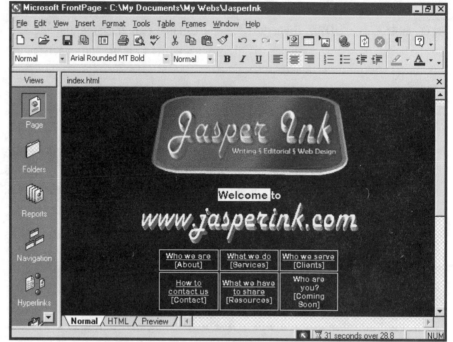

Figure 1.6

Normal view
provides a
WYSIWYG (what
you see is what you
get) view of
your page.

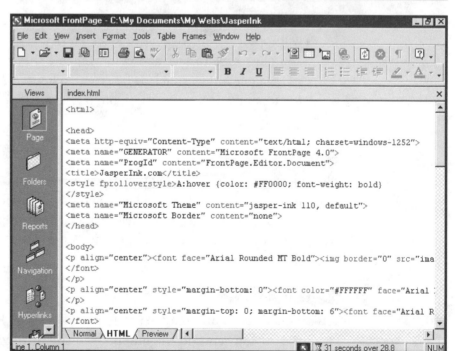

Figure 1.7

You can edit the
HTML code, but do
so with caution—
you might get
unexpected results.

▼ ▼

HTML (Hypertext Markup Language) is the programming language understood by Web browsers. HTML is much easier to learn and understand than typical programming languages.

▲ ▲

● ●

HTML coding employs *tags* to "mark up" the text. Tags are embedded within the Web page text, and they work as on/off toggle switches. HTML tags are surrounded by brackets (<>). Typically, the "on" tag appears before the text being formatted, and the "off" tag (which is the same tag preceded by a /) appears after the text.

For example, to show text in boldface, the HTML code would look something like this:

This is boldface text

The resulting text will appear as:

This is boldface text

● ●

✿ **Preview**. The Preview tab gives you a quick look at how your page will appear in your visitor's browser. Preview saves you a lot of time. You don't have to save and close your file then open it again in a stand-alone browser such as Internet Explorer or Netscape Navigator. It's not a perfect simulator, but it does a great job on most pages (see Figure 1.8).

Folders View

The Folders view, shown in Figure 1.9, gives you Windows Explorer-like access to all the files contained in your Web site. From here, you can keep track of all your files, including renaming, deleting, or copying files. You don't need to worry too much about tracking your files—FrontPage automatically does it for you.

Reports View

You can get detailed information about your Web site in Reports view (see Figure 1.10). You can find the number and size of all your pictures and graphic images. (A large graphic file may be slow to load.)

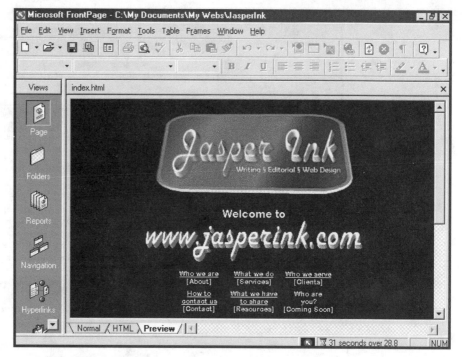

Figure 1.8

The Preview tab
simulates how your
page will look in
a browser.

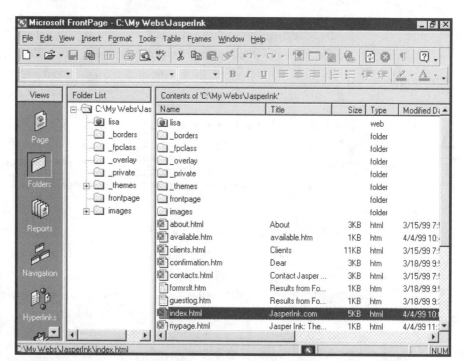

Figure 1.9

The Folders view
helps you manage
the files in your
Web site.

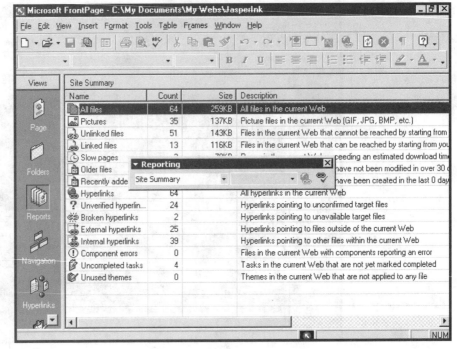

Figure 1.10

FrontPage's generous Reports feature is a Web site manager's best friend.

The first time you go to Reports view, you see the Site Summary, listing 15 different available reports. Double-click any report to open it. Reports are very handy for finding problems and ensuring that everything in your site is complete and working properly.

TIP

Subsequent returns to Reports view takes you back to the last report you viewed on-screen. To return to the Site Summary, select View, Reports, Site Summary.

Navigation View

Use the Navigation view, shown in Figure 1.11, to see or change the structure of your pages and to quickly add navigation bars to some or all of your pages. Drag and drop files from the Folder list, apply the Shared Borders feature, and *voilà*! Instant hyperlinks. You'll learn more about using Navigation view and Shared Borders later.

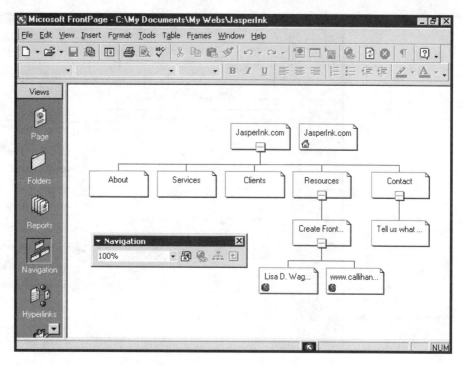

Figure 1.11

The Navigation view is a quick way to link pages of your Web site together.

Hyperlinks View

The Hyperlinks view (see Figure 1.12) gives you a visual map of all the links in your Web site. Click any file in the Folders list to see all the links contained on that page. Click the Expand button (+) to show the links on other pages in the current group. Hyperlinks view makes it easy to see the available paths to and from any page, as well as any external links contained on your pages.

Tasks View

The Tasks view gives you a complete list of all the "to-do" items remaining for your project (see Figure 1.13). This may be one of the handiest features of FrontPage, because it automatically keeps track of the details you need to fix or check later. Once you get a sizable Web site underway, there might be quite a few of these details. On Sunday afternoon, you'll learn just how helpful the Tasks list is as you clean up your site and prepare to publish it online.

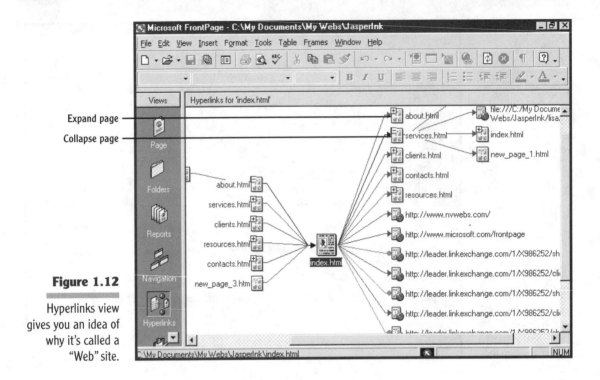

Expand page

Collapse page

Figure 1.12

Hyperlinks view gives you an idea of why it's called a "Web" site.

TIP You might need to click the Views bar's down arrow to see additional Views buttons.

Closing FrontPage

If you were experimenting and exploring as you followed along through the first part of this session, you'll want to close any open documents or webs you might have created. Again, you might find this procedure similar to that of Word, Excel, or other applications.

TIP If prompted to save a file, choose No for now. You'll learn how to save your work later when you finish for the evening.

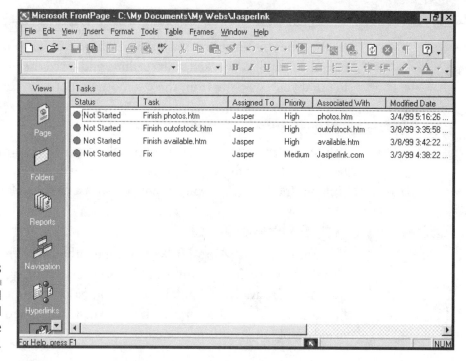

Figure 1.13

If you're forgetful by nature, you'll appreciate the Tasks list.

- To close a single page, click the Close Current Page button. (Remember, this button is at the top of the document, below the FrontPage toolbars.)

- To close an entire web, select File, Close Web.

- To close FrontPage, click the Close FrontPage button or select Exit from the File menu.

Take a Break!

Okay, now you have a basic understanding of how FrontPage works, and you have a general idea of what you want your Web site to look like. What you haven't done yet is any real work. So, take a few minutes to stretch, walk the dog, maybe grab a carrot stick or two, then you'll get down to the business of creating your first Web page!

Creating a Quick and Simple Web Page

By the time you finish this session, you'll have created your first Web page, inserted a graphic, checked your spelling, and saved the file. You'll be ready to build your Web site from there tomorrow morning. Ready? Get to it!

Creating a New Web Page

Before you get started, you'll want to make sure you're starting from a fresh, new page. Open FrontPage from the Start menu as you learned earlier in the evening, and FrontPage will present you with a new, blank document.

Entering and Editing Text

If you've ever used Microsoft Word (or any other word processor, for that matter), you won't have any trouble using the FrontPage editor. All the usual tools are available: bold, italic, and underline buttons, alignment and formatting tools, and so on. Most of the common Word keyboard commands apply to FrontPage as well.

 TIP If you don't remember what a particular button on the toolbar does, point to it with the mouse pointer. In a moment, a ScreenTip appears, providing a brief description of the tool.

 NOTE In this book, I built a Web site for my freelance writing business, Jasper Ink. With the ideas for your own Web site in mind, you're ready to get started.

All you have to do to begin your first Web page is start typing. To enter the text for your first page:

1. Type an opening heading for your Web page and press Enter.

2. Type a short sentence or phrase of introductory text and press Enter.

3. Enter a few subheadings that you want to designate as the main categories for your Web site.

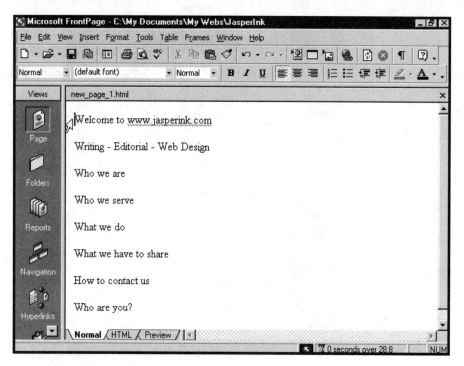

Figure 1.14

The beginnings of
the first Web page

Your screen should look similar to the one in Figure 1.14.

Now apply some formatting to the text:

1. Click anywhere in the main heading to select the paragraph.

2. Click the down arrow next to the Style drop-down list, then select Heading 1 (see Figure 1.15).

3. Select your second line of text and apply the Heading 2 style.

Turn the list of subheadings into a bulleted list:

1. Select the first subheading, press and hold the Shift key, and drag to the end of the last subheading. All of your subheadings should be selected.

2. Click the Bullets button on the Formatting toolbar. FrontPage automatically indents the paragraphs and adds bullets to each item (see Figure 1.16).

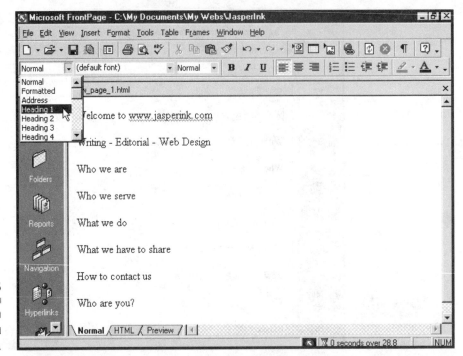

Figure 1.15

Apply a paragraph style just as you would in Word.

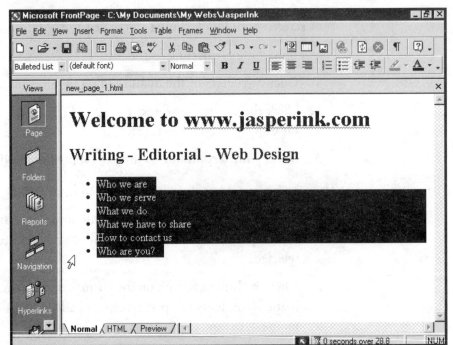

Figure 1.16

One quick click turns these paragraphs into a bulleted list.

You can add, move, or delete text and formatting at any time:

1. Select the last item in your bulleted list and click the Bullet button again to remove the bullet point. The paragraph changes back to Normal text.

2. To delete text, select the text to remove, then press Delete.

3. To add new text, click where you want to insert text and begin typing. Existing text will move to the right, as shown in Figure 1.17.

You can use normal cut-and-paste or drag-and-drop editing procedures to move text around in your document:

1. Select the first item in your bulleted list and press Ctrl+X to cut the paragraph.

2. Right-click at the start of the last bulleted paragraph, then select Paste from the shortcut menu that appears (see Figure 1.18).

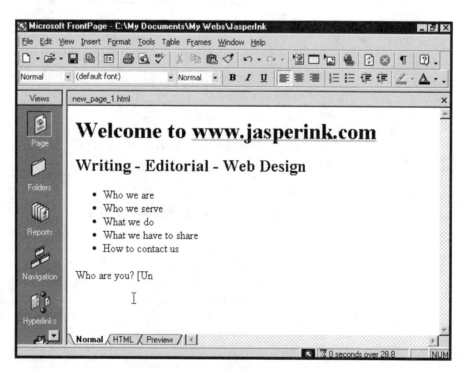

Figure 1.17

Add and delete text as you would in any word processor.

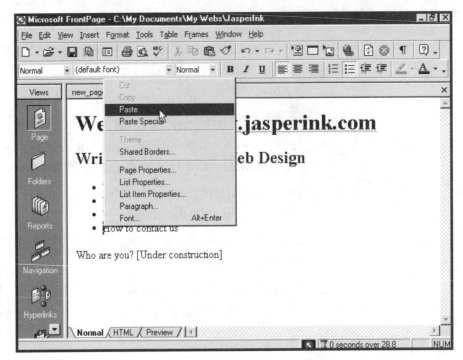

Figure 1.18

Use the shortcut menus for easy cut-and-paste operations.

3. Click to the left of your last bulleted paragraph to select the entire line.

4. Click again on the highlighted text and hold down the left mouse button. When you next move the mouse, the cursor changes to the drag pointer (see Figure 1.19)

5. Drag the highlighted text to the start of the first bulleted paragraph and release the mouse button. FrontPage drops the line of text in its new location.

6. Click at the end of the last bulleted paragraph and press Enter. FrontPage creates a new bulleted paragraph, as shown in Figure 1.20.

7. Changed your mind about that new line? No problem. Press the Backspace key once to remove the bullet, and press Backspace again to remove the line you just created.

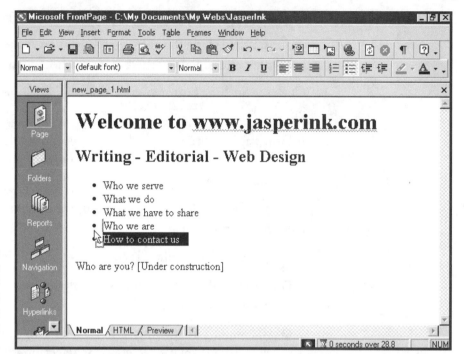

Figure 1.19

Clicking and dragging can be the fastest way to move a large amount of text.

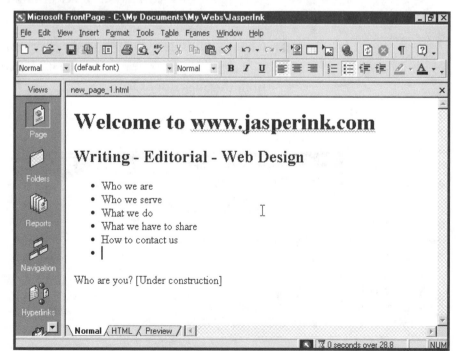

Figure 1.20

FrontPage guessed that the new paragraph you're adding should be another item in your bulleted list.

Checking for Spelling Errors

After you're satisfied with the text, you'll want to make sure you didn't make any typing errors. Follow these steps to check your document:

1. Click the Spelling button on the toolbar. FrontPage begins the spelling check.

2. If FrontPage finds a word it does not recognize, the Spelling dialog box opens and the word in question appears in the box next to Not in Dictionary, as shown in Figure 1.21.

3. You have several choices for correcting words the spelling checker identified as misspelled:

   ○ **Ignore**. The spelling is correct; ignore this instance of it.

   ○ **Ignore All**. The spelling is correct; ignore all instances of the word in this document.

   ○ **Change**. The spelling is incorrect; change this instance of it. Enter your own correction or select one from the Suggestions list.

   ○ **Change All**. The spelling is incorrect; change all instances of it in this document. Enter your own correction or select one from the Suggestions list.

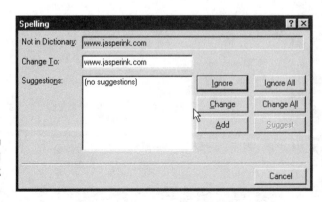

Figure 1.21

Use the spelling checker to check your work.

Figure 1.22

Where would you be today without your trusty spelling checker?

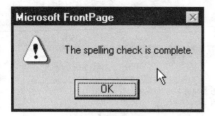

- ✪ **Add**. The spelling is correct; recognize this word in all documents by adding it to the dictionary.

- ✪ **Suggest**. The spelling is incorrect, but none of the suggestions are correct. Select a suggested word, and then click Suggest for alternatives.

- ✪ **Cancel**. End the spelling check.

4. When the spelling check is finished, a message appears (see Figure 1.22). Click OK to close the dialog box.

Inserting a Graphic

Your Web site will be boring without some visual elements. Those image files you collected earlier in the evening will come in handy now. You can insert graphics from files stored on your computer, from FrontPage's built-in Clip Art Gallery, or from another Web site. For this example, I added a file from the FrontPage CD-ROM.

1. Click where you want to insert the graphic.

2. Select Insert, Picture, and then select From File. The Picture dialog box appears. Click the button Select a file on your computer located in the lower left corner and the Select File dialog box opens (see Figure 1.23).

3. Navigate to your file, select the file name, then click OK. FrontPage inserts the picture on your Web page, as shown in Figure 1.24.

4. If you want to change the alignment of your graphic, select the object and then click the Left, Center, or Right Align buttons on the toolbar.

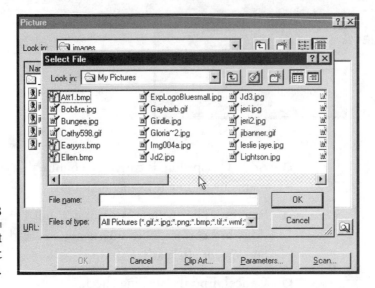

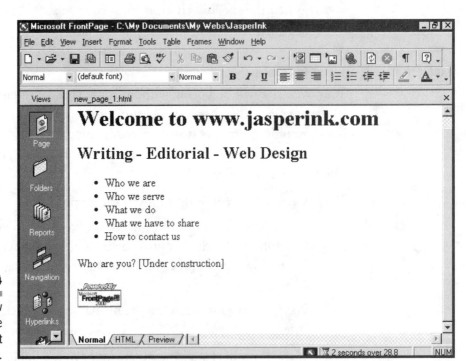

Congratulations—you've just created your first Web page! I told you it was easy. You're far from finished, but you've done enough to get an idea of where you're headed. Enough creativity for now; take a look at the results of your efforts so far, then close up shop for the night.

Saving Your Work

Before you go any further, you need to save your work so you can come back to it later. To save this file to a folder on your hard drive, follow these steps:

1. Click the Save button on the toolbar. If this is the first time you've saved the file, the Save As dialog will appear, as shown in Figure 1.25. (If not, FrontPage will save the file in the background and you can continue working.)

2. Enter the name you want to give the file in the File name box. (FrontPage will suggest a file name, so feel free to use it if you like.)

3. Navigate to the folder on your hard drive where you want to save the file.

4. FrontPage will assign a Page Title to your document based on the first line of text. The Page Title is the name that appears on the title bar of your browser when this page is open. To change the title, click Change and enter the new name in the Set Page Title dialog box, then click OK.

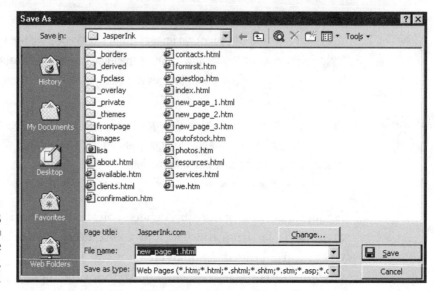

Figure 1.25

Use the file name
FrontPage suggests,
or enter your own.

TIP It's a good idea to be as descriptive with page titles as possible. Some Web search engines display only page titles when reporting a user's search results. If you want a noticeable Web site, you need to give the user a hint about your site's content. You're much more likely to draw a visitor with a title like "Jasper Ink: The Midwest's Premiere Writing and Editorial Service" than the suggested "JasperInk.com."

5. Click Save to save the file. If you have a graphic in the file, FrontPage will prompt you to also save the embedded file (see Figure 1.26). Click OK to close the dialog box.

CAUTION Save frequently, not just when you're finished working. You never know when your computer might crash, or the power will go out, or any number of other anomalies. If something like that happens, all your hard work will go down the drain, and you'll have to start over from the point you last saved the file.

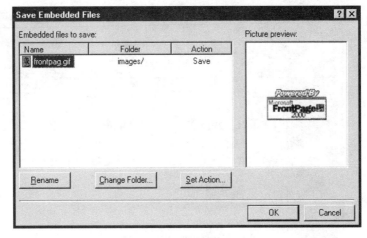

Figure 1.26

FrontPage needs to copy files you've embedded into its file list.

Previewing Pages in a Browser

Although working in FrontPage's Normal view will give you a general idea of how your text will look online, it's not completely accurate.

For a better representation of how a visitor will see your page, click the Preview tab (see Figure 1.27). The differences at this point may be subtle or non-existent. As your site develops, however, the differences will be more obvious as you compare views.

As I said earlier, though, sometimes even the Preview view doesn't tell the whole story. You'll want to check your progress in a real browser (or two or three) from time to time, just to ensure you're getting the results you want. To view your new page, save any changes, then follow these steps:

1. Select File, Preview in Browser. The Preview in Browser dialog box opens, giving you a list of browsers you can use to view the file (see Figure 1.28).

2. To add another browser to the list, click the Add button and enter the browser's name and location in the Add Browser dialog box. Then click OK.

3. Select the browser you want to use, then click Preview. The selected browser will open and display your Web page, as shown in Figure 1.29.

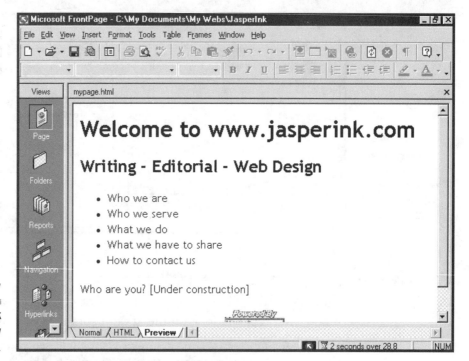

Figure 1.27

Take a quick peek at the browser view on the Preview tab.

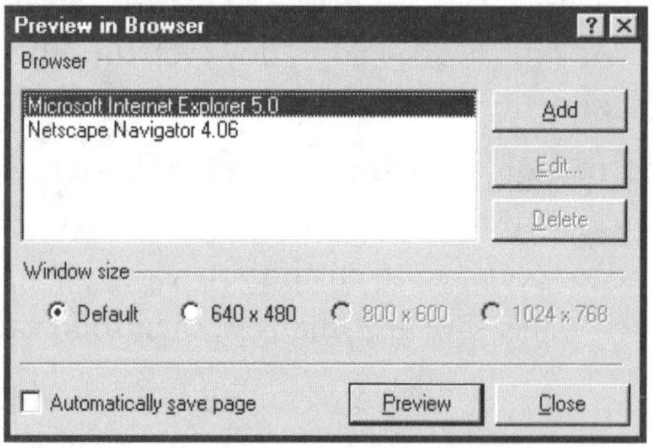

Figure 1.28

You can check the appearance of your page using a variety of browsers.

4. When you're finished, click the browser's Close button to return to FrontPage.

5. Repeat steps 1-4 to view the file in another browser.

Whew! Your Web site is well on its way to becoming a reality, and you've only been working for a few hours. Not bad for an evening's work, eh?

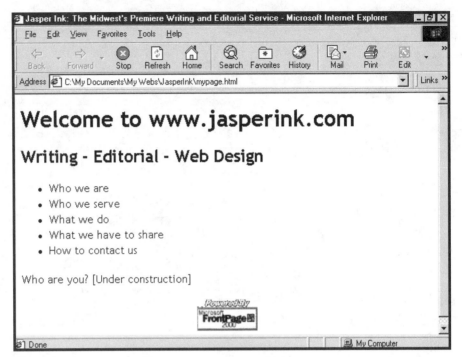

Figure 1.29

Here's how my opening page looks in Internet Explorer 5.

What's Next?

You now have one great-looking page, but you have a long way to go before your Web site is complete. Tomorrow, you'll learn more about enhancing your pages, including how to add common features like links and backgrounds. You'll also explore more advanced Web site design features such as forms and frames. On Sunday, you'll add marquees, hit counters, and a dynamic table of contents that automatically changes as your content changes. Then you'll put on the finishing touches and, at last, publish your Web site online.

For now, save any new work you've done, close FrontPage, shut down your computer, and go relax. You've earned it!

Adding Flair and Function

- Creating a New Web
- Importing Other Webs or Pages
- Giving Your Pages Personality
- All About Lists
- Getting a Cohesive Look with Themes

Good morning! While you were sleeping, another few thousand people logged on to the Internet for the first time. Each one of them is a potential visitor to your Web site, so get rolling!

Last night you learned a lot about planning your Web site and working in FrontPage. You also built your first Web page, added a few embellishments, and saw how your new page looks in a browser. Today, you'll build on what you learned last night. By the end of the day, you will have many new pages to show off your growing skills as a Web designer. So, throw on your favorite baggy sweats, grab a bagel and some juice, and put on some background tunes. You have a lot of exciting work to do today!

Building Your Site

In last night's session, you worked on a single Web page. Most Web sites consist of several pages. FrontPage makes it very easy to manage your entire Web site. You can make the same change to multiple pages, update links, and other tedious chores, but only if you store all the information about your site in one place. That one place is a FrontPage web. Your first task this morning is to create a new web and learn how to import any existing Web sites, pages, or other documents you might already have tucked away somewhere. After that, you'll add the page you created last night and get to work on sprucing it up and adding more pages.

Creating a New Web

A FrontPage web is a collection of Web pages, graphics, documents, and other files needed to operate your Web site. It's also the place where you manage your site by adding or removing pages, updating hyperlinks in one fell swoop, and other changes.

NOTE Depending on your situation, you might be able to manage your FrontPage web directly from your company's network or your *WPP's* server. Most individuals and small businesses, however, store their site on their computer's hard drive and publish the completed site or updates to the server periodically. In this book, I'll assume that's your story as well. If not, you'll want to check out other options in Appendix A, "Publishing Your FrontPage Web Pages".

BUZZ WORD A *WPP*, *Web Presence Provider*, also called *Web Service Provider* (*WSP*) or *hosting service* is the company that you hire to store your Web site so that other users can access it on the Internet. Not to be confused with *ISP*, or *Internet Service Provider*, the company that gives you dial-up access to the Internet, whether or not you have a Web site of your own.

NOTE Your ISP and your WPP may be the same company, but they don't have to be. See more details about ISPs and WPPs in Appendix A, "Publishing Your FrontPage 2000 Web Pages."

You'll want to start every new project by creating a new FrontPage web first. To create a new FrontPage web:

1. Open FrontPage from the Start menu. Close any webs or pages that might open automatically (such as the one you created last night) by clicking Close (for pages) or Close Web (for Web sites).

TIP

If you manage only one Web site, you can tell FrontPage to always open the last web you used. Select Tools, Options to open the Options dialog box, then put a check in the box next to Open Last Web automatically when FrontPage starts. Click OK to close the dialog box.

If you work on several sites, you're better off disabling this option and opening FrontPage to a blank page. Use the Files, Recent Files, or Recent Webs menus to quickly open the desired web.

2. Select File, New, Web. The New dialog box will open to present you with a variety of template options for your new site (see Figure 2.1). Select the One Page Web template and click OK.

3. Tell FrontPage where to store this web by entering the path name in the edit box below. Specify the location of the new web. The default location, C:\My Webs\, is as good a place as any.

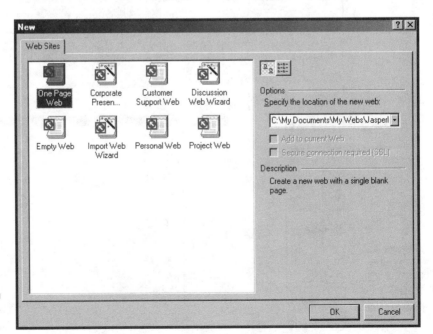

Figure 2.1

Create a basic one-page web in a flash.

NOTE I store my Web files in the My Webs subfolder under My Documents on my computer's hard drive, and the examples in this book reflect that location. It doesn't really matter where you store your files as long as you can easily organize and keep track of them.

4. Click OK. FrontPage will open your new web and create a folder structure. You'll notice that FrontPage has already created a new, blank page called index.htm, as shown in Figure 2.2.

NOTE Name the file containing the opening page of any web index.htm (or other variations, such as index.html, default.htm, default.asp, and so on, depending on your server).

When you type the URL to go to a Web site, you usually just have to type the domain's Web site address to open the site:

www.jasperink.com

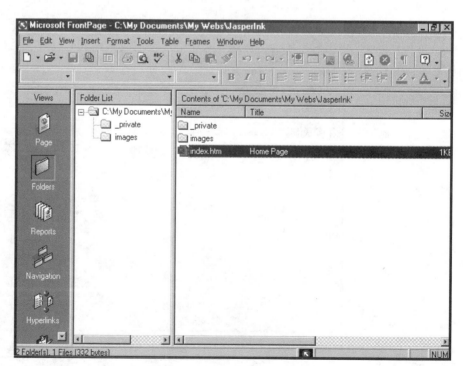

Figure 2.2

Here's your web, with a blank index (home) page to get you started.

The browser knows to automatically open the index or default page if it finds it. In reality, however, the full address you're pointing to is something like:

http://www.jasperink.com/index.html

You might also see index pages with the extension .asp instead of .htm or .html. Pages using this extension are Active Server Pages. Most of the examples in this book use the .htm extension.

Adding New Pages

Unless you have only the most basic one-page Web site in mind, you will want to add new pages to your site. You may need a page of links or a form to get feedback from your visitors.

You can add new pages one at a time as you develop your site, or you can add all your pages at once then develop them individually. The latter method

---

WHAT GOOD ARE TEMPLATES?

FrontPage is all about making your job easier. Templates can save you time by doing some of the development work for you. For example, if you want to set up a discussion-based Web site complete with user submission forms, search capabilities, and reply threads, double-click the Discussion Web Wizard. FrontPage will ask you a series of questions about your intended Web site, and then generate all the pages you need to get started. What's more, you can even choose an overall theme for your web's look and feel (you'll learn more about themes later this evening). All you have to do is customize the content to suit your needs, insert your own graphics, create additional pages needed, and apply any special formatting.

FrontPage saves you the trouble of creating all those fields in a form. You tell FrontPage which ones to include and how you want them to look, as shown in Figure 2.3.

When the wizard completes the setup, it offers to take you straight to the Tasks lists. That's FrontPage's way of saying, "Okay, I did my part, now it's your turn."

It's okay to use these templates if they provide you with what you need. Your work is far from finished, however. You still need the skills you learn in this book to edit the templates, insert advanced features, and personalize the Web site. In the next section, you'll add a new page to your web using a template that's included with FrontPage.

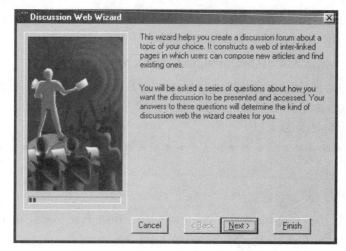

This wizard helps you create a discussion forum about a topic of your choice. It constructs a web of inter-linked pages in which users can compose new articles and find existing ones.

You will be asked a series of questions about how you want the discussion to be presented and accessed. Your answers to these questions will determine the kind of discussion web the wizard creates for you.

Cancel   < Back   Next >   Finish

Figure 2.3

The template wizards are a quick shortcut to creating the basic structure of your web and pages.

works fine if you know exactly which pages you'll need from the start, but chances are you'll add some anyway.

Adding a New Page to Edit Later

If all you want to do is create a blank page now and work on it later, you can. In fact, you can even ask FrontPage to remind you to edit the page later so you don't forget.

It's a good idea to add a to-do item to your Task list any time you need to go back and finish something. After you get several pages in your web, it can be hard to remember all those little details by yourself!

NOTE   You'll work more with the Task list when you finish the web on Sunday afternoon.

1. Click Folders view to see the list of files and folders in your web.

2. In the Folder List pane, click the folder in which you want to add the new page. For now, just select the top-level folder.

3. Click the down arrow next to the New button on the toolbar, and then click Page. FrontPage creates a new page and adds it to the Contents pane of the Folders view (see Figure 2.4). The default file

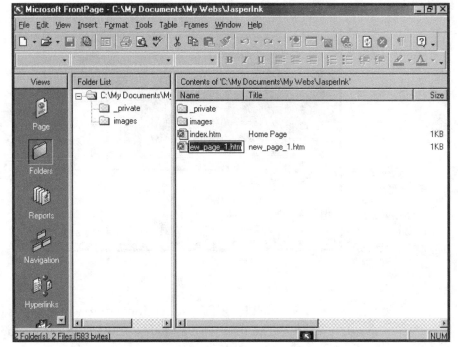

Figure 2.4

Rename your page from the default right here and save an extra step later.

name, new_page_*x*.htm, is highlighted so you can give it your own file name. *X* represents the new page number; each page you create is numbered successively.

4. Type the desired file name, using .htm as the extension. The name you enter here will be part of the URL you will enter or link to when viewing the page online. If you use spaces in the file name, FrontPage will replace them with underscores.

5. Press the Tab key. FrontPage accepts your change and highlights the new page's Title.

6. Type a title for the page. The page title will appear in the title bar of the visitor's browser when viewed online.

7. Press Tab again. FrontPage accepts your new title and highlights the new page's Comments field. Type any comments you want and press Enter.

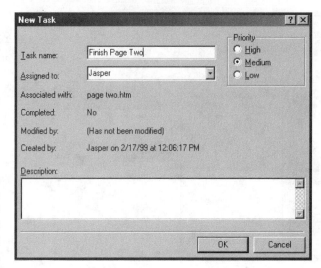

Figure 2.5

If you don't want to edit a new page immediately, add it to your list of tasks.

8. Now tell FrontPage to remind you to work on this page later. Right-click the new page and choose Add Task from the shortcut menu. The New Task dialog box opens (see Figure 2.5).

9. Type a name in the Task name text box and click OK. FrontPage closes the dialog box, adds the task to your Task list, and takes you back to the Folders view so you can continue working.

Adding a New Page to Edit Immediately

Sometimes you'll want to work on a new page as soon as you create it. In the Jasper Ink Web site, I need to create a Frequently Asked Questions page. I think I'll let FrontPage do some of the work, so I'll use a template. You should add a page appropriate to your own content, such as a Guest Book, a Table of Contents, or just a blank Normal page to develop from scratch.

1. Click Page view to change to the editing view.

2. Select File, New, and select Page. The New dialog box opens and displays a list of available page templates, as shown in Figure 2.6.

3. Select the desired page style and click OK. FrontPage creates your new page and opens it for editing.

Add to task list ———

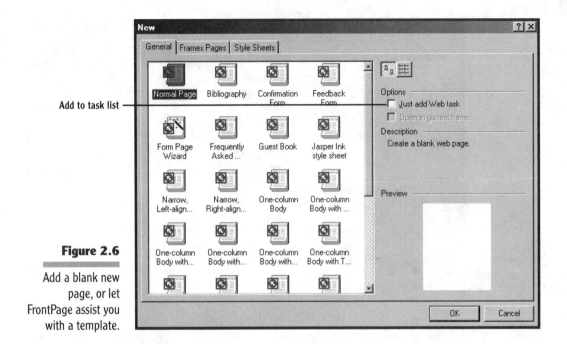

Figure 2.6

Add a blank new page, or let FrontPage assist you with a template.

Type the text you want on this page. It's a good idea to save your work frequently, so do that now. You'll be prompted to save the file and give it a title if you haven't already.

If you used a template, read the comments FrontPage displays on the page. These tips help you edit the template-based page to suit your needs (see Figure 2.7).

TIP If you change your mind and don't want to keep the page you just created, just click the page's Close button. Poof! The page is gone just as quickly as it was created.

By now, you should have a couple of new pages in your web in addition to the index.htm file that FrontPage created for you. They're not very detailed, but that's okay. Next, you'll work on fine-tuning these pages.

In the next sections, you'll focus on importing existing Web pages or Office documents. If all you have to import to your new web is the page you

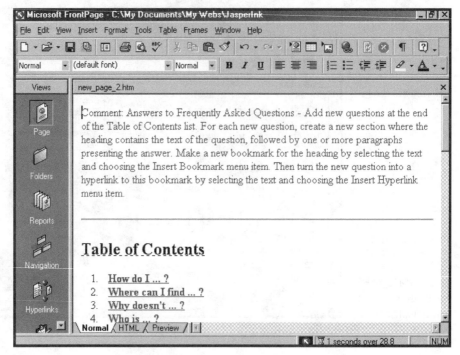

Figure 2.7

FrontPage includes instructions and tips in a template so you can personalize the content.

created last night, skip the next two sections and go straight to "Opening Last Night's Page." Make a mental note that the information is here to help you when you need it.

Importing Other Webs or Pages

You can import existing Web sites and pages into your web. Why would you want to? Any number of reasons:

- ⚙ You want to make changes to an existing FrontPage web but keep an unchanged copy of the site available.

- ⚙ Your existing site was created in another program and you want to begin using FrontPage to manage the site.

- ⚙ You want to take just a few pages of an existing Web site and add them to your new site.

☼ You want to import a sample Web site to study its structure and learn how certain features were implemented.

Whatever the reason, FrontPage makes it easy to import existing Web sites or pages into your new site.

Importing an Existing Web Site

To import an existing Web site for use as a new Web site, use the following steps. For this example, you'll import a sample Web site from the FrontPage installation CD-ROM.

1. Make sure all existing webs and pages are closed.

2. Select File, Import. The New dialog box will open. Click Import Web Wizard and click OK. The Import Web Wizard opens, as shown in Figure 2.8.

3. Enter the location or path name for the site in the appropriate box. I found a sample Web site on the CD-ROM in the folder named pfiles\msoffice\template\1033\webs. Depending on your FrontPage 2000 version, your samples might be located elsewhere on the CD.

Figure 2.8

The Import Web Wizard can help you add existing pages from other sites. In fact, you can import the entire site if you'd like.

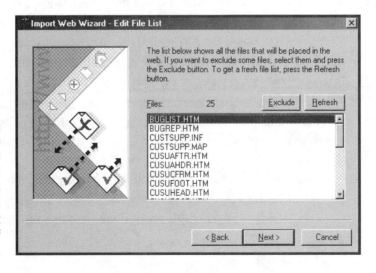

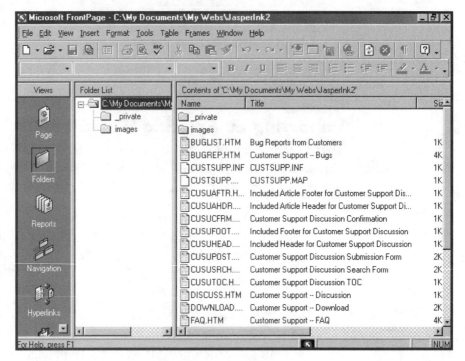

Figure 2.9

Get a jump-start on
your Web site by
importing one from
somewhere else
and modifying it to
fit your needs and
design preferences.

 **CAUTION** Be very, very careful about importing files from someone else's Web site. Web sites are protected by copyright laws just like a written document, and plagiarism is plagiarism. It's acceptable to borrow some basic ideas (who was it that said "there's no such thing as an original design"?) but never, never, *never* publish someone else's work as your own. That goes for photos, graphics, or any other file you might find. If it is not clearly marked that the files can be freely distributed or copied, always ask permission from the site owner. It's not only the law; it's good manners. (Mom would be so proud!)

4. Click Next, then Finish to begin the import. When the import is finished, click Folders view to see a list of the files and folders imported (see Figure 2.9). From there, you can open and edit any file.

Importing an Existing Web Page from Your Computer or Network

You might have some stand-alone Web pages or HTML documents on your hard drive that you want to use in your new Web site. To import just one or two pages into your current web, follow these steps:

1. With your current web open, select File, Import. The Import dialog box appears (see Figure 2.10).

2. To import a file, select Add File. The Add to Import File List dialog box opens.

3. Change the Files of Type to HTML files. Navigate to the desired file and click it to select it. Click Open to add the file to the list.

 TIP ■■■■■■■■■■■■■■■■■■■■■■■■■■■■■■■■■■■■■■■
Use Ctrl+click to select more than one file.
■■■■■■■■■■■■■■■■■■■■■■■■■■■■■■■■■■■■■■■

4. To import an entire folder, click Add Folder, select the desired folder, and click OK. FrontPage will add all the files in the chosen folder to the import list.

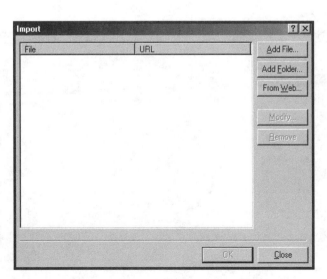

Figure 2.10

Importing single pages from other webs or folders is another way to save time in your site development.

5. Remove any files you don't want to import from the list by high-lighting the file or files and clicking Remove.

6. When you've listed all the files you want to import, click OK to close the dialog box and begin the import.

Importing an Existing Page from the World Wide Web

If you find a page on the Web that you particularly like and want to down-load and modify for your own use, you can do so as long as you're mindful of copyright laws. To import just one or two pages into your current web, follow these steps:

1. With your current web open, select File, Import. The Import dialog box appears.

2. Click From Web to start the Wizard. The Choose Source page appears first (see Figure 2.11). Select From a World Wide Web site, then type the URL of the page in the Location text box. (Be sure to enter the full address including the file name, such as **www.jasperink.com/mypage.htm** or you might end up acciden-tally importing the entire site!)

Figure 2.11

Copying a design is usually okay (you can't copyright a background color, for example), but using someone else's content or graphics without permission is against the law.

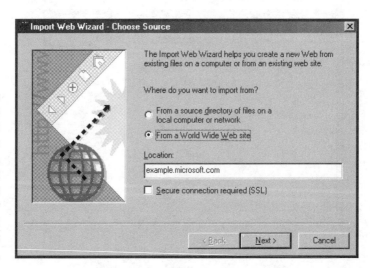

3. Click Next to complete the Wizard's questions, then click Finish to start the import. FrontPage will import the designated file into your web. You may be prompted to connect.

Importing Office 2000 Documents

One of the most exciting developments of Microsoft Office over the last two versions has been its growth in "Web friendliness." All the primary Office applications are fully integrated and Internet-compatible. Create an animated PowerPoint presentation complete with transitions and sound effects. Import that presentation into FrontPage and publish it to your Web site, no tweaking necessary. Anyone using Internet Explorer 4.0 or higher can view the slide show in their browser just as they would see it on the screen. Netscape users can play the slide show in their own installation of PowerPoint or the PowerPoint Viewer. To import an Office 2000 document into your web, follow these steps:

1. With your current web open, select File, Import. The Import dialog box appears.

2. To import a file, select Add File. The Add File to Import List dialog box opens.

3. Change the Files of type to Microsoft Office files (see Figure 2.12). Navigate to the desired file and select it. Click Open to add the file to the list.

TIP Use Ctrl+click to select more than one file.

4. When you've listed all the files you want to import, click OK to close the dialog box and begin the import.

Switch to Folders view and delete any unwanted files you might have inserted as an experiment. Save your work and close all open webs except your main project.

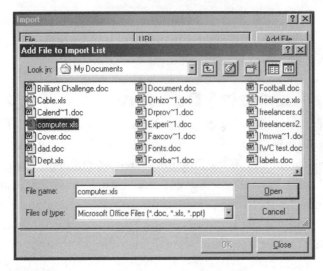

Figure 2.12

Import Office 2000 documents into your web just as you would any other Web page or graphic.

DON'T USE A SCREWDRIVER TO DRIVE A NAIL...

For Web pages that are primarily text-based, it makes sense to use the right tool for the right job. Create your text document in Word so you can take advantage of Word's robust word processing features, and then import the file into FrontPage to publish it on your Web site.

Do the same for complex tables. Use Excel to create a spreadsheet, then select Insert, File to insert the spreadsheet into an open FrontPage Web page. FrontPage will automatically convert the document to HTML format and insert it as a table in your open Web page, as shown in Figure 2.13.

Opening Last Night's Page

When you created your new web this morning, FrontPage automatically added a starter file called index.htm. You already have the starter page you created in last night's session, so you'll just drop it in, literally. Herein lies another quick shortcut for building your site quickly, drag-and-drop. To import last night's page into your new web, try this:

1. Open your FrontPage web and click Folders view.

2. Open Windows Explorer and use it to locate the file you worked on last night. Click the file to select it.

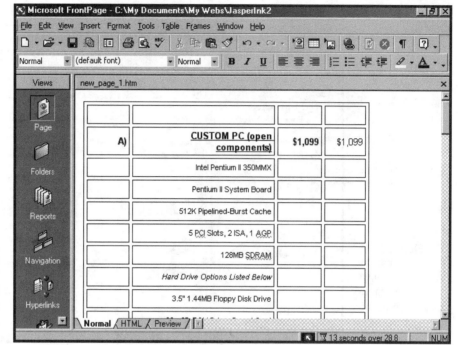

Figure 2.13

Use Insert rather than Import to add an Office document directly to an existing Web page.

3. Drag the file to the FrontPage icon on the Windows taskbar (see Figure 2. 14), but don't release the mouse button. Hold the pointer over the icon. After a moment, the FrontPage window will come to the front. Drag the pointer to the Contents pane and release the mouse button. The page imports instantly.

4. Repeat steps 1-3 to import the graphic file you inserted in last night's page. If you don't import the graphic, you'll get an empty box with an X where the graphic should be.

Remember, however, you must name a Web site's opening page index.htm. You already have one with that name—the blank one installed by the Wizard. You don't need it now, so delete the existing index file and rename last night's page index.htm.

1. To delete a file, just select it and press Delete.

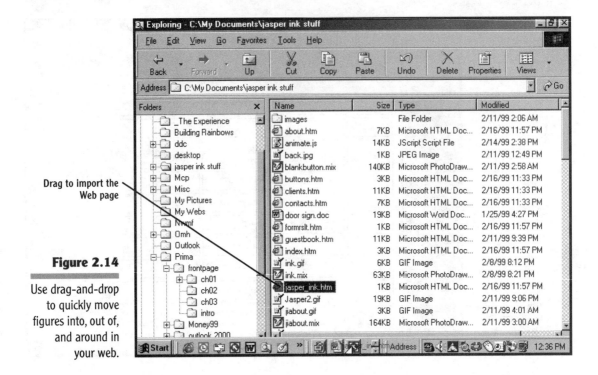

Drag to import the Web page

Figure 2.14

Use drag-and-drop to quickly move figures into, out of, and around in your web.

2. To rename a file, click Folders view, and then click the file you want to change.

3. Right-click the file name and select Rename.

4. Type the new file name and press Enter, as shown in Figure 2.15.

Notice that FrontPage pauses a moment to update not just the file name, but also to update any links or references to that file name in your web (see Figure 2.16). If you have a fast computer, you might miss it. It's more noticeable when your Web site is larger because it takes longer. This is one of FrontPage's most outstanding features. You don't have to "search-and-replace" page-by-page to find all the links to that particular reference.

That long and not-so-exciting lesson on setting up your new Web site is finished (no applause, please). Ready to move on to something a little more creative and fun?

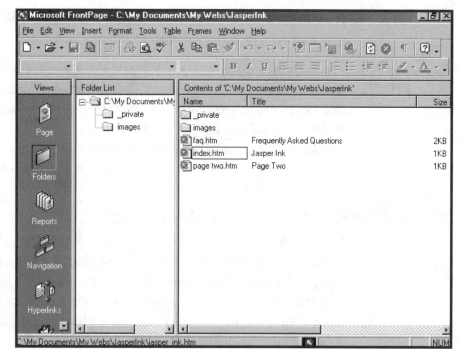

Figure 2.15

Rename the file you created last night to index.htm. That tells browsers to open this page first when the user visits your Web site.

Figure 2.16

FrontPage updates all references and links whenever you move, rename, or delete a page.

Giving Your Pages Personality

Open the index.htm file from Folders view and take a look at the page you created last night. Nice start, but pretty plain so far, eh? Plain black text on a plain white background just isn't very exciting.

The rest of this morning's session will deal with making your pages look good. You'll add background colors and patterns, apply new styles and fonts, and create a sophisticated multi-level bulleted list with graphics in place of the bullets. Finally, you'll learn how to spice up your site's overall appearance by applying a theme.

NOTE Throughout the remainder of this session, I'll demonstrate the techniques using the original page I created last night just so that you can see the difference each treatment has to the same content. Please feel free to continue building new pages as appropriate for your Web site and apply these techniques to any or all of them.

Basic HTML Styles and Headings

HTML began as a very structured programming language without a lot of options. You had a handful of available heading styles, a few styles to make indented lists, and other options. Although the basic styles have not changed, now there's a lot more flexibility in what you can do within the confines of those styles. Nevertheless, you should have a basic understanding of HTML styles, because you will use them.

In a word processor, you have a great deal of control over paragraph and heading styles. You can define exactly how you want them to appear: the font size, the typeface, amount of space between lines, and other styles. HTML styles, on the other hand, are a bit more cut and dried. You can change all these attributes using FrontPage's formatting techniques, but 1) it's a lot more work and 2) not every browser will be able to display your embellishments.

There are six basic HTML heading styles. Each of them is left-aligned, and their individual characteristics are described in Table 2.1. Think of heading styles in terms of an outline. Heading 1 holds your top-level topic; Heading 2 indicates subtopics under Heading 1; Heading 3 for topics under Heading 2, and so on. The lower the level, the smaller the heading. However, unlike 8th grade English class, there are no rules regarding when to use which heading, so use your best judgment and design instincts when assigning a style.

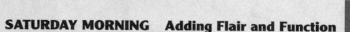

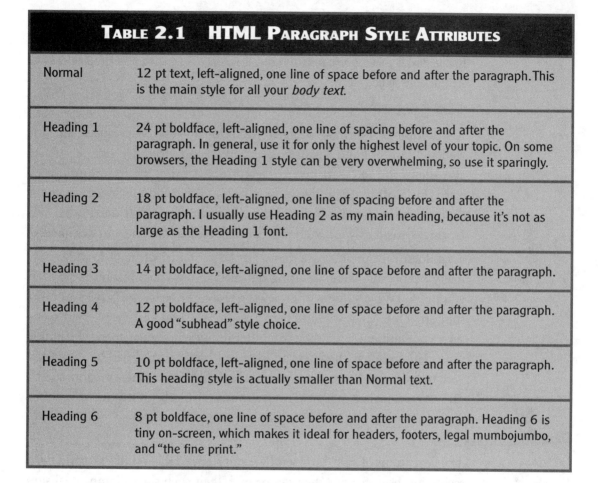

TABLE 2.1 HTML PARAGRAPH STYLE ATTRIBUTES	
Normal	12 pt text, left-aligned, one line of space before and after the paragraph. This is the main style for all your *body text*.
Heading 1	24 pt boldface, left-aligned, one line of spacing before and after the paragraph. In general, use it for only the highest level of your topic. On some browsers, the Heading 1 style can be very overwhelming, so use it sparingly.
Heading 2	18 pt boldface, left-aligned, one line of spacing before and after the paragraph. I usually use Heading 2 as my main heading, because it's not as large as the Heading 1 font.
Heading 3	14 pt boldface, left-aligned, one line of space before and after the paragraph.
Heading 4	12 pt boldface, left-aligned, one line of space before and after the paragraph. A good "subhead" style choice.
Heading 5	10 pt boldface, left-aligned, one line of space before and after the paragraph. This heading style is actually smaller than Normal text.
Heading 6	8 pt boldface, one line of space before and after the paragraph. Heading 6 is tiny on-screen, which makes it ideal for headers, footers, legal mumbojumbo, and "the fine print."

TIP You learned last night how to assign a style, remember? Click somewhere in the paragraph you want to change, then pick a style from the Style drop-down list.

NOTE The default font for most browsers is Times New Roman. The font and sizes may vary depending on the visitor's browser.

In addition to Normal, you may occasionally use other styles, such as Bulleted List, but you'll usually use Normal and Headings 1-6. FrontPage also allows you to create new paragraph styles using the techniques you'll learn this morning, but always keep in mind that older browsers may not support them. Anything the browser can't interpret will default back to Normal style, and your Web page won't look like the one you designed.

That doesn't mean don't use them, just be aware. It's difficult to judge how many people out there are using out-of-date browsers, but it's more than you think. (What's more, even newer versions of Netscape Navigator don't support some Microsoft Internet Explorer features and vice versa.) Consider your audience; are they computer junkies or regular Joes? The junkie most definitely has the latest and greatest browser, and will be impressed with well-designed sites. Joe just wants the information, and probably doesn't care or even realize that he's using a four-year-old browser.

Formatting Text

The limitations of early browsers have not stopped the rest of the world from seeing just how creative they can be with their Web sites. Commercial sites especially are constantly redefining the standards for a cool Web site. So how do you get beyond 12-point black Times New Roman? Read on.

I'm more of a *sans serif* kind of person, so I want to change the main headings of the Jasper Ink Web site to a nice clean san serif font. I'm not sure which one yet, but I'll let FrontPage help me decide. (You can read more about sans serif fonts in the Sidebar at the end of this section.)

1. Select the text you want to change. If you're changing an entire paragraph, click in the left margin next to the paragraph to quickly select it. Otherwise, select the desired words.

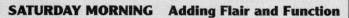

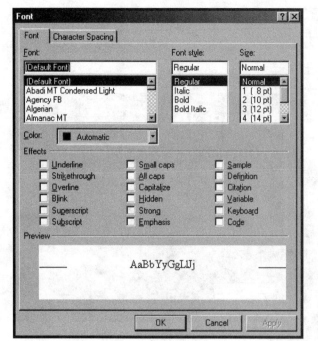

Figure 2.17

Déjà vu? This dialog box looks similar to the Font dialog box in Word.

2. Select Format, Font to open the Font dialog box. This dialog box, shown in Figure 2.17, looks much like the Font dialog box in Microsoft Word, but the available options differ.

3. Select a font in the Font list. Notice in the Preview area that FrontPage gives you a sample of your selection. If you're not sure what a font looks like, that's a big help. After taking a peek at several, I'm choosing Arial Rounded MT Bold. Choose whatever you like—but you might not have that font.

4. Select a Font Style. Some fonts look better in bold, and sometimes italic makes them hard to read. Again, the Preview area is a good marker.

5. The Font Size list includes available sizes 1-7. Size 1 is the smallest (8 point), 7 is the largest (36 point). For reference, Heading 1 is size 6 and Normal style is size 3.

6. Pick a color for your text by clicking the down arrow next to the Color box and selecting a color from the color palette. When choosing a

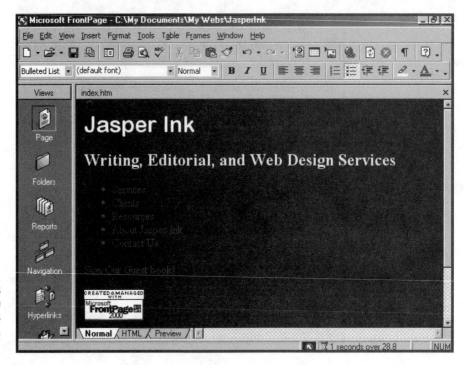

Figure 2.18

High-contrast colors
are much easier to
read onscreen.

font color, keep in mind your background color. Blue text on a black background will be nearly impossible to read no matter how good your monitor is (see Figure 2.18). Stick with high-contrast colors.

7. Choose from a variety of effects. Some you'll recognize, others are holdovers from early HTML days. (Emphasis, for example, is the same thing as Italic.) When applying effects, remember that a little goes a long way. Especially Blink, which makes your text blink off and on in Netscape Navigator.

8. When you're satisfied with your choices, click OK to close the dialog box. Your page is updated to reflect the changes.

Formatting Paragraphs

In addition to the look of the text, you can also control the spacing around it. There's no space between the lines of the bulleted list on my Jasper Ink

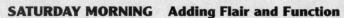

PLAIN OR FANCY, STRAIGHT OR CURLY?

A *sans serif* font style has flat, plain edges rather than fancy tips or flourishes. Sans serif fonts are great for headings, but text-heavy pages in a sans serif font can be more difficult to read than those set in a serif font. Arial is a common sans serif font you've probably used before. Our dear old friend Times New Roman is a serif font.

It's easiest to see the difference when you compare them one-on-one.

This is Arial (sans serif).

Notice the perfectly straight T, I, and i.

This is Times New Roman (serif).

Notice the little points on each end of the T, n, and s. These are the serifs. Thus, sans serif is French for "without little fancy points" (or something like that).

---

page, but I think there should be. (The last line is fine, however, so I won't select it.)

1. Select the paragraph(s) you want to change.

2. Select Format, Paragraph to open the Paragraph dialog box, as shown in Figure 2.19.

3. Again, this dialog box resembles its cousin in Word. In the Alignment drop-down list, you can change from the default left-aligned to right, centered, or justified.

4. To change the indentation of a paragraph, adjust the settings in Before text (to add space to the left) and After text (to add space to the right). To indent only the first line of a paragraph, adjust the number in the Indent first line box.

5. To add or remove space before or after a paragraph, between words, or between lines, adjust the appropriate values in the Spacing area.

6. Click OK when you're finished to close the dialog box and see the changes (see Figure 2.20).

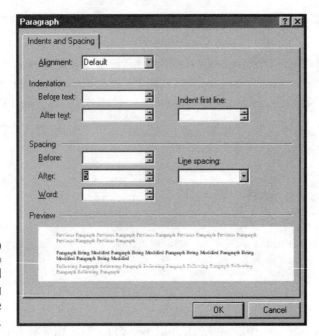

Figure 2.19

Change the line and
paragraph spacing
if you don't like the
default settings.

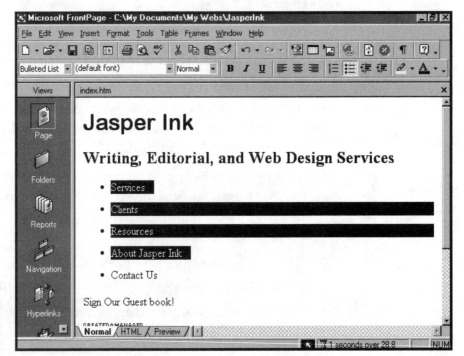

Figure 2.20

A little space
between paragraphs
never hurts.

Applying Borders and Shading

You can apply borders to a line of text, too. In addition to your standard black line, you can be a little more creative. For example, you can use borders to quickly create the illusion of a button onscreen. It's the lazy way out, but it works!

1. Select the paragraph(s) you want to change.

2. Select Format, Borders and Shading to open the Borders and Shading dialog box, as shown in Figure 2.21.

3. Under Setting, select None to remove an existing border, Box to add the border to all four sides, or Custom to select three or less sides. If you select Custom, click the border buttons in the Preview area to choose the sides you want.

4. Select a Style. To make a button, select Inset or Outset. FrontPage will apply a three-dimensional beveled border.

5. Padding refers to the amount of space between the border and the text. Adjust these settings as you see fit.

Figure 2.21

Borders and Shading can enhance your site as long as you don't overuse them.

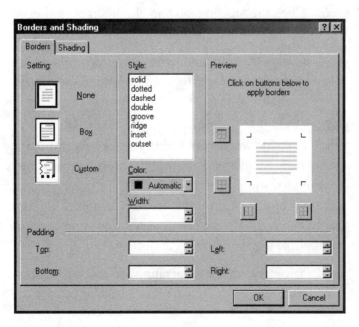

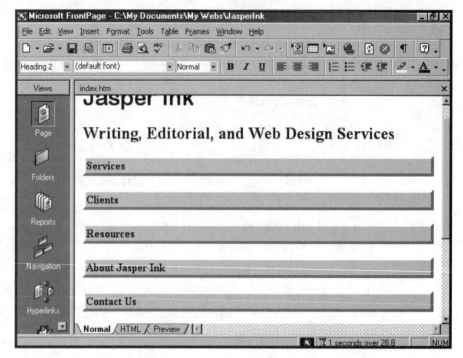

Figure 2.22

Voilà! Instant push button. Now just increase the right-side indent to make the button shorter and add hyperlinks.

6. Click the Shading tab and choose background and foreground colors for your paragraph shading. For the button effect, try a nice gray.

7. Click OK when you've got it the way you want it. The dialog box will close and FrontPage will show you the changes (see Figure 2.22).

Saving Time with the Format Painter

What happens when you decide you like the formatting you just did to one paragraph and want to apply the same formatting to others? Do you have to go through that whole process for every paragraph? Of course not! Take a shortcut and use the Format Painter. The Format Painter copies multiple text and paragraph formats from one selection and applies it to another. To use the Format Painter, just point and click:

1. Select the text or paragraph with the formatting you want to copy.

Format Painter

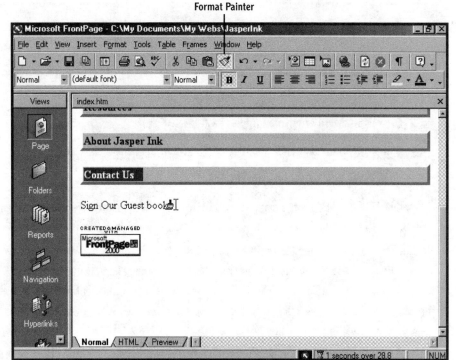

Figure 2.23

The Format Painter copies formatting from one place to another.

2. Click the Format Painter button once to turn it on (see Figure 2.23).

3. Select the text or paragraph to apply the formatting to. The Format Painter will apply the formatting as instructed and turn itself off.

4. To copy the formatting from one selection to several other selections (such as every other paragraph), select the text to copy, then double-click the Format Painter button. This action tells FrontPage to keep applying the formatting wherever you click until you say stop.

5. To say stop, click the Format Painter button again or press Esc.

Easy, huh? You don't know how much time that little tool saves me. Oh, and did you know it's also available in Word, Excel, and the other Office 2000 applications?

WHAT IS DYNAMIC HTML?

Dynamic HTML (DHTML) gives you the ability to add a bit of animation to your text. If you're familiar with PowerPoint, you've probably used transition effects for your presentations. Same idea.

By applying DHTML to a paragraph, you can apply a variety of effects (see Figure 2.24), such as:

- Drop in one word of the paragraph at a time

- Spin or fly in the text until it settles into place on the page

- Change the font color when you click on or point to a paragraph

Dynamic HTML is a Microsoft enhancement to HTML 4.0. It may not work with any version of Internet Explorer or Netscape Navigator older than version 4.0. Results in other browsers may be unpredictable.

If you don't want to be tempted to play with DHTML, leave it disabled and FrontPage won't even make you think about it. To disable DHTML in FrontPage, select Tools, Page Options, then click the Compatibility tab. Clear the Dynamic HTML check box to disable the use of this feature (see Figure 2.25). Enable it again by selecting the check box. Note that you can control the use of a variety of other "compatibility-sensitive" features from this dialog box as well.

To add DHTML effects to a particular page, open the Format menu and select Dynamic HTML Effects. Once enabled, the DHTML Effects toolbar will appear. Select the text and choose your effects from the toolbar. The options are self-explanatory. On Page Load means the effect will occur when the page first opens in the browser. On Mouse over means the effect will occur when the user points to the text with the mouse. You get the idea.

You can experiment on your own with the various options available. Just remember Lisa's rule of design—keep it simple. Lots of special effects can junk up your page, confuse the reader, and sometimes even flake out the browser. It also increases the "overhead" of your page, making it take longer to load in a user's browser (the number one way to lose their interest quickly).

You can apply DHTML to the basic HTML styles Headings 1-6 and Normal. It doesn't work on bulleted lists, for example.

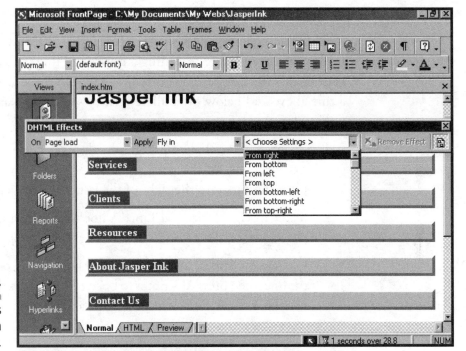

Figure 2.24

Dynamic HTML lets you add animation effects to text.

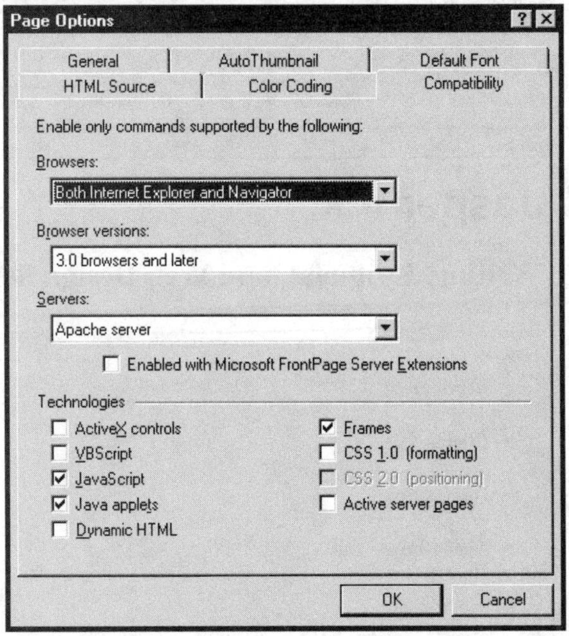

Figure 2.25

If you turn off DHTML, FrontPage won't let you select those options. If you're designing for an audience that might not have current browsers, this is a good idea.

Adding a Horizontal Line

Visual dividing lines help keep your page organized and guide the reader to your points of interest. Adding a horizontal line (also called a rule) to your page is the quickest means to that end. On the sample page, I'll add a rule above and below my bulleted list to set it off visually. Feel free to follow along.

1. To insert a line above a paragraph, place the cursor to the left of the first character in the paragraph. To place it below the paragraph, place the cursor to the right of the last character.

2. Select Insert, Horizontal Line. A line that spans the width of your page appears where you indicated, as shown in Figure 2.26.

3. Change the appearance of a line by changing its properties. Select the line, then press Alt+Enter to open its Properties dialog box. Here you can set the line's width, height, alignment, and color to your

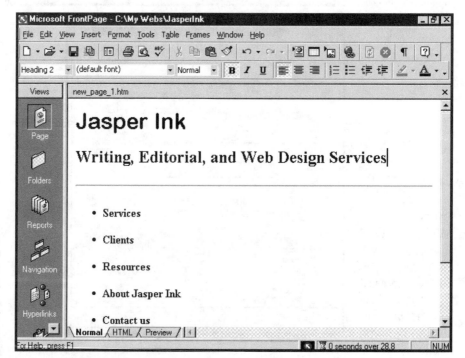

Figure 2.26

A horizontal line gives a visual break to your page, making it easier for visitors to focus on one area at a time.

WHERE TO FIND WEB ART

You can also use graphics as horizontal lines. Instead of inserting a line, insert the graphic as you did in Friday night's session. You can find artwork appropriate for lines and borders in the Office 2000 Clip Gallery or on hundreds of Web sites that give away Web art images. Here are a couple of good image sites to start with.

FIND IT ON ▶
THE WEB

✿ **www.cpsweb.com/cliphome.htm**

✿ **www.clipartconnection.com**

✿ **www.caboodles.com**

If you don't find what you like here, try searching the Internet from Yahoo! or your favorite search engine.

Also, if you decide to use a theme for your Web site (coming up later this morning), FrontPage will automatically use a graphic line that coordinates with your web's overall look.

liking. You don't get a Preview area in this dialog box, so you might have to experiment a little to determine the best settings.

Adding Colors and Backgrounds

Even with colored text and graphics, your page still might seem like it has too much white space. Unless white is what you want (which is just fine for some designs), the background of your Web pages should be just as attractive as the text and images. As you might suspect by now, it's an easy thing to do.

Adding a Solid Color Background

A solid-color background is crisp and simple, and it doesn't add a lot of download time to a page. If you want to add a colored background, follow these steps:

1. Open the page with the background you want to change.

2. Right-click any blank space on the page (not on text or a graphic) to open the shortcut menu.

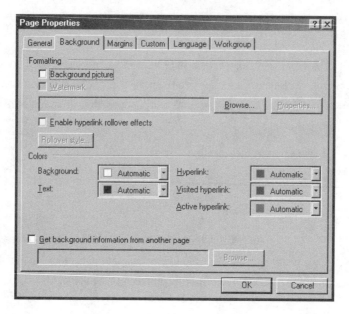

Figure 2.27

Apply a solid color background to keep your page less cluttered.

3. Click Page Properties. The dialog box contains several tabs of options and controls for your page. Click the Background tab to bring it to the front (see Figure 2.27).

4. Select a color from the Background color palette, which you'll find in the Colors section of the dialog box.

5. Next select a color for the text from the Text color palette. Remember the discussion about legibility and color contrast—make sure your color choices enhance your Web page, not detract from it.

6. Click OK to close the dialog box and see your changes, as shown in Figure 2.28.

Adding a Pattern or Graphical Background

Sometimes a nice subtle image or pattern in the background is more appropriate for your design. If that's the effect you're looking for, follow these steps:

1. Open the page with the background you want to change.

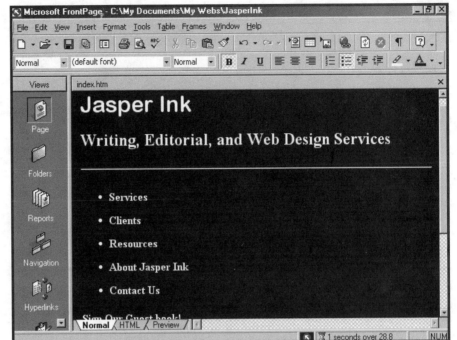

Figure 2.28

White text on a black background has a rather dramatic effect.

2. Right-click any blank space on the page (not on text or a graphic) to open the shortcut menu.

3. Select Page Properties. The dialog box contains several options and controls for your page. Click the Background tab to bring it to the front.

4. You can choose to add a file from your computer, from the Clip Art Gallery, or from a Web address. Try adding some clip art.

5. Select Browse, Clip Art to open the Clip Art Gallery. Type **web background** in the Search for clips box and press Enter. The Clip Gallery presents you with a number of lovely pictures from which to choose (see Figure 2.29).

6. Right-click the picture you want (always a tough decision, there are so many good ones) and select Insert from the shortcut menu. Remember the subtlety factor—busy backgrounds make your text hard

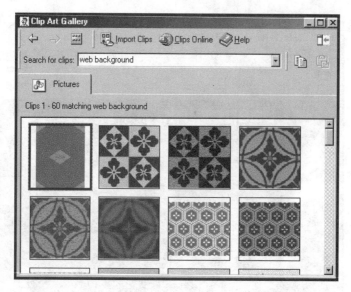

Figure 2.29

Microsoft includes quite a few Web images in the Clip Art Gallery; you might not need to look any further.

to read, so stick with something "quiet." FrontPage enters the path and file name in the edit box.

7. FrontPage offers a couple of interesting options for your background:

- ❖ **Watermark**. When Watermark is selected, your background picture or pattern does not scroll up and down with the text, it remains fixed. Try viewing your background both ways in the Preview window to understand the significance of this effect. The side-by-side examples in Figure 2.30 demonstrate this effect.

- ❖ **Hyperlink rollover**. You can use a little "mini-DHTML" effect on your page by telling FrontPage to Enable Hyperlink rollover. In English, this means that when the user points to a hyperlink, the link's color, font, or size change (see Figure 2.31). The text returns to normal when you move the pointer. Select Rollover Style to choose the rollover font effects.

8. Click OK to apply the changes and close the dialog box.

9. To see the changes to your page and to view the effects onscreen, preview the page in your browser by clicking the Preview in Browser button.

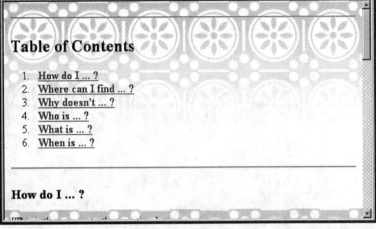

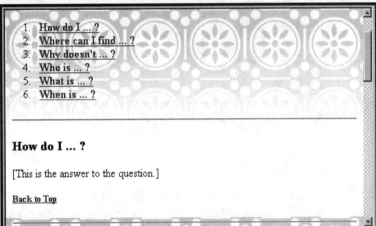

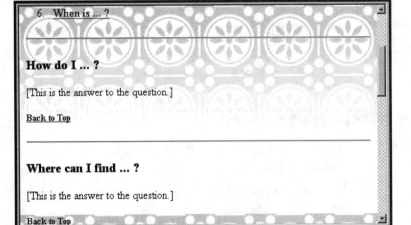

Figure 2.30

A watermark background doesn't scroll, it stays in one place while your text and images move up and down in the browser.

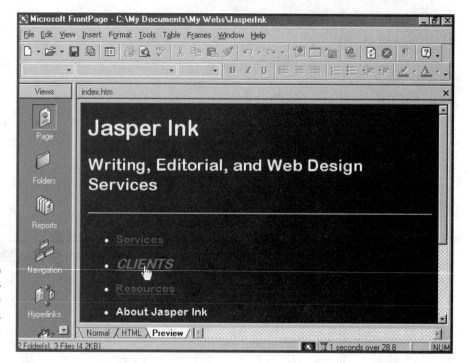

Figure 2.31

Hyperlink rollovers
are an easy way to
liven up the user's
interactivity with
your Web site.

 NOTE To use the same background settings on all of your pages, select Get Background Information From Another Page. Enter the file and path name for the page you want to match. FrontPage will mimic all the settings in this dialog box for each page you set. This is an easy way to keep a consistent look from page to page. What's more, if you make changes to the "base" page's background properties, those changes are carried over to the other pages as well.

Take a Break!

You've been sitting for a while now, so you're probably ready to take a quick break. Take the dog for a walk, give your sweetie a peck on the cheek, or check on the kids. Get some more coffee, too. When you're ready to get back to it, I'll be right here.

Before you break for lunch, you'll spend some time working with bulleted and numbered lists, then add some real splash to your Web site by applying a theme that ties together all your headings, text, and backgrounds with one overall look. Go on, I'll wait...

All About Lists

Lists can make a text-heavy page easier to navigate, and help your visitors quickly identify areas on your Web site that might be of interest to them. Multi-level lists can work as a content outline for your readers. When you use lists as a pseudo table of contents, with hyperlinks attached to each list item, your visitor can quickly scan a list and go to the area they want to see. In general, lists also help to break up a page visually and give your site more "curb appeal."

Several list styles are available in FrontPage, but the ones you're most likely to use are bullets and numbers. You created a simple bulleted list on your main page last night by selecting the paragraphs and clicking the Bullets button, but that's just the beginning of what you can do with them.

Bulleted Lists and Collapsible Outlines

Try something a little more complex since you already did a simple bulleted list. First, you'll need to enter some text for your list. Include both main list items and sub-level items. I've included Writing, Editing, and Web Design as topics under my main item called Services, and two subheadings under Writing.

I want to create a three-level bulleted list, with each level set off by a different bullet style. I also want users to see only the top-level items when the page loads, and let them click on a bullet item to expand the list. Sound tricky? Try it yourself:

1. In Normal view, select the entire list and click once on the Bullet button on the toolbar. All the selected items will be bulleted identically.

2. Select the second- and third-level items and click the Increase Indent button twice. The selected items will indent to the next level and show a new bullet style (see Figure 2.32).

Increase Indent button ————

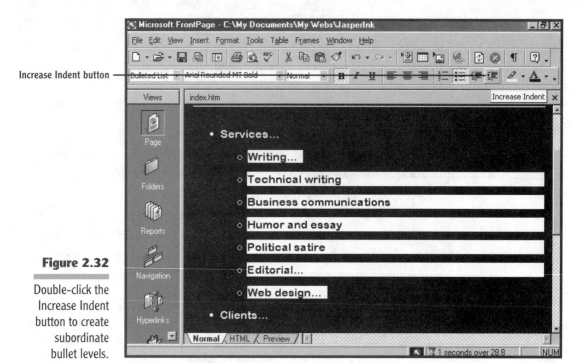

Figure 2.32

Double-click the
Increase Indent
button to create
subordinate
bullet levels.

3. Repeat step 2 on just the third-level list items to create the third level of bullets.

4. To enable the expand-on-click feature, select the entire list again. Right-click the selection and select List Properties. The List Properties dialog box will appear with the Plain Bullets tab showing.

5. Select the option Enable Collapsible Outlines and the option that goes with it, Initially Collapsed, then click OK to close the dialog box.

6. Switch to Preview and check out your list. Click the main heading that you know has sublevels to reveal the second-level bullets, and then do the same for the third level. Your results will look something like Figure 2.33.

Pretty slick! You can see now how collapsible lists can come in handy. Incorporate some graphic bullets, hyperlinks, bookmarks, and forward and back buttons, and you have a nice navigational tool for your visitors. (Don't worry; by the end of the weekend, you'll know how to do all that.)

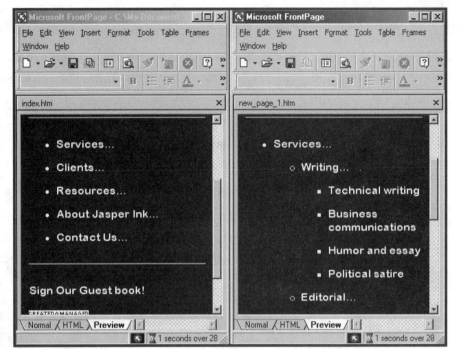

Figure 2.33

Click a list item to expand it and reveal subordinate levels.

NOTE You can even use collapsible outlines to expand a list to something more detailed, like a descriptive paragraph of text or a table of numbers. Use the same formatting steps above, handling the table or text as just another list item. One idea where this would be handy would be an online product catalog. Click once to see a description of the item, click again to see the price, available sizes and colors, and shipping details. You get the picture.

Numbered Lists

A numbered list can be helpful in a variety of situations. You can use them to give users step-by-step instructions; give a visual cue for the number of items in a lengthy list; or give a structured multilevel outline format to legal documentation posted online.

To create a quick bulleted list, just select the paragraphs you want to number and click the Numbering button on the toolbar.

USING PICTURES AS BULLETS

A popular design technique is to replace regular bullets with small graphics or pictures. This adds some visual interest to your page and gives you a little more opportunity for artistic expression.

The procedure for creating graphic bullets starts with the same six steps above. Once you've got that accomplished, delve deeper into the List Properties dialog box using these steps:

1. In Normal view, right-click a top-level bullet item.

2. Right-click the selection and select List Properties from the shortcut menu.

3. Click the Picture Bullets tab to bring it to the front.

4. Select Specify Picture to enable the feature and type the picture's path and file name in the text box (or use Browse to import a file from your computer, the Clip Art Gallery, or the Internet).

5. Click OK. The graphic is applied to all bulleted items at that level (see Figure 2.34).

6. Repeat steps 1-5 for each level of your list.

TIP Keep in mind that most graphic images designed to be used as bullets are very small—usually about 5x5 pixels. If you want to use an image of your own, be sure to resize it before importing. Otherwise, each of your graphic bullets will appear as a full-sized image.

Create a multilevel outline the same way you would a multilevel bulleted list. (You can also use the Collapsible Outline feature for numbered lists.) To customize the numbering system for your list, follow these steps:

1. In Normal view, select the entire list and click once on the Numbering button on the toolbar. All the selected items will be numbered sequentially.

2. Select the second- and third-level items and click the Increase Indent button twice. The selected items will indent to the next level and be numbered sequentially at that level. The top-level numbers will renumber themselves accordingly, as shown in Figure 2.35.

3. Repeat step 2 on just the third-level list items to create the third level of numbering.

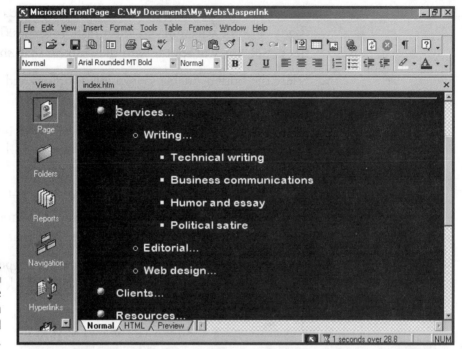

Figure 2.34

Replace those boring bullets with graphics to add visual variety.

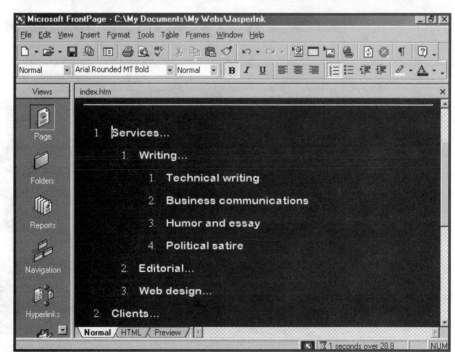

Figure 2.35

Create a multilevel outline using FrontPage's numbered list format.

4. To enable the expand-on-click feature, select the entire list again. Right-click the selection and select List Properties. The List Properties dialog box will appear with the Numbers tab showing.

5. Select the option Enable Collapsible Outlines and the option that goes with it, Initially Collapsed, then click OK to close the dialog box.

6. Switch to Preview and check out your list. Click the main heading that you know has sublevels to reveal the second-level bullets, and then do the same for the third level.

7. To use a different numbering style on a sublevel, right-click a list item at the level you want to reformat and select List Properties. The List Properties dialog box will appear with the Numbers tab showing.

8. Select the numbering style to use for that level (perhaps letters or Roman numerals?), as shown in Figure 2.36. Click OK to close the dialog box.

9. Repeat steps 7 and 8 for each sublevel of your list.

Figure 2.36

Apply a different number style to each list level to create a formal outline.

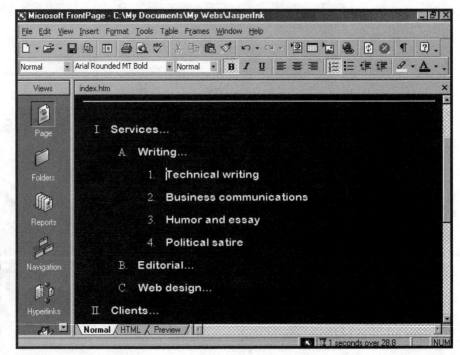

Other Lists

FrontPage also supports some other types of lists, but their usage is rare. In fact, of the three, most browsers only support one.

- **Definition list**. This style is convenient for presenting a list of terms and their definitions. Terms are displayed flush left, the definitions block-intended, as shown in Figure 2.37.

- **Directory list**. Use this style to present a sequence of short terms without bullets or numbering. Most browsers ignore the style. You can create the same effect by selecting the list items and clicking the Increase Indent button.

- **Menu list**. This list presents an unordered list of short entries. You tell me the difference between that and a directory list. I'm stumped. Most browsers also ignore this style, so I guess it doesn't matter.

Figure 2.37

A definition list can come in handy when you have a list of terms and lengthy descriptions that accompany them.

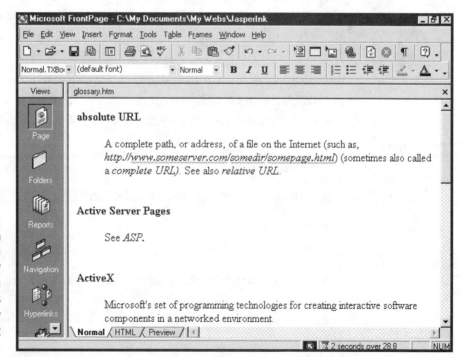

Getting a Cohesive Look with Themes

All these formatting tools are great for a few lines of text or a few Web pages at a time, but it sure is a lot of work to format entire webs one line at a time! Wouldn't it be nice if you could apply a whole battery of formatting at one time—background patterns, bullet styles, even fonts? You can. Apply a theme with a couple of clicks, and presto! It's done.

Applying a Theme

A theme includes a plethora of built-in page and paragraph formats, all tied together in a professionally designed color and graphic scheme. Themes can go a long way in helping you convey your message to visitors. Use a playful theme such as Loose Gesture or Citrus Punch for a festive feel. The Kids theme is perfect for Web sites designed for children, and Chalkboard for a school or classroom page. Automotive would be great for a car collector's Web site (see Figure 2.38).

You can apply themes to an entire Web site or just to individual pages. Mix and match themes depending on each page's content, or use just one for a cohesive look across all pages. By default, each of FrontPage's built-in themes apply formatting to the following items:

- Backgrounds
- Paragraph styles (including colors and fonts)
- Page banners
- Lists
- Navigational buttons (Home, Top, Back, Next, etc.)
- Horizontal lines

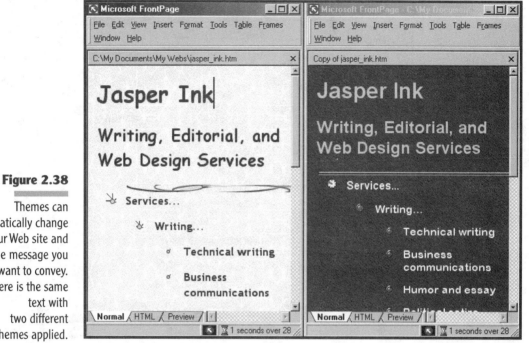

Figure 2.38

Themes can dramatically change your Web site and the message you want to convey. Here is the same text with two different themes applied.

It's truly amazing the difference a theme can make, both in the appearance of your Web site and the time it takes you to design it. To apply a theme, open your web and follow these steps:

1. From Normal view, select Format, Theme. The Themes dialog box will appear with a list of available themes on the left and a large preview area on the right, as shown in Figure 2.39.

TIP   To apply a theme to more than one page but not the entire web, select the desired pages in Folders view, and then open the dialog box.

2. At the top of the dialog box, choose whether you want to apply the theme to All pages or just the Selected page(s).

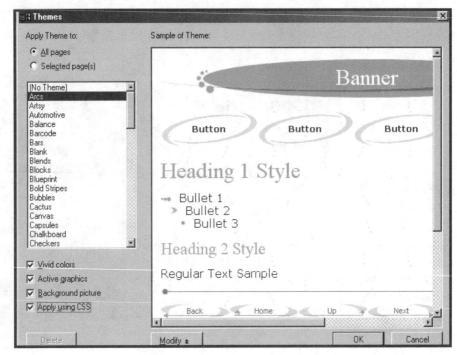

Figure 2.39

Use the preview area to sample various themes until you find one you like.

3. Click on various themes to see the way they look in the preview area. Most of their names give you an idea of the concept. Tabs and Folders has that manila envelope look and feel. Technology uses buttons that look like computer boards. Sweets uses lollipops and candy canes.

4. If you're designing for high-end users who are likely to have up-to-date browsers, check the Vivid Colors and Active Graphics options at lower left. Vivid colors enhances the theme's color scheme by using a higher color mix and greater number of colors. Active graphics replaces plain buttons and navigation bars with animated page elements, such as hover buttons. Remember that not all browsers support these features.

5. After you've made your selections, click OK to apply the theme. Use Preview or click the Preview in Browser button to inspect the impact the new theme has on your web, as shown in Figure 2.40.

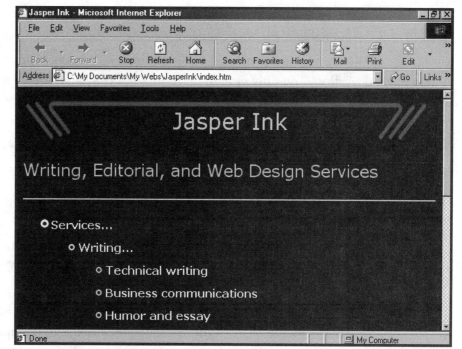

Figure 2.40

Like a well-orchestrated symphony, a theme applies all the right instruments to make beautiful music.

If you don't like the theme you've chosen, follow these same steps to change to a new theme. To completely remove a theme from your site or page, click (No Theme) at the top of the list of themes.

FIND IT ON ▶ THE CD
You'll find a great collection of bonus themes and backgrounds on the CD that accompanies this book. See Appendix F, "What's on the CD-ROM?" for more information.

Modifying a Theme to Your Liking

Sometimes you'll find that a theme is *almost* what you want, but not quite. Fortunately, you don't have to bag the idea altogether. Instead, you can customize the theme and save it with a new name.

For the Jasper Ink site, for example, I started with the Neon theme and modified a few items. I removed the background pattern and just went with a solid black; substituted my own graphics for bullets and navigational buttons, and changed the color of some heading styles.

Modifying a theme takes a little time to figure out, but it can be worth the effort. You only have to do it once to create a personalized theme you can use for all your pages (or all your Web sites, if you have more than one). To customize a theme, follow these steps:

1. Select Format, Theme to open the Themes dialog box.

2. Click the Modify button. FrontPage will reveal three new settings buttons: Colors, Graphics, and Text, as shown in Figure 2.41.

3. Click Colors to apply a different color scheme but keep the theme's graphics intact. You can only apply a new overall color scheme, not customize individual styles. Click OK after you've applied the new scheme.

4. Click Graphics to use different graphics in your theme. Most commonly, you'll want to change the background graphic, but you can

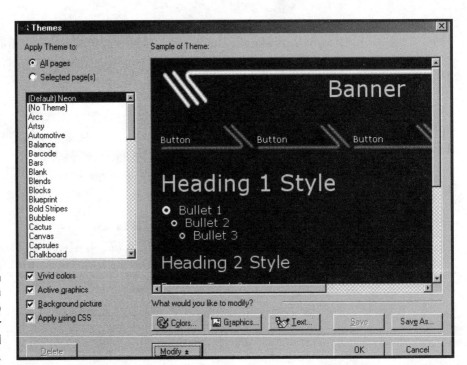

Figure 2.41

You can customize a theme to incorporate your own graphics and color preferences.

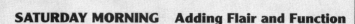

also insert your own button graphics, bullets, and horizontal lines. To change an individual item, select it from the Item drop-down menu, and then enter your changes.

5. Click Text to apply new fonts to your Normal (Body) and Heading styles. Select an item from the Item list and click a new font.

6. When you're happy with the theme as modified, click Save As to give your theme a new name (see Figure 2.42). Type the name of your new theme and click OK. You can't save changes to FrontPage's built-in themes; you can only modify then rename them.

Wrapping Up

Wow! Is it lunchtime already? Just look at all you've accomplished so far today. You created a new web, imported the page you created last night, applied background patterns, fonts and colors, bullets and numbers, and inserted horizontal lines on your pages. You have likely already developed

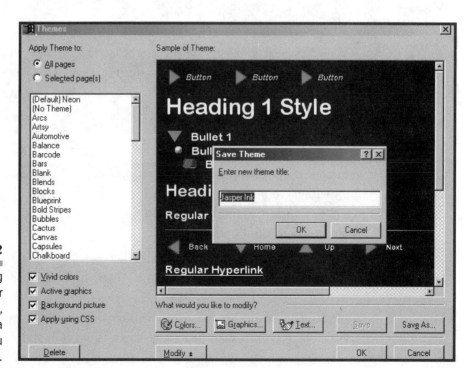

Figure 2.42

Modify an existing theme to your heart's content, then save it with a new name so you can use it again.

STYLE SHEETS & CSS

You've probably heard about a new feature in FrontPage 2000 called cascading style sheets, or CSS for short. A CSS gives you a great deal more control over your Web site's appearance, and creates additional special effects. Each CSS defines styles you can apply to your pages or text items. Use them to create non-standard styles that you can apply to any item in your Web site. Following are just a few of the items you can add to a CSS:

✿ **Font**. Apply attributes such as All Caps or Italic as part of a heading style.

✿ **Paragraph**. Customize the indentation, line spacing, and spacing before or after a paragraph.

✿ **Borders and shading**. Add special effects such as boxes to your text.

✿ **Positioning**. Control attributes like text wrap and layering of graphic elements.

CSS is an up-and-coming power feature of FrontPage 2000 and other Web design tools. Like all things HTML, the World Wide Web Consortium (W3C) governs the technical specifications for cascading style sheets. This organization maintains standards for Web site design. Also, keep in mind that CSS is purely a Microsoft standard, so even the newest version of Netscape Navigator will not display cascading style sheets properly.

FIND IT ON ▶
THE WEB
A comprehensive study of cascading style sheets is beyond the scope of this book. For a thorough discussion and examples of how to implement cascading style sheets for your pages or Web site, the FrontPage 2000 Help system is a great place to start. You can read more about CCS and the W3C at **www.htmlhelp.com/ reference/css/**.

(or at least started on) several of your site's pages. No wonder your stomach's growling! Go now and take a nice leisurely lunch break. If you need to run a few errands, this might be a good time. Maybe peek ahead in the book to see what's coming up later.

Grab a snack and rest for a while, and then you'll move on to what makes the World Wide Web live up to its name—hyperlinks. Links connect your page to other parts of your pages, to other pages within your Web site, and to pages on other sites anywhere on the Internet. It is truly a web of information available to visitors with just a few clicks. See you in an hour or two!

Putting the "Web" in World Wide Web

- ✿ All About Hyperlinks
- ✿ Working with Bookmarks
- ✿ Adding Shared Borders and Navigation Bars
- ✿ Testing Your Work
- ✿ Verifying Links

Before the days of the World Wide Web, Internet users relied on tools such as Gopher and Archie to find the information they needed. There were no cool search engines that spoke to you in plain English, no easy-to-read pages that directed you to the information you wanted to find, and no pretty pictures to entertain you along the way. These old Internet tools were difficult to understand and use, let alone to get results. It's no surprise that the Web has become so popular. It took the phenomenal potential of the Internet out of the hands of the experts and brought it down to a level that the rest of us can understand and utilize.

Hyperlinks are the guts of the Web. In fact, they are the whole *point* of the Web. Rather than digging around like a gopher and not knowing what you'll come up with, hyperlinks let you quickly zoom from one page to another (or from one Web site to another). You can click on what you want to see details about and ignore the rest.

All About Hyperlinks

I don't think I've seen a Web site yet that did not include some kind of hyperlink, except maybe those one-page "billboard" sites. Because hyperlinks are an integral part of the Internet, you need to know how to create, edit, and work with them in detail. In this session, you'll work with three types of hyperlinks:

- ❖ **External links**. Hyperlinks that point to another Web site

- ❖ **Internal links**. Hyperlinks that point to another page in your Web site (Internal links might also include navigation bars and shared borders.)

- ❖ **Bookmarks**. Hyperlinks that point to a specific place or object on a page in your Web site (or sometimes on another Web site)

You'll also learn about image maps and hotspots, multiple hyperlinks that are built into graphic images.

Text-based links are generally referred to as *hypertext*. Any type of hyperlink, whether text or graphic, will point your browser to a different URL or Universal Resource Locator (the Web address or path of a particular Web page or site). As Figure 3.1 illustrates, every Web page has a unique URL, just as every home has a unique street address or phone number.

▼ ▼

Hypertext documents are electronic documents that contain links to other documents, allowing non-sequential viewing of large amounts of information. Users can choose their own path through the material by clicking the link to the topic that interests them. A Web site is a collection of hypertext documents.

▲ ▲

There are two methods for creating hyperlinks. You can create your pages and then add links to the existing pages (within your own web, or create the hyperlink and the new page at the same time. Either method is fine, it just depends on your development style. You'll probably find, in fact, that you do a lot of both.

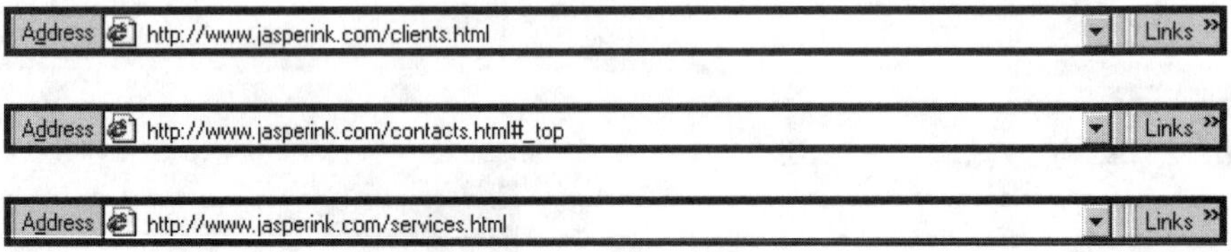

| Address | 🗐 | http://www.jasperink.com/clients.html | ▼ | Links » |

Figure 3.1

| Address | 🗐 | http://www.jasperink.com/contacts.html#_top | ▼ | Links » |

No two Web pages
have the same URL.

| Address | 🗐 | http://www.jasperink.com/services.html | ▼ | Links » |

FIND IT ON ▶
THE WEB
You can download files that contain several examples of all the hyperlinks discussed here at **www.prima-tech.com/frontpage2000** or **www.jasperink.com/frontpage**. You can open these files directly from the site, or import them into a FrontPage web on your hard drive.

Creating Links to Existing Pages

The easiest links to add are those that connect to pages within your own Web site. To create a link to an existing page in your Web site, follow these steps:

1. In Page view, type the text to be used as the link if it doesn't already exist. Then select the text. Whatever you select will appear underlined on your Web page after you create the link.

TIP You can use the literal URL name to identify the link, or something more descriptive and creative. You've probably seen links handled in a variety of ways. For example:

- ○ "Click **here** to download."

- ○ "Download a trial version at **www.microsoft.com**."

- ○ Or, more simply: "**Download now!**"

2. Select the text you just typed (you can select as little or as much of the text as you want), and then right-click to open the shortcut menu (see Figure 3.2).

3. Click Hyperlink to open the Create Hyperlink dialog box.

4. You can create the hyperlink four different ways:

- ○ Use the Look in drop-down list to navigate to an existing page in your Web site, and then click the file you want to link to (see Figure 3.3).

- ○ Click the Folders button to link to a page currently stored on your hard drive or network but not yet in your Web folder. Navigate to the file location and click the file you want to link to.

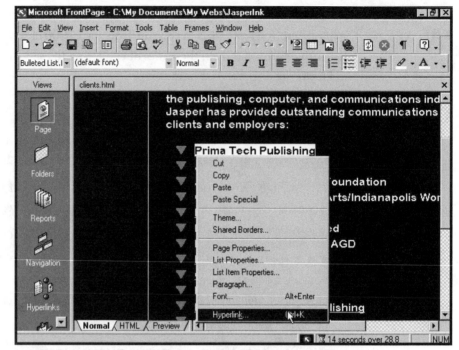

Figure 3.2

Any text or object
can become a link
by creating a
hyperlink.

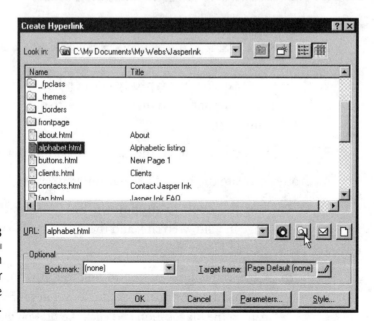

Figure 3.3

You can link to an
existing page or
create a new page
on the fly.

NOTE If you link to a file you have not yet imported, FrontPage will prompt you to import the file the next time you save your work.

      ✿ Click the Web Browser button to link to a page on the Web. When your browser opens, navigate to the Web address, and then close the browser.

TIP If you're linking to the main home page of a Web site, you don't need to enter a specific page or file name. Just type **www.sitename.com** and leave it at that. As you learned this morning, most browsers automatically look for the default or index file if none is specified.

      ✿ Type the URL or the path and file name in the URL text box.

5. When the address for the link appears in the URL text box, make sure it is complete, as shown in Figure 3.4. External links to other Web pages must begin with **http://** followed by the site's URL (such as **www.microsoft.com**), followed by any subdirectories or specific file names. The complete URL will look something like this: **http://www.microsoft.com/frontpage/sample.html**

NOTE Internal links use a normal path name like the ones you've seen in DOS or Windows Explorer. If the file is in a different directory, be sure the full path name is given:

images/logo.jpg or **../about.html**

You don't need the file:///c: etc. garbage that might appear unless you are linking to a file stored on your hard drive or network. These files will only be accessible if your visitor also has access to your hard drive or network—not likely.

6. Click OK. The dialog box will close.

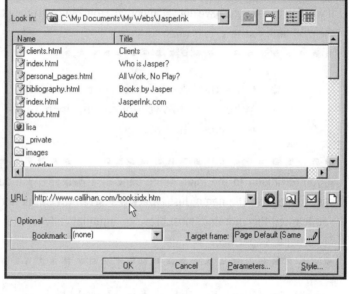

Figure 3.4

Do you just want to go to the site's home page, or a different page within the Web site?

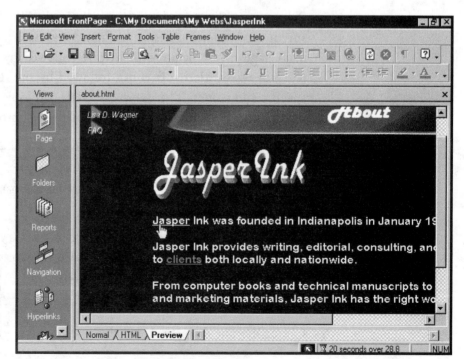

Figure 3.5

Links should be easy to distinguish from other elements on your page.

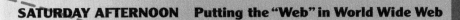

Presto! You can tell that the link was created because the text is now under-lined and colored blue (unless your theme or template uses a different color for links. Mine leaves them white, but underlines them). Figure 3.5 shows the results.

FIND IT ON ▶
THE CD

If you're linking to a file the user can download, be sure the file is compressed as small as possible so the download does not take any longer than necessary. The CD that accompanies this book includes a copy of WinZip, the popular file compression utility from Nico Mak Computing, Inc. See Appendix F, "What's on the CD-ROM?" for more information.

Creating Links to New Pages

If you don't want to wait until you have all your pages done to create some hyperlinks, you can create the link and ask FrontPage to remind you to add the necessary information later. (The first few steps are the same.)

1. In Page view, type the text to be used as the link.

2. Select the text, and then right-click to open the shortcut menu.

3. Select Hyperlink to open the Create Hyperlink dialog box.

4. Click the New button on the far right. FrontPage will open the New dialog box and ask you to select a template, as shown in Figure 3.6. Select the one you want to use.

5. In the Options area, select Just add Web task to tell FrontPage you want to create an item for the task list.

6. Navigate to the appropriate folder, and then click Save. FrontPage creates the hyperlink on your existing page and adds a task to the Task list.

That's it! Adding your collection of linkage to the millions has never been easier.

You'll work through some "to-do" tasks on Sunday afternoon, but you can go back to that task anytime. Just click the Tasks view, double-click the

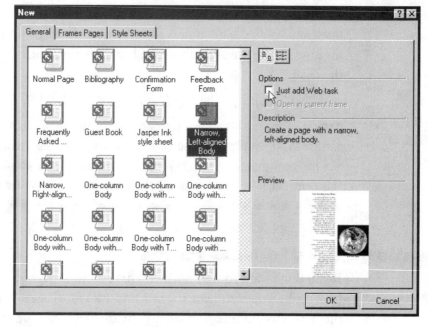

Figure 3.6

FrontPage will let you link to a page that doesn't exist yet, as long as you remember to create it later.

task on the list, and click Start Task to get rolling (see Figure 3.7). FrontPage will open a new page using the template you requested and the file name you entered. You can then edit the page as you would any other.

Figure 3.7

A Webmaster's work is never done.

TIP ■ You can attach a hyperlink to any selectable object, not just text: an image, a table—virtually anything on a page the user can point to or click on except background images. ■

Creating E-mail Links

In addition to Web page links, you can create links that enable the visitor to contact you via e-mail. When clicked, a *mailto:* hyperlink opens a blank e-mail message in your visitor's e-mail software. The message will already be addressed to you. All they have to do is type the message and click Send. To create an e-mail link, follow these steps:

1. In Page view, type the text to be used as the link.

2. Select the text, and then right-click to open the shortcut menu.

3. Select Hyperlink to open the Create Hyperlink dialog box.

4. Click the E-mail link button. The Create E-mail Hyperlink dialog box will open (see Figure 3.8).

5. Type the e-mail address and click OK. The URL will appear as:

   mailto:jasper@jasperink.com

6. Click OK to close the dialog box. Your link will be added to the page, just like that.

TIP ■ You can add a subject line to the message link (see Figure 3.9) by adding the "syntax":

?subject=*subject*

to the edit box, so the link resembles:

mailto:jasper@jasperink.com?subject=Great book! ■

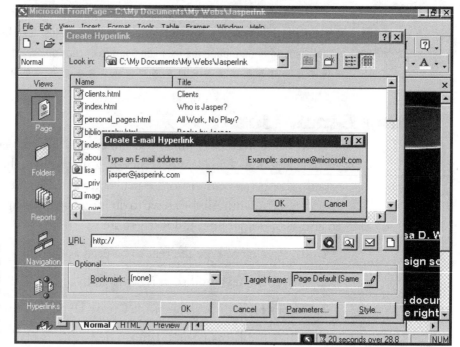

Figure 3.8

A mailto: hyperlink opens a new message in your visitor's e-mail program.

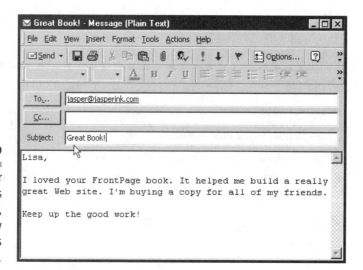

Figure 3.9

Unless the sender manually edits the subject line, you'll automatically know where this message originated.

ALIASES: E-MAIL *INCOGNITO*

It's always a good idea to give your visitors a way to get in touch with you, especially if you're running a business Web site. If you're worried about giving out your private e-mail address, ask your WPP if they offer free e-mail *aliases*.

▼▼▼▼▼▼▼▼▼▼▼▼▼▼▼▼▼▼▼▼▼▼▼▼▼▼▼▼▼▼▼▼▼▼▼▼▼▼

BUZZ WORD   An *alias* is an e-mail address that has no Inbox of its own, but instead works as a forwarding address. A common alias you'll see on the Internet is:

webmaster@domain.com.

▲▲▲▲▲▲▲▲▲▲▲▲▲▲▲▲▲▲▲▲▲▲▲▲▲▲▲▲▲▲▲▲▲▲▲▲▲▲

Most often, the Webmaster address actually points to the e-mail address of the person who is in charge of managing the Web site. At Jasper Ink, for example, mail sent to webmaster@jasperink.com is actually delivered to jasper@jasperink.com. (That's me.)

You can sign up for free e-mail aliases from a number of online services as well. Here's just a few to check out:

FIND IT ON ▶ THE WEB
   www.hotmail.com

   www.yahoo.com

   www.iname.com

I always think of an e-mail alias as a post office box number. Your street address may change, but your PO box doesn't. You can move anywhere and you'll still get your mail (as long as you go pick it up, of course). If I change my e-mail address, the alias webmaster@jasperink.com can be redirected to whatever my new e-mail address might be.

Working with Bookmarks

The hyperlinks you worked with a few minutes ago take you from page to page and Web site to Web site. If you want to move to a specific location within the Web site, you'll need to use a bookmark. *Bookmarks* are URLs that direct the user to an exact location on a page. Bookmarks help you move quickly to the information you're looking for without wading through irrelevant material. Like other hyperlinks, a bookmark takes two to tango—the link to the bookmark, and the bookmark tag itself.

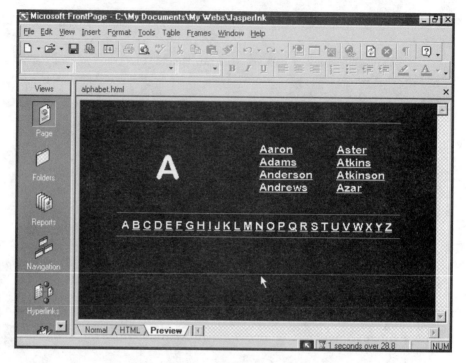

Figure 3.10

Use bookmarks to save your visitors time when perusing your Web site.

A typical use of bookmarks is to create alphabetical "tabs" at the top of a page (see Figure 3.10). Want to see something listed under M? You could scroll halfway down a very, very long page, or you could click once on the M bookmark and be there instantly.

Defining a Bookmark

Before you can create a link to a bookmark, you must have a bookmark to link to, *n'est ce pas?* To define a bookmark on a page, follow these steps:

1. In Page view, select the text or object that you want to link. You can select an entire line, just a word, or even a graphic. Headings and subheadings, for example, are usually likely candidates for bookmarking.

2. Select Insert, Bookmark. The Bookmark dialog box will open (see Figure 3.11).

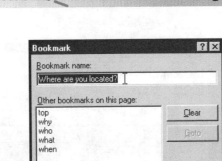

Figure 3.11

FrontPage will suggest a name for the bookmark.

3. Give your bookmark a brief but meaningful name. Click OK to close the dialog box and create the bookmark.

TIP Bookmarks are invisible to the reader, therefore they don't have to make sense to a reader, but they should make sense to you. If you have many bookmarks on a page, it might become difficult to remember what's what. FrontPage will suggest your entire selection as the name. Use it if you want.

In Page view, your bookmark will appear as a dotted underline (see Figure 3.12). In Preview or in the browser, however, you won't see them.

TIP If you take a peek at the HTML code behind the link, you'll see something like this:

```
<a name="help">How can we help you?</a>
```

The **<a name="x">** tag is what to look for when you're trying to decipher the bookmarks on someone else's pages.

Linking to a Bookmark

You can link to a bookmark from any spot on any Web page. It is just another URL, after all. Ready to try it? It's just like creating any other hyperlink.

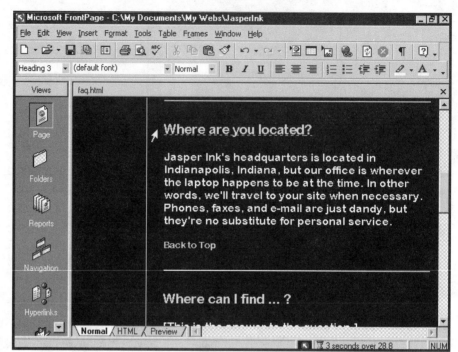

Figure 3.12

You can see the
bookmark, but
visitors can't.

1. In Page view, type or select the text or object that will serve as the link.

2. Right-click on your selection and choose Hyperlink from the short-cut menu.

3. Select the file that contains the bookmark just as you did in "Creating Links to Existing Pages".

4. When the URL text box contains a file name that includes bookmarks, you can see them by selecting the Bookmark drop-down arrow (see Figure 3.13). Select the bookmark you want to target. FrontPage will add a # plus the name of the bookmark to the URL text box, so you end up with:

   ```
   guestbook.html#help
   ```

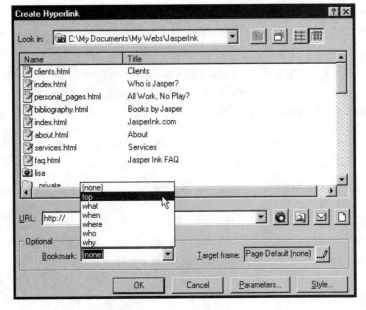

Figure 3.13

You can have a number of bookmarks on the same page.

5. Click OK to close the dialog box. The new bookmark link will look like any other hyperlink, underlined and blue (by default, anyway).

TIP There are a few automatic bookmark codes built into HTML. For example, selecting a bookmark coded **#top** will automatically take you to the top of the current page, even if there's no bookmark defined there. This is handy when you have a long page. You can give the reader a ride "Back to Top" and save them the trouble of scrolling.

In this evening's session, you'll learn about tables. Using a table to organize and align a lot of bookmarks or links is an easy way to keep big lists neat and tidy. The example you saw in Figure 3.10 was created with a table and a set of bookmarks.

GRAPHIC LINKS AND IMAGE MAPS

You've seen them: those big flashy graphics that splash across your browser when you land on a particular Web site. There is no text, just a picture. If you were confused at first, you probably quickly realized that you could click on the image itself and go somewhere. Is that a hyperlink? Yes, of course it is. It's just well disguised as a *hotspot* on an *image map*.

▼ ▼

A *hotspot* is a hyperlink that is attached to a graphic on a Web page.

An *image map* is a graphic that has one or more hotspots.

▲ ▲

Although they are much easier to make than they used to be, you still need special software to work on image maps. The details of creating elaborate image maps are beyond the scope of this book. On the other hand, FrontPage gives you some limited hotspot capabilities, and that may be all you ever need. To create a hotspot on a graphic, follow these steps:

1. In Page view, select the graphic you want to use. The Drawing toolbar will open.

2. Click the Hotspot button that corresponds to the shape you want for the hotspot: rectangular, circular, or polygon shaped (see Figure 3.14).

3. Draw the shape on the graphic where you want the hotspot to be present. For polygons, click where you want the polygon to start, click on the location for each corner of the polygon, and then double-click to complete the drawing. When the shape is complete, the Create Hyperlink dialog box will open, as shown in Figure 3.15.

4. Use the usual navigation methods to locate and enter the URL of the link, including any bookmarks if appropriate.

5. Click OK to close the dialog box and create the hotspot.

To test your hotspot, switch to Preview view and point to the hotspot. The pointer will change to a pointing finger, indicating the presence of a link (see Figure 3.16). Click the link to make sure it operates as intended.

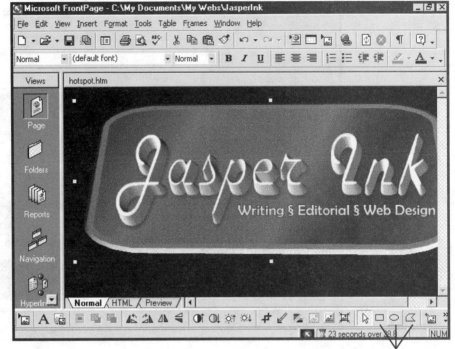

Hotspot tools

Figure 3.14

You can create simple hotspots for your image files.

Figure 3.15

You can have a number of bookmarks on the same page.

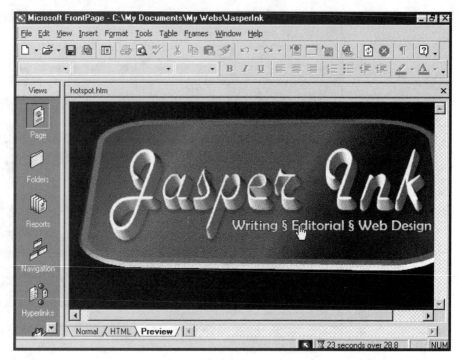

Figure 3.16

Click the hotspot to go to the link described, just as you would a text link.

Take a Break!

Well, that was fun. Ready for a stretch? Take a stroll out to the mailbox—maybe there's a letter from an old friend (or maybe just Ed McMahon) waiting to be read. When you come back, you'll wrap up the daylight hours with some more advanced kinds of links: shared borders and navigation bars. These features help you add an easy-to-follow mapping system to your Web site so that your visitors don't get lost, and so that they can find everything easily. See ya in a few! (Don't eat too many of those cookies; it's almost time for dinner.)

Adding Shared Borders and Navigation Bars

A relatively recent development in Web design is the use of *shared borders*. Each page's shared border is slightly different in content, but maintains a very similar look and feel.

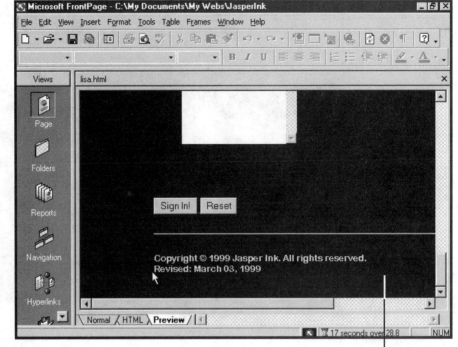

Figure 3.17

Use shared borders for information that is the same on every page. If it changes, you only have to edit one page instead of all of them.

shared border

▼ ▼

A *shared border* is an area down or across the edge of a page that is reserved for boilerplate information common to all or some of the pages in a Web site.

▲ ▲

On these particular borders, you see a group of buttons (or hyperlinks). The buttons are clearly links to other pages in the Web site, all nicely listed and grouped together for easy access. Although they work similarly, there's no clear dividing line on a shared border as often as there is in a framed Web site (and no clumsy invisible pages to keep track of).

You can use shared borders to add a common header or footer (like the copyright information shown in Figure 3.17), to include your company logo and contact information in the same place on every page, or to add a navigation system to your Web site.

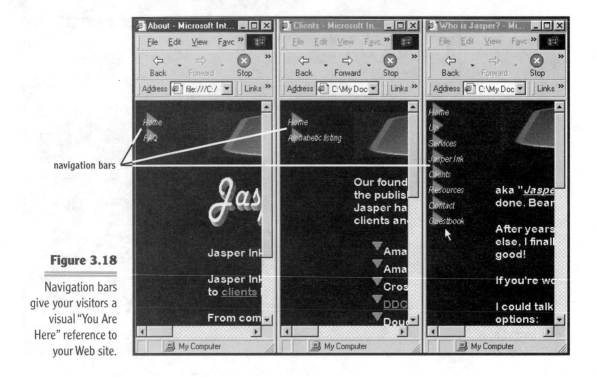

Figure 3.18

Navigation bars give your visitors a visual "You Are Here" reference to your Web site.

Navigation bars, as shown in Figure 3.18, move the reader through your Web site. A navigation bar can easily guide the reader forward and backward within a group of pages on a similar topic, from one topic to the next, back to the beginning, and so on. The best part is that FrontPage keeps track of the "you are here" point automatically and updates the items in the border as the user moves from page to page.

▼▼▼▼▼▼▼▼▼▼▼▼▼▼▼▼▼▼▼▼▼▼▼▼▼▼▼▼▼▼▼▼▼▼▼

BUZZ WORD

Navigation bars are a structured group of buttons or text links that move the reader through your Web site.

▲▲▲▲▲▲▲▲▲▲▲▲▲▲▲▲▲▲▲▲▲▲▲▲▲▲▲▲▲▲▲▲▲▲▲

Organizing Your Pages in Navigation View

To implement navigation bars, you need to tell FrontPage how you want your Web site to be structured. You can click and drag pages around in the Navigation view, creating an organizational chart of sorts.

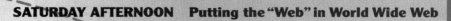

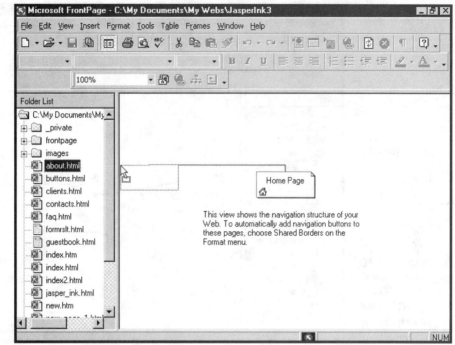

Figure 3.19

Drag pages from
the Folder List to
create your
navigational
structure.

1. Click the Navigation view button on the Views bar. FrontPage reveals an open canvas with a single page icon (your index or home page) showing, as shown in Figure 3.19.

2. Think of your Web site in terms of a corporate organization chart. The home page, at the top of the chart, is the company president. All other pages are of some subordinate level below the president. To create your navigational structure, click the Folder List button on the toolbar to reveal the list of files in your Web site.

3. Click one of your second-level (vice-presidential, if you will) files in the Folder List and drag it just below the Home page icon. When you get close to the icon, a connector will appear (see Figure 3.20).

4. Release the mouse button when the page is correctly positioned below the home page. FrontPage will add the page to the navigation structure.

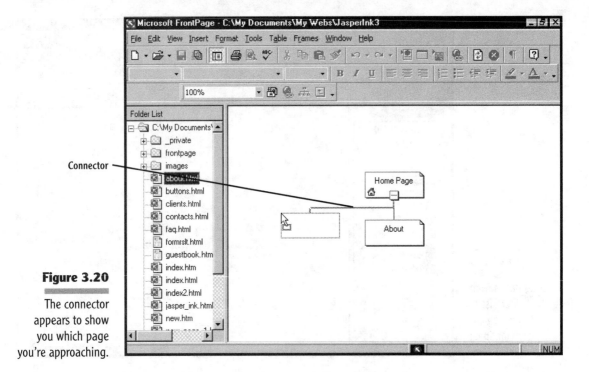

Connector

Figure 3.20

The connector
appears to show
you which page
you're approaching.

5. Continue dragging your second-level pages. The left-most pages will be listed first in the navigation bar. When you've completed the second level structure, do the same with the third and any additional levels. (Alternatively, you can build one branch or "department" at a time. It depends on how you want to do it.)

TIP   If the canvas begins to get too cluttered, you can collapse branches by clicking the – button. Click the + sign to expand the branch again.

6. There may be some instances in which you need a page in the navigational structure for organizational purposes, but don't necessarily want it to appear as a link on the navigation bars. If so, right-click on the file icon and select Included in Navigation Bars on the shortcut menu to remove the check mark. FrontPage will disable the page

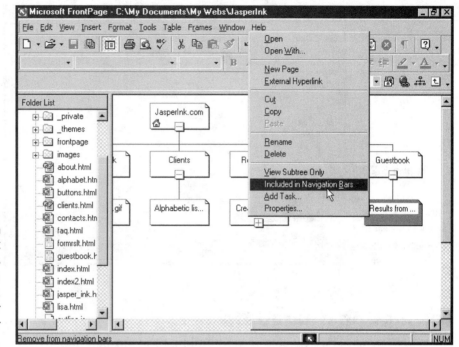

Figure 3.21

You probably don't want a form results page to appear in the navigation bar, since the reader only gets to it after submitting a form.

and change its icon to gray, shown in Figure 3.21. (It also disables any subordinate pages from the navigation bars.) You can still access these pages using normal hyperlink procedures; they merely won't have automatic links built into the navigation bar.

NOTE   You can add external links to your navigational structure too. In Navigation view, right-click on the file you want to add to the external link, and then choose External Hyperlink from the shortcut menu. Type in or navigate to the link's URL and click OK, just as you would to create a link directly on a Web page. This also works for other pages within your own Web site that are not in the same branch of the navigational structure (see Figure 3.22).

7. When you're satisfied with the organizational structure, you should print a hard copy for later reference (you'll need it in just a moment).

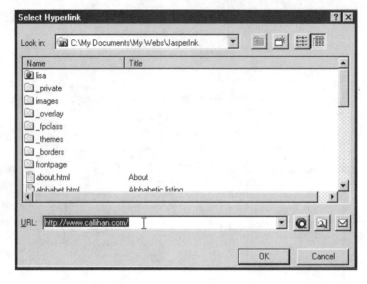

Figure 3.22

Sometimes you
want an external
link to appear in
your navigation
bars as well.

Formatting Shared Borders

The next step toward building the navigation bar is to tell FrontPage the
type of information to include on each page. Here's where the shared borders feature comes into play.

I'm also going to use this feature to add a footer of legal stuff to every page
on my site. I'll start there—it's a little less complicated.

1. Click the Folder List button on the Views bar. FrontPage presents
   your collection of pages and files.

2. Select Format, Shared Borders. The Shared Borders dialog box opens
   (see Figure 3.23). The small preview area in the dialog box will give
   you a basic idea of what to expect with each selection.

3. To add a footer to the entire Web site, select All pages, and then put
   a check mark in the Bottom check box. (You might have to check
   the box more than once to make the check mark appear.) Don't
   change any other items that might be selected or partially dimmed.
   Click OK to close the dialog box.

4. Double-click any Web page in the file list. It will open in Page view.
   Scroll to the bottom of the page and notice the section separated by

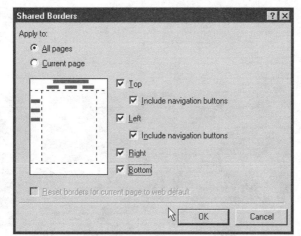

Figure 3.23

You can have shared borders on all four sides if you want, but don't forget to leave room for your content!

a thin border. That's the shared border area. Use this area to insert your boilerplate text or objects (see Figure 3.24).

5. Type, format, and arrange the footer text as you want it to appear. Insert tables, graphics, or whatever you want. When you're finished, click on Preview to check the results.

6. Open another page and notice that it contains the same footer text. You now have a running footer that appears at the shared bottom border of every page.

7. To add a navigation bar on the left, right, or top of every page, repeat this same process, selecting the appropriate check box for the border you want to include. You can customize the type of navigation links included on groups or individual pages, but you must enable the shared border on a page before it will appear.

NOTE If you have attached a theme to your Web site, you also have the option of displaying your navigation links as buttons (see Figure 3.25). FrontPage will use buttons that coordinate with the overall look of the theme, inserting text labels on the buttons. You might need to experiment with this setting for best results. Some buttons take up more room on the page than they really should, eating up precious real estate on the main portion of your page. They do enhance your site, though.

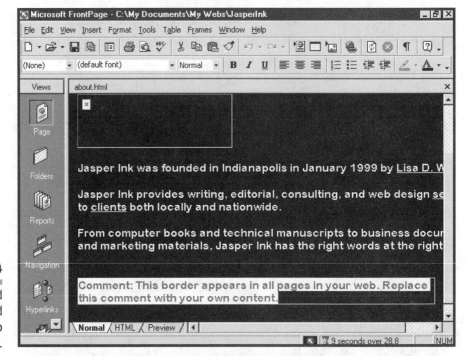

Figure 3.24

The bottom shared border is a good place for your Web site's legal notices.

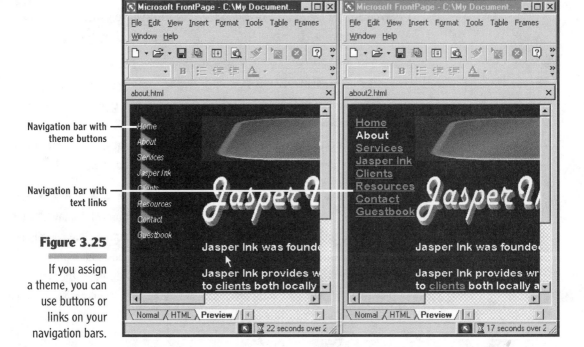

Navigation bar with theme buttons

Navigation bar with text links

Figure 3.25

If you assign a theme, you can use buttons or links on your navigation bars.

Configuring Navigation Bars

With your navigational structure in mind, think about how you want folks to be able to navigate your Web pages. You might want a different set of links for each level of your site. For example, on your home page, you might want to show links only to the second-level pages. On the second-level pages, you might want to show not only links to the other pages on that level (using Forward and Back links), but to all of the subordinate or "child" pages under that branch of the structure. Perhaps throw in an "Up" link back to the next highest level and a "Home" link back to the main page as well. Before diving in, take a moment to examine the Navigation Bar Properties dialog box:

1. In Page view, open any page you've designated to have a navigation bar, and then right-click on the text in the shared border area.

2. Select Navigation Bar Properties from the shortcut menu. When the dialog box opens, it presents a variety of configurations for that page's navigation bar, as well as a legend explaining the meaning of the various symbols in the dialog box (see Figure 3.26). The thumbnail (or miniature) of a site structure changes depending on which options you select.

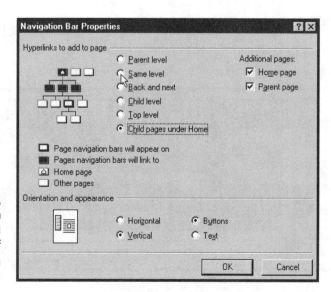

Figure 3.26

FrontPage helps you decide which set of pages to include on the navigation bar.

 NOTE Here's another place where you might want to experiment with the various settings on different levels of your Web site structure. Even with the legend onscreen and your Navigation view printout in hand, it might be difficult to determine exactly what you'll get without seeing it in the actual pages.

3. Select an option or two, and then click OK to implement the change. Notice which page links appear with each setting.

4. Repeat steps 1-3 a few times until you're comfortable with the impact of each variation.

5. When you're ready, select one of the pages you've designated to share borders and assign the navigation properties you want.

6. Repeat step 5 to customize settings for individual pages if necessary. See Figure 3.27 for the results.

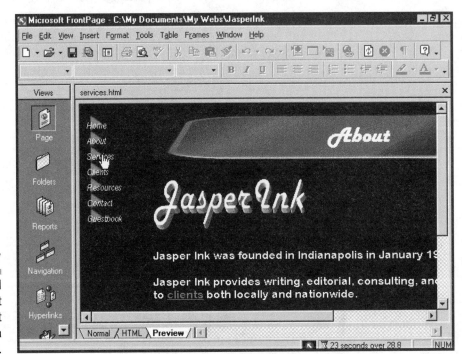

Figure 3.27

A well-designed Web site won't let your visitors get lost among the plethora of pages.

Assuming you survived all of that unscathed, you're ready to take a break from creating and check out what you've accomplished today.

Testing Your Work

No matter how hard you try, no one is perfect. It's entirely possible that you've made some typing errors in a few of those many links you've recently added to your Web site. Fortunately, FrontPage is a very forgiving program, and makes it easy to check for errors and verify the integrity of your links. (This is one of my favorite features, because I'm a lousy typist.)

Navigating Hyperlinks in FrontPage

The most obvious way to check if your links work properly is to click on them. Using FrontPage's Preview view, you can breeze through your Web site to admire your work and find out what's not working like it should. To navigate your hyperlinks from within FrontPage, follow these steps:

1. From Page view, open your home page (index.htm*) file, and then click the Preview tab. Your home page will appear in the FrontPage browser.

TIP You can check links from the Normal view tab by pressing Ctrl and clicking the link.

2. Click on any internal link on your home page. Your browser should take you to the intended destination. If it does, keep clicking links. Test as many as you can find. Don't worry about external hyperlinks for now; you'll check them next.

TIP Remember that the Preview browser does not include a Back button, so if you get stuck somewhere and can't get back, click the Normal tab to go back to the home page and start over.

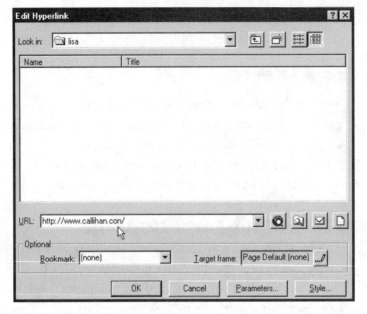

Figure 3.28

Hmmm...why isn't
this one working?
Let me guess—
I made a typo.
Me? Never!

3. If you find a link that doesn't work as expected, you can fix them on the fly. Switch back to Normal view, right-click on the link and select Hyperlink Properties to open the Edit Hyperlink dialog box again and investigate the problem (see Figure 3.28).

4. Edit the link as needed, close the dialog box, and then click the Preview tab again to retest the link.

5. Save all your files to the hard drive before you run the automated link verification test. Save your work and let FrontPage import any files requested. Close the web, but don't exit FrontPage.

TIP After you've saved your pages, you can also test your links by opening the home page and clicking the Preview in Browser button on the Standard toolbar, and navigating through your pages in a real browser.

Verifying Links

One of FrontPage's collections of Web site management tools is the Broken Hyperlink report feature. Start the report and sit back while FrontPage checks each link in your Web site for you.

 NOTE   You must be connected to your Internet Service Provider or network server to run this report (assuming you have included some external links in your Web site).

1. Reopen your web by selecting File, Recent Webs, and then selecting the web name from the list that appears.

2. Select View, Reports, Broken Hyperlinks. FrontPage will open to show a list, in table format, of any links that are already known problems as well as those that have not yet been verified (see Figure 3.29).

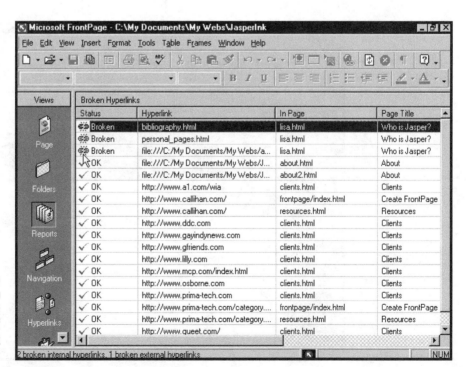

Figure 3.29

FrontPage is the Sherlock Holmes of broken link detectors.

3. Select the Status column heading to sort the links by verification status. Most will say either Broken or Unknown.

4. Click once on the first Unknown link listed, press and hold the Shift key, and select the last Unknown link in the list. Release the Shift key.

5. Right-click anywhere in the selection to open the shortcut menu. Select Verify. FrontPage will "reach out and touch" all the selected links to make sure they work (see Figure 3.30).

● ●

NOTE If you have a lot of links (and/or a slow connection), this might take a few moments. As it verifies each link, it will change the status to OK or Broken. When the test is finished, you may have a rather lengthy list. Don't panic. Most often, one wrong URL can cause errors on several pages at one time. Fix it once and they will all be correct.

● ●

Figure 3.30

Often the same link will cause a problem in more than one page.

Status	Hyperlink	In Page	Page Title
Broken	bibliography.html	lisa.html	Who is Jasper?
Broken	clients.html	about.html	About
Broken	clients.html	index.html	JasperInk.com
Broken	clients.html	about2.html	About
Broken	clients.html	buttons.html	New Page 1
Broken	personal_pages.html	lisa.html	Who is Jasper?
Broken	file:///C:/My Documents/My Webs/a...	lisa.html	Who is Jasper?
OK	file:///C:/My Documents/My Webs/J...	about.html	About
OK	file:///C:/My Documents/My Webs/J...	about2.html	About
OK	http://www.callihan.com/	frontpage/index.html	Create FrontPage 200
OK	http://www.callihan.com/	resources.html	Resources
OK	http://www.prima-tech.com/category...	frontpage/index.html	Create FrontPage 200
OK	http://www.prima-tech.com/category...	resources.html	Resources

Microsoft FrontPage - C:\My Documents\My Webs\JasperInk

File Edit View Insert Format Tools Table Frames Window Help

Views / Broken Hyperlinks

Page / Folders / Reports / Navigation / Hyperlinks

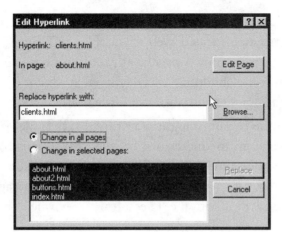

Figure 3.31

Which method to use? Try repairing the URL first. If it still doesn't work, edit the page to change or eliminate the link.

6. To fix a broken link, double-click on the link in the Reports view. The Edit Hyperlink dialog box will open. You can choose to fix the link by editing the page on which it is found or by editing the URL in the dialog box. If you edit the URL, you have the option of applying the changes to all the affected pages, or just one (see Figure 3.31). After you've repaired a link, the FrontPage report will read Edited.

7. When you've finished the manual repair process, run the verification test again as you did in steps 4 and 5. Keep repeating this process until all the links check out OK. If one remains stubborn and just won't verify, consider eliminating it and replacing it with one that's more cooperative.

What's Next?

At this point, you have enough of a Web site to consider it publishable. It now has several pages, graphics, lists, and most importantly, lots of links. It's nicely decorated, too. You could post it now and leave it at that. However, why limit yourself to just a basic Web site? FrontPage leveled the playing field between professional developers and the rest of us by making it very easy to build in advanced features and special effects, so why not take advantage of it? The session coming up is optional, but you won't

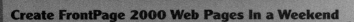

want to miss it. Tonight after dinner, you'll work with two common features of more sophisticated Web sites: tables and frames. Tables help you organize information on a page neatly and efficiently. Frames are an advanced method of building a navigational structure into your Web site (useful for a large site with lots of information).

If you skip the session tonight, you can always come back to it another time. If you're up for more tonight, then by all means, go have a nice dinner with your family or friends and relax for a while. Tuck the kids in and come back for a few more hours of fabulous FrontPage fun. (Okay, so that was corny. Bear with me. I get a little crazy when I'm hungry.)

Bonus Session: Adding Tables and Frames to Your Pages

- ✿ Tables Are Your Friends
- ✿ Importing Data from Excel or Word to a Table
- ✿ Editing and Formatting a Table
- ✿ Designing with Frames
- ✿ Editing Frames

I f all you're interested in is a simple Web site with a few graphics and some links, you're done. However, if you're up to the challenge of building a more sophisticated site, stay tuned. In tonight's session, you'll learn how to take your site to the next step by implementing tables and frames.

Tables Are Your Friends

You're probably familiar with tables in general. You know that tables come in handy when you need to organize information. What you might not know is that FrontPage makes it easy to add tables to your Web pages.

The first time I tried to design a table for a Web site (in the days before Microsoft FrontPage), it took me hours, and it wasn't a very complicated table. Writing the HTML code by hand was a chore, and keeping track of all the rows and columns nearly drove me nuts. Boy, was I delighted to find the great table design features in FrontPage! Now you can create tables in a snap. You can use tables to:

- ✪ Organize text and graphics on your page in rows and columns
- ✪ Line up links or buttons
- ✪ Give your pages a multiple-column layout (like a newspaper)
- ✪ Display more than one page at a time

You can create the table and then fill it in, or you can convert existing text to a table. In addition, FrontPage includes some very friendly table-based templates to get you started with multicolumn layouts.

The popular shareware Web site "Tucows" (The Ultimate Collection of Winsock Software) uses a table-based design to organize the data for the hundreds of shareware applications available on its site. For some superb examples of table usage, visit **www.tucows.com.** It's also a great place to poke around for Web tools and utilities.

FIND IT ON ▶
THE WEB

In the Jasper Ink Web site, I'll create a table—from scratch and from existing text—to organize the major links on the home page. Next, you'll pull in some text from Word and Excel documents and create a table on the fly. Then I'll show you how to format your tables, add or remove rows and columns, and add headings or captions. You'll have this table thing down in nothing flat. Given my early table design experiences, I envy you.

Creating a New Table

You'll start by creating a simple table to use as a navigational tool. (I'm putting it on my index page. Yours can go wherever you prefer.)

1. In Page view, open the file you want to edit. Click the Normal tab to ensure you're in editing mode.

2. Create a new paragraph at the point where the table will be inserted.

3. Click the Insert Table button on the toolbar. The Table palette will appear, enabling you to tell FrontPage how many rows and columns to include in your table (see Figure 4.1).

4. Select the box that represents the number of rows and columns you want in the table. I have six major topics, so I'll need 2 rows and 3 columns. Your empty table, with default borders, will appear at the insertion point, as shown in Figure 4.2.

Now just fill in the cells with the text for each of your Web site's main areas. You can insert text or graphics in each table cell, and link to each object as usual.

Insert Table button ———

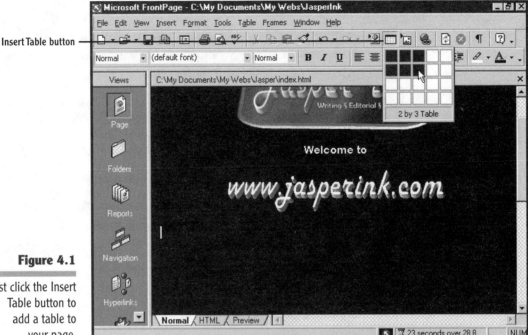

Figure 4.1

Just click the Insert
Table button to
add a table to
your page.

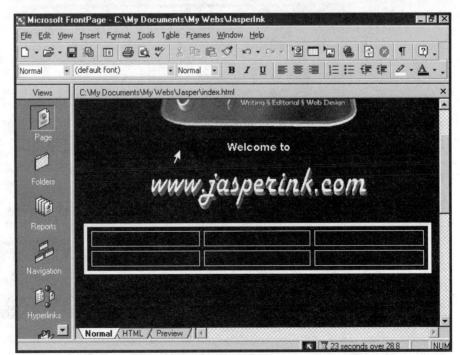

Figure 4.2

FrontPage creates a
table based on the
number of rows
and columns you
selected from
the palette.

Converting Text to a Table

You might have organized some information as a list, but decided later it might work better as a table. No problem, it's easy to make changes. To convert existing text to a table, follow these steps:

1. In Page view, open the page you want to edit. Click the Normal tab to ensure you're in editing mode.

2. Select the text you want to convert to a table.

3. Select Table, Convert, Text To Table. The Convert Text To Table dialog box will appear (see Figure 4.3).

4. If the text for your table is a simple list of short paragraphs, select Paragraphs to separate the text into individual table cells. If you have text with tabs (as shown in Figure 4.3), select Tabs.

5. Click OK. FrontPage draws the table as you requested and adds the default border style.

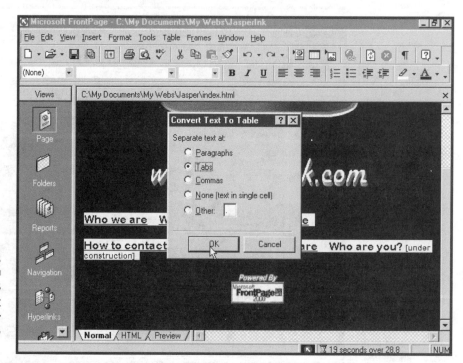

Figure 4.3

Sometimes it's faster to convert existing text rather than type in new information.

TIP   To change a table to text, select Table, Convert, Table To Text.

Importing Data from Excel or Word to a Table

So far, tables have been a breeze. But what if you want to do something like import spreadsheet data into a Web page? Or maybe you have a table created in Word that you want to use. Don't worry, it's still easy. It just takes a few more steps to get there.

Importing Microsoft Excel Data

Don't waste your time retyping all those numbers on your Web page when you have perfectly good data already available. To import data from Excel as a Web page table, follow these steps:

1. In Page view, open the file you want to edit. Click the Normal tab to ensure you're in editing mode.

2. Place the insertion point where the table will be inserted and create a new paragraph.

3. Open Excel and open the worksheet that contains the data.

4. Select the cells you want to copy to your Web page, and then click the Copy button from the toolbar, as shown in Figure 4.4. Your data will be in the Windows Clipboard, ready for pasting.

5. Switch back to FrontPage, click the insertion point, and click the Paste button from the toolbar. FrontPage will insert the copied data, as shown in Figure 4.5. (It won't pick up some of your worksheet's formatting properties, but you can fix that in a minute.)

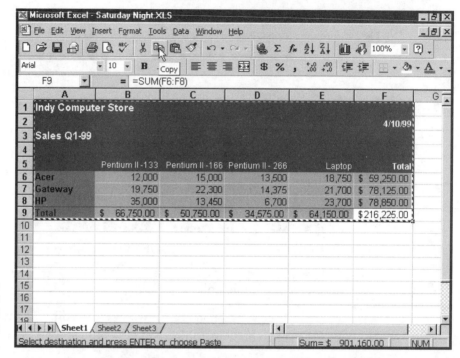

Figure 4.4

Copying data from Excel can save you time.

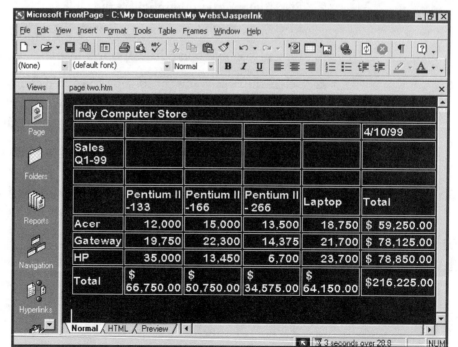

Figure 4.5

This table needs some cleanup, but it beats starting from scratch.

NOTE The data you've inserted is static. It is not linked to the original spreadsheet and thus won't be updated if you change the spreadsheet.

You can insert a dynamic spreadsheet that links directly to Excel using the Office Spreadsheet component. Keep in mind that these components are not visible in some browsers, including Netscape 4.0 and lower. For more information on working with this component, open FrontPage's Help system and type **add an office spreadsheet component** in the Answer Wizard.

Copying a Table from Microsoft Word

You might have used Word to create tables in word processing documents, and now you want to use that same information on your Web page. To import data from Word as a Web page table, follow these steps:

1. In Page view, open the file you want to edit. Click the Normal tab to ensure you're in editing mode.

2. Place the insertion point where the table will be inserted and create a new paragraph.

3. Open Word and open the document that contains the table.

4. Select the table or the portion of the table that you want to copy to your Web page, and then click the Copy button on the toolbar. Your table will be in the Windows Clipboard, ready for pasting.

5. Switch back to FrontPage, click the insertion point, and click the Paste button on the toolbar. FrontPage will insert the table at the place you indicated, as shown in Figure 4.6.

TIP If you have a rather complex table that includes lots of merged cells, special formatting, and so on, you might want to save yourself some formatting work in FrontPage. To more closely match the original formatting of your Word table, select Insert, File, and choose the Word document in the Select File dialog box. When you click OK, FrontPage will insert the document, with the table designed more closely to the way you intended.

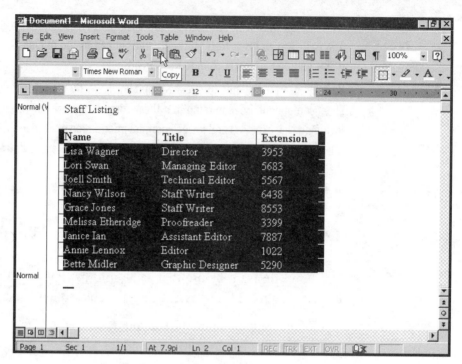

Word tables can be copied or inserted into your Web pages.

Editing and Formatting a Table

Now that you have your table inserted, it probably needs a little sprucing up. FrontPage has a very generous array of table formatting tools. You'll find many ways to control the appearance of your table. You can:

- Add or change the borders

- Control the color of the table's foreground and background

- Change the alignment of the table and the amount of space it uses on the page

- Determine how much space or *padding* to use between the cell borders and the text within the cells

- Add and delete columns and rows

- Merge cells together

- Format the first row or column into headings so they look different

▼ ▼

Cell *padding* is the amount of space between the inside border of a cell and the outer edge of the text. It's easy to confuse cell padding with cell spacing. Cell spacing is the amount of space between the outside borders of two cells, rows, or columns.

▲ ▲

Adding Rows and Columns

As you work with your table, you may decide you need more space for text or data. You might want to add more rows or columns. To add a row or column to your existing table, follow these steps:

1. In Normal view, click in the cell next to where you want to make the addition. The addition you're about to make will be relative to the position of the insertion point.

2. Select Table, Insert, Rows or Columns. The Insert Rows or Columns dialog box opens (see Figure 4.7).

3. To insert a row, click Rows, press Tab, and then type the number of rows to insert. In the Location section, indicate whether you want to insert the row(s) above or below the insertion point. Click OK.

4. To insert a column, click Columns, press Tab, and then type the number of columns to insert. In the Location section, indicate whether you want to insert the column(s) to the left or right of the insertion point. Click OK.

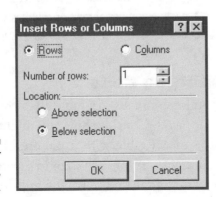

Figure 4.7

Insert a new row or column anytime, anywhere.

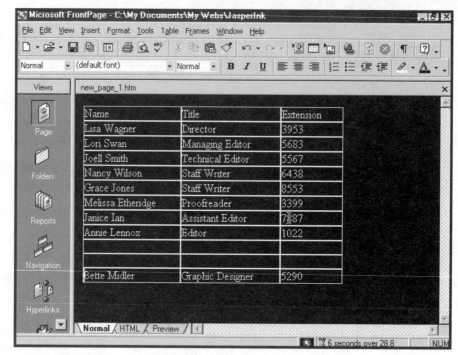

Figure 4.8

It's easy to insert rows or columns in your table.

NOTE Use the shortcut menu to add a new row or column quickly. Select a cell next to where you want to make the insertion, and then right-click to open the shortcut menu and select Insert Row or Insert Column.

By default, the Insert Row command adds a row above the selection; the Insert Column command adds a column to the left of the selection. If you select more than one row or column, FrontPage will insert the same number of rows or columns you selected.

Merging and Splitting Cells

The capability to split and merge cells in a table gives you a great deal of design flexibility for your pages. Consider how you might design a product catalog. You could create a table with a picture of the product, a description, price, and dimensions for each item in separate cells. Figure 4.9 shows a table with split and merged cells. The following steps enable

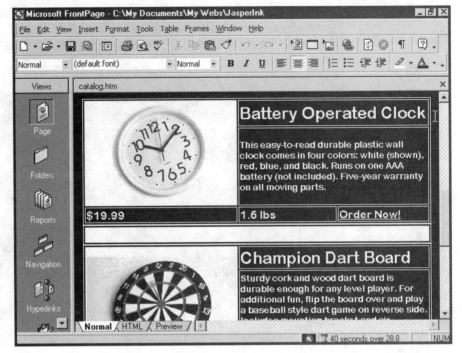

Figure 4.9

Use a table with split and merged cells to create an online catalog like this one.

you to combine merging and splitting procedures to produce a table similar to the one shown in Figure 4.9:

1. In Normal view, click Insert Table on the toolbar and insert a blank table with four rows and three columns.

2. Select the first three cells in the first column. Right-click the selection and select Merge Cells from the shortcut menu. The three selected cells merge into one cell that is three rows high (see Figure 4.10).

3. Select the bottom row of the table (point to its border to grab the whole row). Right-click the selection and select Merge Cells from the shortcut menu. The bottom row is now one cell that spans the width of the table.

4. Right-click in the third cell in the second column and select Split Cells from the shortcut menu. The Split Cells dialog box appears (see Figure 4.11).

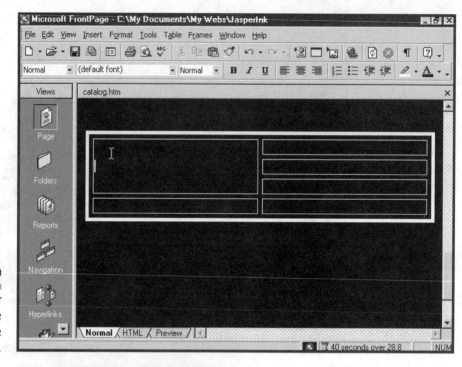

Figure 4.10

Merge cells together
to design more
creative table
layouts.

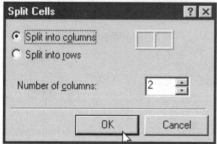

Figure 4.11

No table design is
set in stone thanks
to FrontPage's
flexible editing
features.

5. Make sure Split into columns is selected, and change the number of columns to 3. Click OK to perform the split.

6. Select the last row of the table again. Select Table, Split Cells (you may need to expand the menu). In the Split Cells dialog box, tell FrontPage to split the cell into 2 rows.

7. Click OK. The original row now has an identical twin.

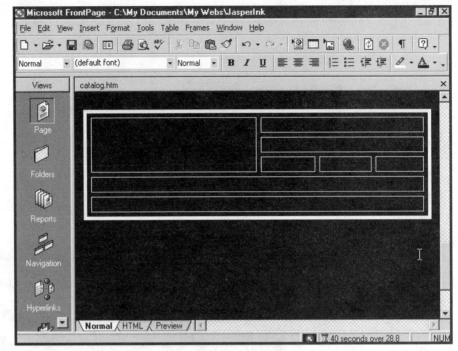

Figure 4.12

This is a table with merged and split cells. Looks harder than it is, doesn't it?

The results of your work should resemble Figure 4.12. How'd it go? Not bad for a rookie.

Deleting Rows, Columns, and Cells

If you added rows, columns, or cells that you no longer need, just get rid of them! To delete a table row, column, or cell:

1. Click in the extraneous cell, and then select Table, Select. A submenu appears (see Figure 4.13).

2. Choose the command appropriate for what you want to delete; the entire table, the entire row or column, or the individual cell. (For this example, select Row.) FrontPage highlights the selection.

3. Select Table, Delete Cells, and the cell is removed. Figure 4.14 shows the results.

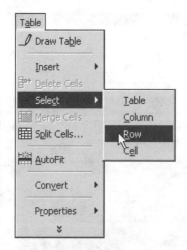

Figure 4.13

You'll need to use the Select menu to be sure you're selecting the right cells after merging and splitting a few times.

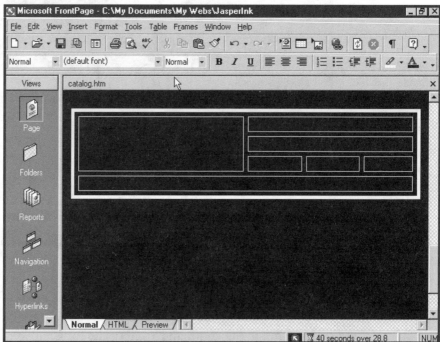

Figure 4.14

Now add text and graphics and you're all set!

YOU CAN'T ALWAYS GET WHAT YOU WANT

Selecting the cells you want in a table can be tricky, especially after you've split and merged cells. The original rows and columns may have been manipulated in such a way that it's not always clear to FrontPage (or you) which cells belong in which row or column. Here are a few tips for selecting cells in a table:

⚙ To select an entire row or column, point to the border at the start of the row or column until the pointer changes to a small black arrow, and then click to confirm the selection.

⚙ If your selection area includes merged or split cells, the highlighted results may or may not be what you expected. Use the commands on the Table, Select submenu to see how FrontPage responds to the Select command from any given cell.

⚙ To select an individual cell, use Alt-click.

⚙ To select more than one row, column, or cell, use Shift+click (or simply click and drag).

⚙ To select non-adjacent items (every other row, for example), use Ctrl+click.

Before you go on, be sure you've completed the table content as much as you can, including any graphics and hyperlinks. You can always add to it later, but a nearly completed table is easier to format.

Formatting Borders, Backgrounds, and Foregrounds

By default, your table uses the same colors as your Web page's default background and text. With a few simple steps, you can change the table's border style as well as the colors used for the cells' backgrounds, foregrounds, and the spacing around and within cells. You can even use a graphic for the background.

NOTE Some of FrontPage's table formatting options are not compatible with some browsers. For example, no version of Netscape Navigator will support graphic backgrounds in tables.

You can make your tables stand out on a page, or you can make them virtually invisible to the visitor. To change the look of your table, follow these steps:

1. Click anywhere in the table, and then select Table, Select, Table. This ensures that the entire table will receive the same treatment.

2. Select Format, Borders and Shading. The Borders and Shading dialog box appears, as shown in Figure 4.15.

3. On the Borders tab, select Box to add or change the border on all four sides of the table.

TIP For no border, select None. For borders on three or less sides, select Custom, and then use the Preview area to select which borders to include.

4. Select a border style. You can use the spin button to adjust the border to the desired width.

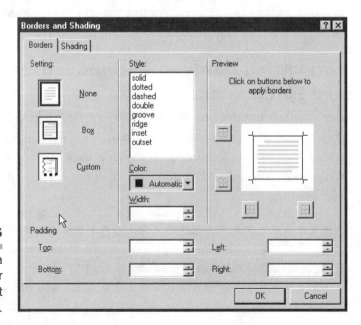

Figure 4.15

You can add a border to all four sides or to just a few.

5. Select a color for the border from the drop-down palette.

6. Now determine how much spacing the cells should have. In the Padding area, click in the Top box and enter a number. (The number represents *pixels*, or screen dots.) For now, enter 5. Press the Tab key and enter the same number for the Bottom, Left, and Right padding. This tells FrontPage to add 5 pixels of space between the inside border and the cell's content, as shown in Figure 4.16.

7. Click OK to see your progress thus far.

8. Select the entire table. Select Format, Borders and Shading. Click the Shading tab on the dialog box. The Shading options come to the front, as shown in Figure 4.17.

9. In the Fill area, select a color for the background from the palette. The background is the fill color of the cells.

10. Select a color for the foreground. The foreground color affects the color of the text in the cells, as well as the "front" face of a three-dimensional border (such as Groove or Inset).

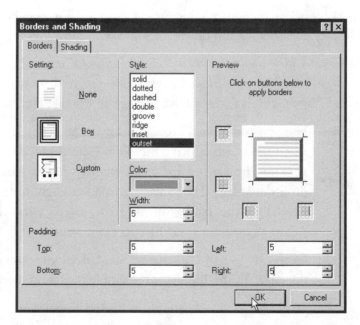

Figure 4.16

You can control the amount of space between the inside border and the cell's content by using Padding.

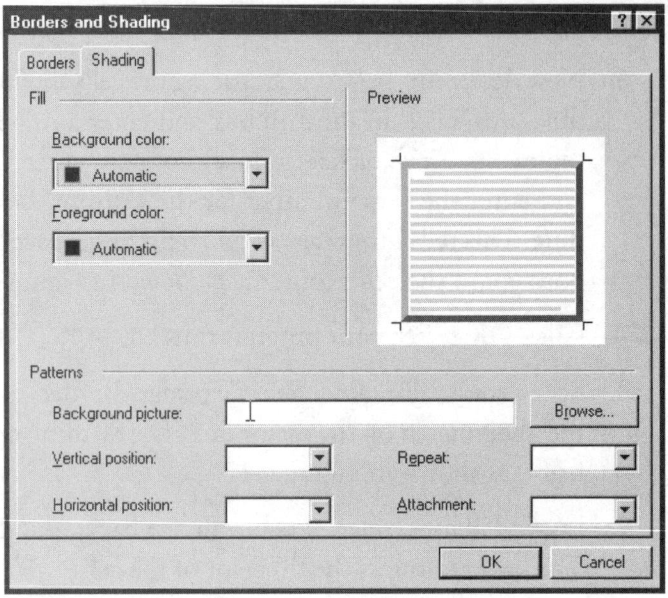

Figure 4.17

Control the
table's foreground
and background
colors with the
Shading settings.

11. Click OK to see your progress.

12. Select the entire table. Select Format, Borders and Shading. Click the Shading tab on the dialog box.

13. To use a graphic as the cell background, select the Background picture text box under Patterns. Type or navigate to the image file so that its full path or URL appears in the text box.

14. You may want to tell FrontPage how to align and handle the graphic. Align the graphic in the middle by selecting Center in the Vertical position drop-down list and Center from the Horizontal position drop-down list. If the image is small enough, it can be tiled or repeated in the background. Experiment with the Repeat and Attachment lists to get the effect you want.

15. Click OK to close the dialog box. Check your work by previewing the page. Your table should resemble the one shown in Figure 4.18.

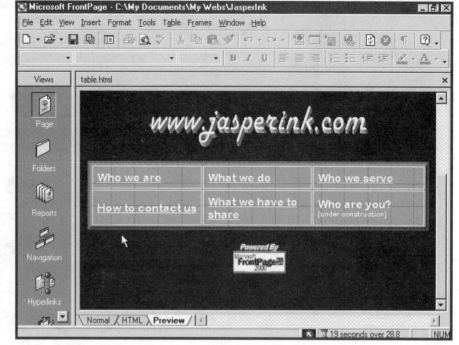

Figure 4.18

Add a patterned background to set off the table from the page.

  TIP To apply the same steps to individual rows, columns, or cells, use the Table, Select submenu to grab the right cells. This comes in handy when you want to give your individual cell borders a different style than the overall table border.

Controlling Table Size, Alignment, and Position

By default, your table fills the width of the page. If you change the size of your FrontPage or browser window, the table columns automatically resize themselves proportionately across the page, as shown in Figure 4.19. You can change the way your table fits on the page using the following steps:

1. Select the entire table, and then select Format, Properties. The Table Properties dialog box appears (see Figure 4.20).

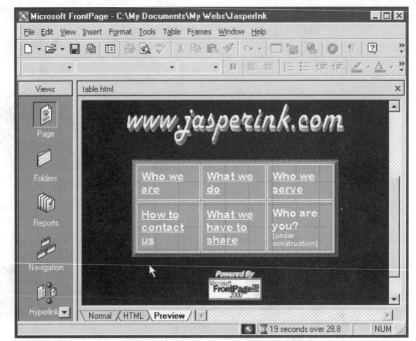

Figure 4.19

By default, tables automatically adjust their column size to fit the page.

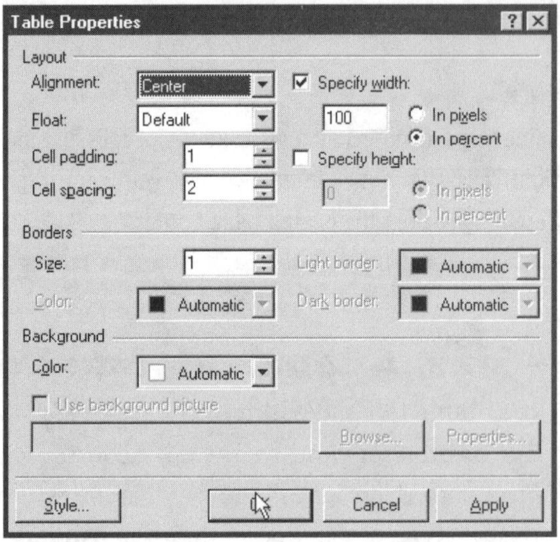

Figure 4.20

You'll find even more ways to customize your table in the Table Properties dialog box.

2. Set an exact width for the table by selecting the Specify width check box. Type a number in the box, and then select In *pixels*. To make the table a specific width in relation to the overall page width, select In percent.

▼ ▼

A *pixel* is a unit of measurement, short for picture element. A pixel identifies a "point" in a graphic. One pixel equals one "dot" on the computer's display screen. The number of pixels does not determine the size of an image, but only the resolution of the image. The size of the image (whether printed or displayed) is determined by the *DPI* (dots per inch) combined with its pixel dimensions, such as 300x400.

▲ ▲

3. Repeat step 2 to specify an overall height for the table and select the Specify height check box.

4. Choose an alignment to control the position of the table on the page (left, right, centered, justified, or default).

5. Float controls how adjacent text flows around the table. The Default setting actually means none. Select Left or Right to allow text to wrap around the table, as shown in Figure 4.21.

● ●

The Float and Alignment settings work hand in hand; changing one option may automatically change the other.

● ●

6. To add more space between cells (as opposed to padding within a cell), adjust the number next to Cell spacing.

Experiment with these settings until you get the effect you want.

Controlling Row Height and Column Width

When FrontPage inserts a new table for you, it assumes you want all the columns and rows to be the same size. FrontPage allows you to adjust the size of individual rows and columns. You can also set a default size for the entire table. There are three quick ways to make these adjustments within a table:

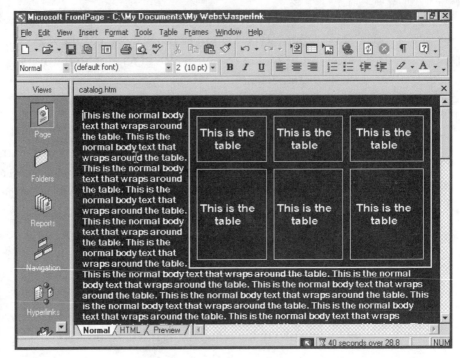

Figure 4.21

Use Float to wrap
text around a table
or graphic.

○ Point to the border to the right of the column or below the row you want to adjust. The pointer will change to a double-headed arrow. Click and drag the border to the desired new width or height, as shown in Figure 4.22.

○ Right-click on the row or column you want to change and select Cell Properties. This opens the Cell Properties dialog box. Select In pixels and enter the specific dimensions.

○ Right-click on the table and select Distribute Rows Evenly or Distribute Columns Evenly to restore the cells to identical sizes.

Formatting Row and Column Headings

Sometimes you want the first row or column of a table to stand out as the headings that identify the information in the table. To create a header row from existing text in the table, follow these steps:

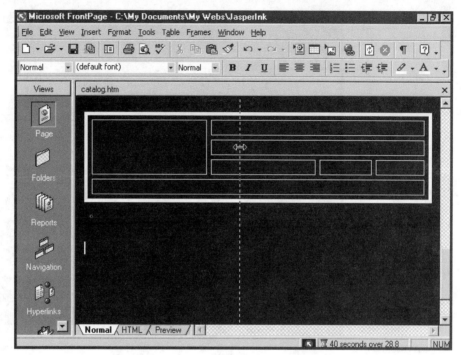

Figure 4.22

Just drag a column
border to change
the column width.

1. Click in the first row of the table, and then select Table, Select, Row.

2. Select Format, Properties. The Cell Properties dialog box opens.

3. Select the Header cell check box.

4. Click OK to close the dialog box. FrontPage will format the row a little differently than the others. By default, the heading text will be bold.

TIP The steps are identical for creating a header for columns, except that, obviously, you select the first column rather than the first row.

From here, you can make more formatting changes; center the headings, change the font size or color, or add background shading. Figure 4.23 shows one such example.

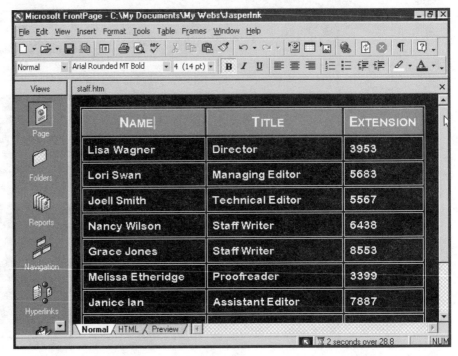

Figure 4.23

Row and column
headings give
your tables a
polished look.

Adding Captions

A table caption identifies your table. Unless you say otherwise, a table caption will appear centered above the table, outside of the border. To add a caption, follow these steps:

1. Click anywhere in the table, and then select Table, Insert, Caption. An empty paragraph and blinking cursor will appear above the table, outside of the border.

2. Type the text for the caption. Add a graphic, if you want. No matter how you resize or realign the table, the caption will remain intact, nicely centered across the width of the table, as shown in Figure 4.24.

3. To show the caption below the table rather than above it, right-click inside the caption and select Caption Properties from the shortcut menu. The Caption Properties dialog box will appear.

Figure 4.24

You can use table captions for a lot more than just an identifying label.

4. Select Bottom of table and press Enter. The dialog box will close and the caption will jump to the bottom of the table.

5. After further consideration, the caption looks better at the top, don't you think? Select Edit, Undo to erase the change you just made. The caption returns to the top of the table.

Take a Break!

You probably zipped through that section in no time, but it's still a good idea to take a short break now to absorb what you've learned. While you trot to the kitchen for a refill, think about the world of design options available to you. When you come back, you'll tackle frames, another optional but useful page layout option. Frames help you organize your Web site into "windows" within a browser, letting visitors scroll through one part of the page while the rest remains static.

Designing with Frames

Web sites that use *frames* have become popular in recent years because they make navigation easy for visitors. You can display several framed pages in one browser window. This makes design tactics more flexible. Use frames to display navigation bars or logos. The possibilities are endless. Keep in mind, however, that some older browsers don't support frames, so think about your audience before you take the plunge.

▼ ▼

A *frame* allows multiple HTML documents to be displayed at the same time in separate frame windows within a browser.

▲ ▲

Frames work a little like shared borders in that you can use them to display a running header or footer or a navigation bar. They're a lot more powerful than that, however. Each frame window contains a different page. You can move around within one frame window, scrolling, clicking, even opening new pages or Web sites, while the other windows within the frame stay put.

Figure 4.25 shows a variation of the original Jasper Ink layout using a simple frame. On the left, you see a narrow column containing a button bar designating the major topics of the Web site, on the right is the main informational page. Notice that each window has a scroll bar so visitors can scroll to see more content in either window if it doesn't all fit within the confines of their browser window.

What you're actually seeing here are three pages, not just two. Every frame consists of at least three pages:

✪   The frame page is the page that "contains" the other embedded pages (the *frameset*). This page is invisible to the visitor.

Figure 4.25

Click a button on the left to display a page on the right. Scroll down either window to see more.

▼ ▼

The foundation for a frame is the *frameset*, a Web page that contains the HTML codes (defined within a FRAMESET tag) defining the layout for a framed Web site. If you use frames on your entire Web site, the page containing the frameset should be your default index page.

▲ ▲

✿ Two or more different content pages, one for each window of the frame

If you have more than two windows in your frame, then you'll have that many more pages included as part of the frame. You can even embed or nest frames within frames, but why complicate a nice, clean layout just because you can?

Preparing the Frame Content

Before you create the frame itself, decide what type of frame you want to use and how many windows it should have.

Switch to Page view to look at some common frame layouts, and then select File, New, Page. When the New dialog box opens, click the Frames Pages tab. Click once on each of the available frame templates and check out their description and layout preview. You'll begin to see possibilities for your own pages. Click Cancel when you're done perusing the templates. (Don't actually open a new frame yet.) Here are some things to consider before creating frames:

- ✿ Do you want a window across the top or bottom that displays an overall header or footer for your Web site?

- ✿ Will two side-by-side windows be enough to display the information?

- ✿ Should the windows work independently of one another, or will one serve as a (static) navigational tool and the other the (dynamic) main display area?

- ✿ Shared borders and navigation bars might not work as expected. Carefully consider when and where to use them on your frame's content pages, if at all.

Once you've decided on a layout, you can design your content pages accordingly. As you're designing them, keep in mind where in the frame the page will appear, and how its content will affect the layout. If you're going for a basic two-window design like the example, you know that the left "table of contents" window is narrow. You don't want this window to take up a lot of screen real estate, and you don't want the visitor to have to scroll too much on this side of the frame. Keep any such pages as short and clean as possible.

Running the Frame Wizard

Once you have your frame content pages developed, as well as the no-frames support page, you can begin setting up the frame. So that you don't mess up your web currently in progress, start with a fresh web. You can import the files back into the original site, or vice versa, later. After that's done, you'll step through the Frames wizard, a very important tool that will take all the pain out of creating a framed page (or most of it, anyway).

SUPPORTING OLDER BROWSERS

Visitors using a browser older than Internet Explorer 3.0 or Netscape Navigator 2.0 cannot view framed Web pages. What's more, some browsers that do support frames enable the user to disable their use. Until the day all the masses are using frames-friendly browsers, you'll want to consider adding "no-frames" support to your frame-based Web site. The no-frames page is actually a fourth "page" that should be considered a vital part of every frame unless you're certain the vast majority of your target audience will only be using frames-friendly browsers.

To support these older browsers, you need to design an alternate "page" that can appear in place of the frame page. If it's simple enough, you can use your same main content page as long as that page contains links to your other pages. Otherwise, the visitor will be stuck once he clicks past the first page and he'll have to step back out of the page using the browser's Back button.

If you're really slick, you can use the FrontPage component called Include Page to automatically display the contents of an existing page, in its entirety, in your no-frames support page. See Sunday morning's session, "Putting the Power of Components to Work" for more information on working with the Include component.

1. Close any open webs, and then select File, New, Web. The New dialog box will appear, as shown in Figure 4.26.

2. Specify the location of the new web in the Options area of the dialog box.

3. You don't need a bunch of extra pages here. Click the Empty Web template, and then click OK. FrontPage will create the new web and open it in a separate window.

4. Switch to Page view if you're not already there, and then select File, New, Page. The New dialog box will open.

5. Click the Frames Pages tab to reveal the available frame templates, as shown in Figure 4.27. Click the template style you want to use, and then click OK. For the example, I'm choosing the Contents template. FrontPage will create your frame "skeleton" and display two command buttons in each frame window.

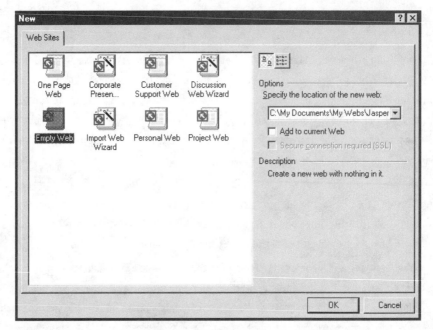

Figure 4.26

Start a frames-
based web from
the Empty Web
template.

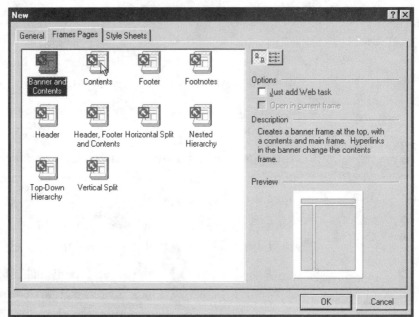

Figure 4.27

There are a wide
range of Frames
Pages templates
available in
FrontPage.

6. Import the content pages you developed from your original web by selecting File, Import. Select the files via the Add Files to Import dialog box.

NOTE To use frames on the opening page of your Web site, your frame skeleton (or container) page must use the default home page file name (index.* or default.*). If one of your content pages uses that name, rename it by selecting Modify in the Import dialog box and entering the new file name. When you save the frame page, name it index.html or whatever your server requires. If you're not sure, use index.htm (you can always change it later).

For the sake of clarity, it might behoove you to name these files based on their targeted positions. Name the page for the left-side frame left.htm and name the main window page main.htm.

Don't forget to import any graphics, subfolders, or other items that are included on your content pages.

7. Now tell FrontPage which pages go where. In the left window, click the Set Initial Page button. In the dialog box, select the file to include in the left side of the frame (the window called Content). If you're following the example, that would be the page named left.htm. Click OK. If you'd rather create a new page on the fly, click the New Page button instead.

8. Repeat step 7 for the right-side window (the window called Main). Both content pages should now be showing in the frame windows as shown in Figure 4.28.

   Notice that there are some extra tabs in the FrontPage editing view:

   ✪ **No Frames**. Click this tab to see how your frames page looks in a browser that doesn't support frames. Right now, it should be empty except for a line that reminds the visitor, "This page uses frames, but your browser doesn't support them."

   ✪ **Frames Page HTML**. Use this tab to view and edit the frames page code (good luck!). It's nice that FrontPage keeps track of the frame coding when you do need to work with it manually.

Figure 4.28

If you click the No Frames view tab, you'd see only one window.

9. To add your no-frames support page, click the No Frames tab. Delete the existing line of text, and then select Insert, File, and choose the file to display.

NOTE This is not really a page unto itself, just an alternate view of the framed page. Each view is hidden from the other. Your visitors will see either the frames page or the no-frames page. There won't be a separate file to name and save for the no-frames support text.

10. When you're finished, preview the page to see your frame (see Figure 4.29). If there are problems or the frame doesn't work as expected, it's likely due to some frame-related settings you'll need to adjust. You'll do that in a moment.

Figure 4.29

Figure 4.29

This two-window design is only the beginning of what you can do with frames.

NOTE   You can only view the No Frames page in editing mode, or in a browser that does not support frames. You won't be able to see it in FrontPage's Preview view or in any browser that supports frames by default.

That's about the size of it. Frames can be a little tricky, but not too confusing.

Editing Frames

You can rework a frame layout any way you choose: delete, remove, or resize frame windows, substitute different content pages, even add nested frames, or frames within frames. Take a quick look at how to accomplish these feats.

Changing the Initial Page in a Frame Window

Just as your index or home page automatically appears when the user types your domain name in their browser, each window of a frame automatically displays a default initial page until the user clicks on a link to see something new. If you want a different initial page to display in one of your frame windows, follow these steps:

1. Right-click in the frame, and then select Frame Properties on the shortcut menu. The Frame Properties dialog box will open, as shown in Figure 4.30.

2. In the Initial page text box, type or navigate to the new page so that the path and file name or URL of the page appears in the text box.

3. Click OK. The frame page will reappear with the replacement page in place (see Figure 4.31).

TIP You can control other details of your frame setup in the Frame Properties dialog box, including:

♦ Spacing between frames

♦ Showing or hiding borders between frames

♦ Margins inside frames

♦ Whether or not visitors can resize the frame pages in their browser

♦ Whether or not scroll bars should appear

For details on these controls (as well as a detailed overview of designing and working with frames), read the information contained in FrontPage's Help system.

Creating a Link to a Framed Page

If you're using frames as a navigational method for your Web site, you need to tell FrontPage what to do when the visitor clicks on a link in the navigation window. Should it open the requested page in the main window, the footer, or a new browser window altogether?

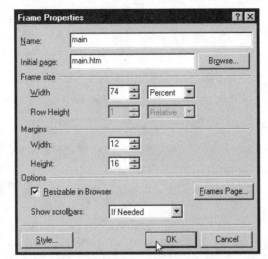

Figure 4.30

You can change
which page
displays in a frame
window in the
Frame Properties
dialog box.

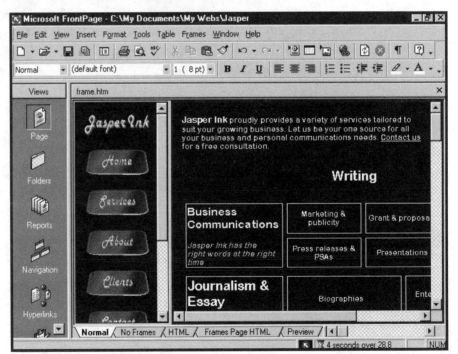

Figure 4.31

The initial page
is changed in a
Frame window.

The frame window you want to use to display a page is called the *target*. Each target has a different name. You use the target name to tell FrontPage where to open the page. In my contents window, I'm actually attaching the links to graphics (the navigation buttons I created in PhotoDraw 2000). To set a target for a hyperlink, follow these steps:

▼ ▼

When creating a link to display a page within a frame, the "window" in which you want a particular page to appear is called the ***target***.

▲ ▲

1. Right-click the hyperlink and select Hyperlink Properties from the shortcut menu. The Edit Hyperlink dialog box opens.

2. Click the Change Target Frame button at the lower right. The Target Frame dialog box appears (see Figure 4.32). Here you'll see a small diagram of your frame page, along with a list of common targets available.

3. Click on a window in the Current Frames Page diagram. Notice that the contents of the Target setting text box changes. To display a page in the left frame window, click the left pane of the diagram.

Figure 4.32

You can tell FrontPage to open a page in the current window, a different window in the frame, or even open a whole new browser window.

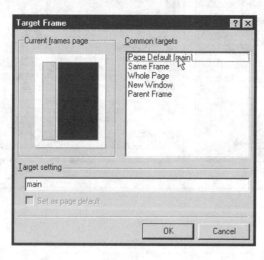

To display it in the right window, click the right pane. No matter how many windows you have in your frame, they will all be available in this dialog box.

NOTE You'll notice some additional targets in the Common Targets area of the dialog box. These pre-defined targets are understood by all frames-friendly browsers. Here's what they mean:

- ✪ **Same Frame (_self).** Open the linked page in the same frame window the current page uses. Leave the other frame windows in the frameset as they are.

- ✪ **Whole Page (_top).** Close the current frameset and all of its windows. In its place, open the linked page in the full browser window.

- ✪ **New Window (_blank).** Leave this current frameset and its windows as they are. Open the linked page in a new instance of the browser.

- ✪ **Parent Frame (_parent).** *(For nested frames only)*. Close the current nested frameset and all of its windows. Open the linked page in the next highest frameset.

4. Select your target window and click OK. You'll return to the Edit Hyperlink box. Click OK again to see the changes.

What's Next?

Now, wasn't that worth sticking around for? As you now know, tables and frames are powerful design tools you can employ to give your Web site a professional, easy-to-use interface. Tables help you include lots of information on your pages, and frames help you include many pages into your Web site without losing your visitors in a maze of links and bookmarks.

Well, it's getting late—save your work and close FrontPage. Tomorrow morning's session is "Putting the Power of Components to Work." You'll really start to feel like a pro when you learn how to add features like hit counters, hover buttons, and search forms. If you think those features sound hard to pull off, you'll be pleasantly surprised. But…that's tomorrow, and tomorrow is another day. *¡Hasta mañana!*

Putting the Power of Components to Work

- Adding a Hit Counter
- Adding a Hover Button
- Adding a Search Form
- Creating a Table of Contents
- Using the Banner Ad Manager

Y ou had a big day yesterday, especially if you finished all of the Saturday sessions. If you didn't get everything done on Saturday, that's okay. You can always go back later and do the optional material.

You have a lot to cover this morning, so if you haven't had breakfast yet, go get that bowl of cereal, have some toast and jam, or boil an egg. You have to stoke the furnace if you want to have the energy. Go ahead and pour that second (or third) cup of coffee, if that's what you need to get a jumpstart in the morning.

In this morning's session, you'll learn how to put FrontPage 2000's components to work for you. The term "component" in FrontPage actually is short for "*WebBot* component." FrontPage's components allow you to easily add many features to your FrontPage Web pages that otherwise only experts at HTML coding could manage to do.

▼ ▼

 A **WebBot** (derived from "robot"), as the term implies, automates the execution of what would otherwise be very complex Web page features.

▲ ▲

There are more components in FrontPage 2000 than you'll have time to tackle this morning. This morning's session covers several of the most useful components. These include:

- ✿ Comment
- ✿ Hit Counter

- Hover Button
- Include Page
- Date and Time (Timestamp)
- Scheduled Picture or Include Page
- Search Form
- Table of Contents
- Banner Ad Manager

If this seems like a long list, don't worry—the Search Form, Table of Contents, and Banner Ad Manager components are optional for this session. Also, most components are not difficult to implement. So, depending on your learning style and speed, you should be able to learn how to use many of these useful components before the morning's up.

Save your initial blank page as components.htm, in your local web folders (C:\My Webs, or any other FrontPage web you want to work in) for this session. Some of the components require that the page be saved before the component can be previewed in a browser.

NOTE The files listed in your Folder List may not match what you see in the figure illustrations. You may have added files and folders to your web during previous sessions that aren't shown in the figure illustrations for this session.

Adding Comments

You can add comments to your FrontPage Web pages that won't be displayed when the page is opened in a Web browser window. They *are* visible to anyone who looks at the page source in a browser. Comments are also visible in various views in FrontPage. Comments are displayed in a different font color in FrontPage's Normal view. Comments are also visible if you view the page in HTML view. Therefore, even though they won't appear in a Web browser's window, you shouldn't put anything into a comment that you wouldn't want others to see.

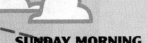

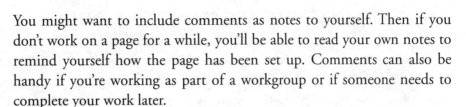

You might want to include comments as notes to yourself. Then if you don't work on a page for a while, you'll be able to read your own notes to remind yourself how the page has been set up. Comments can also be handy if you're working as part of a workgroup or if someone needs to complete your work later.

To insert a comment, you'll need to open your FrontPage web (C:\My Webs, if you used the default when you created your local web). Use the new_page_1.htm page that opens automatically when you first run FrontPage 2000 and open your local web. To insert a comment into your FrontPage 2000 Web page, do the following:

1. Select Insert, Comment.

2. Type your comment in the Comment box (see Figure 5.1). Click OK.

You'll notice that your comment text is in purple at the top of your page to set it apart from other regular text. It is also prefaced by "Comment:"

If you click the HTML tab, you can see the actual code that FrontPage inserts in your page when you add a comment. The codes, `<!--` and `-->`, are the standard HTML codes used for inserting comments into HTML pages. They are used here to keep the WebBot codes from being displayed in a browser, in addition to indicating a comment.

Adding a Hit Counter

One of the most commonly asked question from Web publishing neophytes is "How do I add a *hit counter*?" Without FrontPage, you'd have to run a script on your server (a "CGI script") to add a hit counter. Most Web presence providers provide hit counter scripts that you can use. Some even

Figure 5.1

Inserting a
FrontPage
Comment is easy.

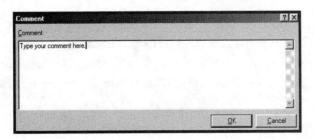

ADDING HTML COMMENTS

You can add a regular HTML comment to your FrontPage Web page. Open the HTML view, click the mouse where you want to add the comment, then type your comment bracketed within the HTML "comment" codes (`<!--`*Type your comment here.*`-->`). Unlike a FrontPage comment, a regular HTML comment won't show up in FrontPage's Normal view. You can view HTML comments in the HTML view, or by viewing the page source in a Web browser (View, Source in Internet Explorer 5.0; View, Page Source in Netscape Navigator 4.5).

let you run your own custom scripts, but it's best to leave that for the experts. Other providers won't let you run custom hit counter scripts at all.

▼ ▼

A *hit counter*, as the name implies, counts the number of "hits" to a Web page. Each visit to a Web page is a hit.

▲ ▲

FrontPage 2000 makes adding a hit counter a snap. There is no need to contact your server administrator or create your own scripts. FrontPage 2000 can do it all for you. To add a hit counter in FrontPage 2000, do the following:

1. Click the mouse where you want to insert the counter, then select Insert, Component, Hit Counter (see Figure 5.2).

2. Select the Counter Style you want to use.

3. If you want to start the hit counter at a number other than "1," select the first check box (Reset counter to) and type the number you want the counter to start with in the box to the right.

4. Select the second check box (Fixed number of digits). Type the number of digits you want displayed in the box to the right (if you type **5** for the number of digits, then the number for your hit counter will be displayed as "00005," for instance, instead of as "5").

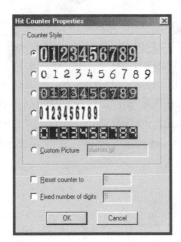

Figure 5.2

The Hit Counter
Properties dialog
box lets you choose
what kind of hit
counter you want to
add to your page.

5. Click OK. You'll see "[Hit Counter]" inserted in your page.

Before you can actually see your hit counter, you need to save and then publish your page. (If you already saved the page at the start of this session, just press Ctrl+S to resave it.) To be able to publish your page, you'll need to have either a Web space account on a FrontPage Web server (with the FrontPage 98 or 2000 server extensions installed) or a personal web server on your local hard drive.

If you already have an account on a FrontPage Web server, publish your web to your Web server as you normally would. When your web is published, FrontPage will provide a link you can click to preview your site. For information on finding a FrontPage Web presence provider and publishing your pages to a FrontPage server, see Appendix A, "Publishing Your FrontPage Web Pages."

 NOTE You can also install a personal Web server on your local hard drive. This will allow you to publish and preview your FrontPage web locally, before publishing to a remote server on the Web. For instructions on installing Microsoft Personal Web Server 4.0 (MS PWS 4.0) and the FrontPage 2000 server extensions, see Appendix E, "Implementing Special Features."

To preview components.htm (if that's what you've named the page), click the link you're provided at the end of the publish process. You'll need to type the file name (**components.htm**) at the end of the URL in the address box (http://yourserver/components.htm, for instance) and press Enter to see your components page. Or you can open your web that's on your server in FrontPage 2000, double-click on components.htm in the Folder List to open it, and then click on the Preview tab. (You can also select File, Preview in Browser.)

Formatting Your Hit Counter

Most Web designers add some text above a counter, such as "You're visitor number." Many also add text below a counter, such as "since July 1, 1999." (You would substitute the actual starting date for your counter.) To center the text and hit counter, select the two lines of text and the counter. Then, click the Center tool on the Formatting toolbar.

See Figure 5.3 to see what a hit counter will look like in a Web browser published to a FrontPage Web server. (This hit counter uses the first counter style, with the number of digits set to 5.)

Creating a Hover Button

I'm sure you've run across buttons in Web pages on the Web that change colors, display alternate images, or emit sound effects when the mouse is passed over them. "I'd sure like to put some of those in my Web pages," you probably thought, but then immediately decided that only professional

Figure 5.3

You won't be able to see your hit counter until you publish it to a FrontPage Web server.

CREATING YOUR OWN CUSTOM COUNTER

If you don't like any of the counter styles that come with FrontPage 2000, create your own! Use a graphics program, such as Image Composer 1.5 or PhotoDraw 2000, to create an image including the numbers 0 1 2 3 4 5 6 7 8 9. Space the numbers equally. If your image editor has rulers, use them to make sure that every number takes up an equal amount of space (don't forget that space also has to be added in before the "0" and after the "9"). Choose whatever font face and color you want to use and add other special effects, like a drop shadow, for instance. If you're using PhotoDraw 2000, you could even create a 3-D hit counter.

Save your hit counter graphic in the FrontPage Web folder that contains the page you want to use your custom counter in. Next, in the Hit Counter Properties dialog box for your counter, select the Custom Picture radio button and type the name of your new counter graphic in the box to the right. Click OK. Then publish your web to see what your new counter looks like. (If your numbers don't line up exactly, you may need to go back to your image editor and reposition the numbers in your counter graphic.)

Web programmers could figure out how to do it. Not so! Using FrontPage's *Hover Button* component, anybody can easily add dynamic buttons to their Web pages.

▼ ▼

A *hover button*, as its name implies, comes to life when the mouse hovers (or passes) over it. The Hover Button component actually inserts a Java applet into your page to which you can assign various properties, such as visual and sound effects. In addition, a hover button usually specifies a hypertext link to activate when the button is clicked.

▲ ▲

For this example, you'll be creating a text-based hover button. When the mouse passes over the button, a Glow effect will display behind the button text. To add a hover button to your page:

1. Click the mouse where you want to insert the hover button. Then select Insert, Component, Hover Button (see Figure 5.4).

2. In the Button text box, type the text you want to include in your button. For instance, you might type **My Home Page**, if you're creating a button that will loop back to your home page.

Figure 5.4

In the Hover Button Properties dialog box, you can specify the text, effect, colors, and size for your button.

3. To select a font for your text, click the Font button (see Figure 5.5).

4. For this example, leave the Font setting (MS Sans Serif) as it is, but select Bold for the Font style and 24 for the Size. To select a color for your text, click the Color box (try the bright yellow color). Click OK.

5. In the Link to box, type the URL of the file your button will link to when clicked. For this example, type the file name of any other file (an HTML, JPG, or GIF file) that is saved in the same folder as components.htm. You can leave the Link to box blank, if you wish. You could also type the full URL of any page out on the Web that you want to link to (**http://www.microsoft.com/frontpage**, for instance). For information on using the Link to box's Browse button to link to a file located elsewhere in your web, or to create a mailto link, see the next section, "Selecting Hover Button Hyperlinks Using the Browse Button."

Figure 5.5

In the Font dialog box, you can specify the font, style, size, and color for the button's text.

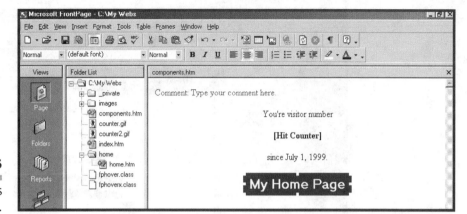

Figure 5.6

The hover button is added to the page.

 **CAUTION**   Hover buttons are Java applets, so file names (and other URLs) are case sensitive. If a file name is listed in the Folder List as MyFile.htm, for instance, you need to type it exactly as it appears (and *not* as myfile.htm).

6. To change the color of your button, click the Button color box. For this example, leave the color set as navy blue.

7. To change the effect you want to use, click the Effect box. For this example, leave Glow set as the effect. (After creating and previewing your hover button, feel free to try out any of the other effects, such as Bevel In or Bevel Out.)

8. To change the color of the effect, click the Effect color box. For this example, leave the effect color set as blue.

9. Since you increased the size of the font, you'll need to also increase the dimensions of the button. Type **200** as the Width and **40** as the Height. Click OK (see Figure 5.6).

Previewing Your Hover Button

You must save your file in order to preview your hover button. Save your file (Ctrl+S). Then click the Preview tab to preview your hover button. Try out

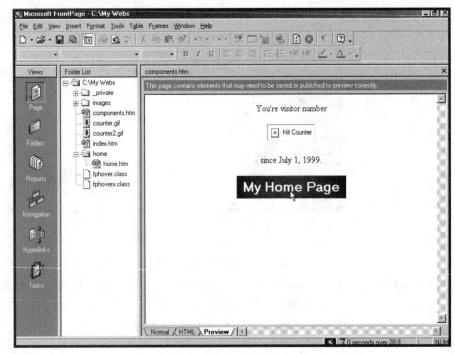

The glow effect
activates when the
mouse passes over
the hover button.

the hover button by passing the mouse over it (see Figure 5.7). If you added a link to the hover button, click on the link to jump to the linked page.

To edit the properties of your hover button in Normal view, double-click the hover button object.

Selecting Hover Button Hyperlinks Using the Browse Button

In the last section, you typed a file name in the Link to box for your hover button hyperlink, or just left it blank. To learn other ways you can link files or pages to your hover button, double-click your hover button to open the Hover Button Properties dialog box. Then click the Browse button (next to the Link to box). In the Select Hover Button Hyperlink dialog box, you can then select to:

○ Link to a file within the currently open FrontPage web

○ Link to a file on the Web

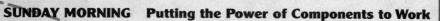
- Link to a page located elsewhere on your computer

- Link to your e-mail address

- Create a new page and link to it

- Link to a bookmark or a frame target

To link to a file or page in an open web, open the folder where the file or page you want to link to is located, and then click the file you want to link to. For example, to create a relative URL (home/home.htm), select a page (home.htm) in a subfolder (\home) that is located in your web's root folder. (The linking page, components.htm, must also be in the root folder.)

To link to a file or page on the Internet, click the first icon to the right of the URL box. Connect to the Internet if necessary and then use your browser to browse to the URL that you want to use. When you close your browser, the URL you last browsed to will be inserted in the URL box.

To link to a file or page that is located on your local computer, but outside of your open web, click the second icon to the right of the URL box. In the Select File dialog box, browse to and click the file you want to link to. When you resave your page, FrontPage will automatically prompt you to resave the file within your open web.

To create an e-mail link, click the third button to the right of the URL box. Type your e-mail address and click OK. This will allow someone to click the hover button to send you an e-mail message.

To create a new page and then link your hover button to it, click the fourth button to the right of the URL box. Double-click the Normal Page template (or any other template you want to use) to open a new page. Close the Hover Button Properties dialog box. Create and save your new page. Reopen the page where your hover button is (components.htm, for instance). Double-click the hover button to edit its properties. You'll see that the name of your new page has been inserted into the Link to box.

The Browse button also lets you specify a bookmark or a frame target for your link. To link to a bookmark within the page you're linking to, first select the page. Then select the bookmark you want to link to from the Bookmark pull-down list. To link to a frame target, select the "pencil" button to the right of the Target frame box.

Adding Sound to Your Hover Button

You can add a sound effect to your hover button that will play when the mouse moves over or clicks on it. However, since hover buttons are actually Java applets, you are limited to using only one type of sound file: 8-bit, 8000 Hz, mono, u-law *.au sound files. To add an *.au sound effect to your hover button:

1. In the Hover Button Properties dialog box, click the Custom button.

2. If you have a compatible *.au file, click the Browse button (next to On click). If the *.au file is outside of your web, click the second icon to the right of the URL box to browse for it.

FIND IT ON ▶
THE CD

You can use Cool Edit 96, available on the CD-ROM, to convert other sound formats to 8-bit, 8000 Hz, mono, u-law *.au sound files. First open the sound file you want to convert and then select Edit, Convert Sample Type, and 8000 (as the Sample Rate). Select the Mono radio button and the 8-bit radio button. Click OK. Select File, Save As. In the Save as type box, select Next/Sun (*.au,*.snd). Click the Options button and select the mu-Law 8-bit radio button. Click OK.

Select the folder where you want to save your sound file. Click Save.

---

3. To select an *.au sound file that will play when the mouse is passed over the button, click the Browse button next to the On hover box.

4. Click OK.

After you add sound effects to a hover button, you cannot preview the button in the Preview view. Instead, you will see a grayed-out box in place of the button when you view the page in Preview view. After saving your page, you need to publish your web to a FrontPage server to preview your hover button. (If you've installed a personal web server on your local hard drive, you can preview your hover button's sound effects after publishing to your personal web server.)

Using Images in Hover Buttons

You don't have to stick to creating text-only hover buttons. You can specify image files for both your button and the button's hover effect. The primary

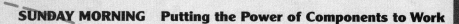

advantage of using images for your hover button is that you can use any font you have installed for creating your button text. You can also use other effects, such as drop shadows, gradient fills, patterns, and 3-D effects.

You'll need to first create the images you want to use in an image editor (such as Image Composer 1.5 or PhotoDraw 2000). Once you've created and saved the images you want to use, follow these steps to include them in your hover button:

1. In the Hover Button Properties dialog box, click the Custom button.

2. Click the Browse button to the right of the Button box to select the image file you want to use for your button. (Click the second button to the right of the URL box to browse your computer's files, if the image file is not in one of your web's folders.)

3. Click the Browse button to the right of the On hover box to select the image file you want to use for your button's hover effect. Click OK.

4. Delete any text that's displayed in the Button text box (otherwise, it'll be displayed over your images).

5. In the Width and Height boxes, type the width and height (in pixels) of your images. Click OK.

   Before you'll be able to preview your new hover button, you need to save your file and then publish your web to a FrontPage server. Figure 5.8 shows an example of an image-based hover button as it appears

Figure 5.8

When previewing an image-based hover button in a Java-enabled browser, before the mouse cursor passes over the button, the first image is displayed.

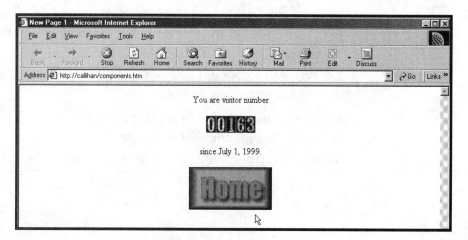

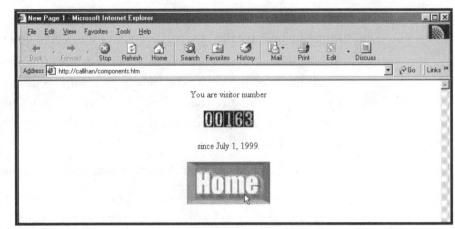

Figure 5.9

When the mouse cursor passes over an image-based cover button, the second image is displayed.

in Internet Explorer 5.0, with the mouse cursor not yet passing over the button. Figure 5.9 shows the same hover button, but this time with the mouse cursor passing over it. If you've assigned any sound effects, they'll also play when you pass the mouse over or click the hover button.

Take a Break!

So far this morning, you've learned to add comments, hit counters, and hover buttons to your pages. Feel free at this point to get up and take a break. If you haven't had your breakfast yet, go ahead and fix yourself a bite. You've got lots more to do today, so you don't want to short yourself on energy. If the morning has stretched on towards noon, break for lunch. The rest of this session is optional, so feel free to skip ahead at this point to the Sunday Afternoon session.

However, if the morning is still young and you're ready to go, I'll see you back here in ten minutes or so. In the next section, you'll learn how to use more of FrontPage 2000's handy components.

Using Include Pages

You may want to repeat information on many different pages, or on all of your pages. You can create a separate page that includes the information you want to use repeatedly, and then use FrontPage 2000's Include Page component to easily add it to your pages.

Creating a Page to Be Included

An include page is just a regular Web page that is included in another page. For this example, you'll be creating a separate page that will hold your address block—your name, e-mail address, URL, and any other information you'd like to include at the bottom of your pages. To create this page:

1. If you're continuing from the previous example, create a new page (select File, New, Page, and double-click the Normal Page icon). If you've restarted FrontPage 2000, a new page should already be open (new_page_1.htm).

2. To add a separator above your address section, insert a horizontal line. Select Insert, Horizontal Line. (To edit the properties of your horizontal line, double-click the line.)

3. From the Style list on the Formatting toolbar, select Address. Type your name (since you've applied the Address format style, the text should be in italics). Don't add a hard return (by hitting the Enter key). Instead, add a line break (select Insert, Break, and OK). This adds a single-space, rather than a double-space, between the lines.

4. Add a link to your e-mail address. Type **E-Mail:** followed by a space, and then type your e-mail address. Select your e-mail address with the mouse. Select Insert, Hyperlink. Click the third icon to the right of the URL box (the icon with the envelope on it, as shown in Figure 5.10). Type your e-mail address and click OK. Click OK again. Add another line break. (Click the mouse at the end of the line, then click Insert, Break, and OK.)

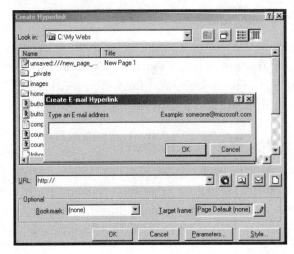

Figure 5.10

In the Create
E-mail Hyperlink
dialog box, you can
create a link to your
e-mail address.

NOTE Some browsers, including some earlier versions of Internet Explorer, can't handle e-mail links. To allow for those browsers, it is a good idea to always include your actual e-mail address as your linked text, instead of using something like "Click here to e-mail me," and so on. That way, even if their browser won't handle mailto links, a visitor to your site will still be able to contact you using their regular e-mail client.

5. On the next line, add the URL for your home page, if you have one. Type **Home Page:** followed by a space, and then select Insert, Hyperlink. Following "http://," type the rest of your home page's URL and click OK. Click the space bar once, and then add another line break (see Figure 5.11).

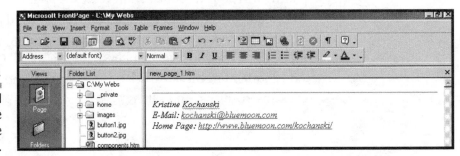

Figure 5.11

Add a name, e-mail
address, and home
page URL to the
address section.

6. Type anything else you want to include, such as your address, phone number, and so on. Add line breaks, rather than hard returns, at the end of each line.

7. Save your file as address.htm.

Adding the Date and Time

Including the date and time when a page was last updated can be helpful to visitors of your site. This is also called a timestamp. If you keep your page updated on a regular basis, it will tell them that the info on your page is the latest and the greatest. Manually doing this, however, at the bottom of every page that you edit or update can be a royal pain, to say the least. The trick here is to use FrontPage 2000's Date and Time component to add the date and time to your address page. Then you only need to include this page at the bottom of all your other pages and they will automatically be stamped with the date and time when you last made changes to them. To add a date and timestamp to your address section:

1. If you haven't done so already, add a line break at the end of the last line you added to your address section.

2. Type **Last Updated:** followed by a space, and then select Insert, Date and Time.

3. In the Date and Time Properties dialog box, leave the first radio button (Date this page was last edited) selected (see Figure 5.12).

4. From the Date format list, select the format you want to use to display the date.

Figure 5.12

You can stamp your page with the date and time when the page was last edited or updated.

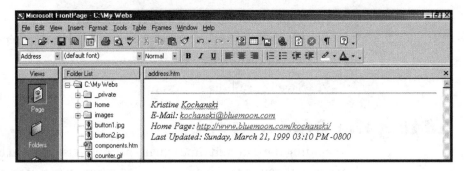

Figure 5.13

The date and
timestamp has been
added to the
address section.

5. From the Time format list, select the format you want to use to display the time.

6. Click OK (see Figure 5.13). Press Ctrl+S to resave address.htm.

Including Your Address Page

Now, all you have to do is include your address page (address.htm) at the bottom of any other page you create. You should never have to create an address section again for any of your pages. They will be automatically stamped with the new date and time whenever you make update changes to them. Follow the steps listed below to insert address.htm at the bottom of components.htm:

1. In the Folder List, double-click on components.htm to open it.

2. To include your address page at the bottom of your components page, place your cursor at the bottom of the page, select Insert, Component, Include Page.

3. In the Include Page Properties dialog box, type **address.htm** (or you can click the Browse button to select the file, as shown in Figure 5.14). Click OK.

As shown in Figure 5.15, your address page should now be included at the bottom of components.htm. Now, whenever you make any editing changes to the page, the date and timestamp will update automatically.

You can add your include page in any other page you create in your web, even if your include page and the page where you want to add it are not in

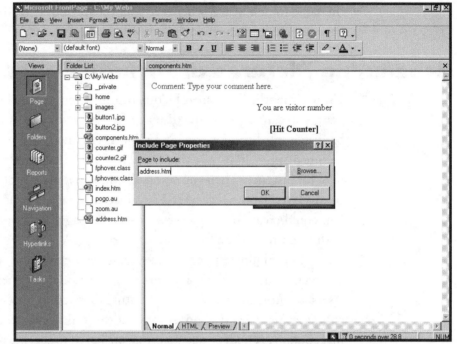

Figure 5.14

The page, *address.htm*, will be included at the cursor location in the current page.

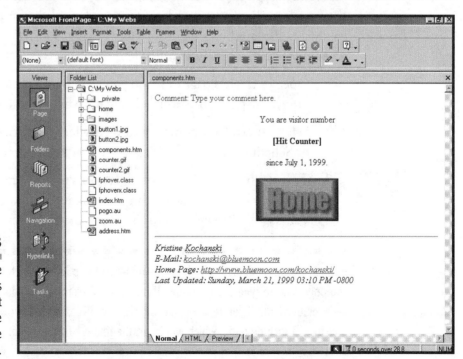

Figure 5.15

The address page (*address.htm*) has been included at the bottom of the current page (*components.htm*).

the same folder. Then, whenever you update your include page, all of the pages where it has been included will also be automatically updated.

Scheduling Pictures or Include Pages

Using either the Scheduled Picture or the Scheduled Include Page component, you can schedule the display of a picture or page so that it will only be displayed during a specified period. For instance, you could create a picture or an include page that is tied to a particular holiday, such as Christmas, for instance. Then you could schedule that picture or page so it would be displayed from December 15 to December 25, but not before or after. You could create other pictures or include pages that would be displayed leading up to and on other holidays, such as Valentine's Day, Easter, the 4th of July, Halloween, or Thanksgiving. You could also schedule pictures and pages that would display only on the birthdays of friends, relatives, or associates. You could also use this feature to schedule articles, press releases, announcements, and so on. Another idea would be to create include pages that contain agendas or calendars that are keyed to specific months or weeks. You would only need to update, save, and publish the pages, and they would be displayed automatically only during their relevant periods. To schedule pictures or include pages:

1. Open or create a page in which you want to insert a scheduled picture or include page. In Normal view, click where you want to insert it.

2. Select Insert, Component, and then select either Scheduled Picture or Scheduled Include Page, as shown in Figure 5.16.

3. Type the file name (or relative URL) of a picture or include page you want to schedule in the During the scheduled time text box. You can also use the Browse button to select a picture or include page.

TIP If the file to be scheduled is in the same folder as the page in which it will be displayed, you only need to type the file name. If it is in a different folder, you'll need to type the file's relative URL. If you're hazy on using relative URLs, use the Browse button to select a picture or include page, which will insert the relative URL for you.

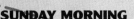
Figure 5.16

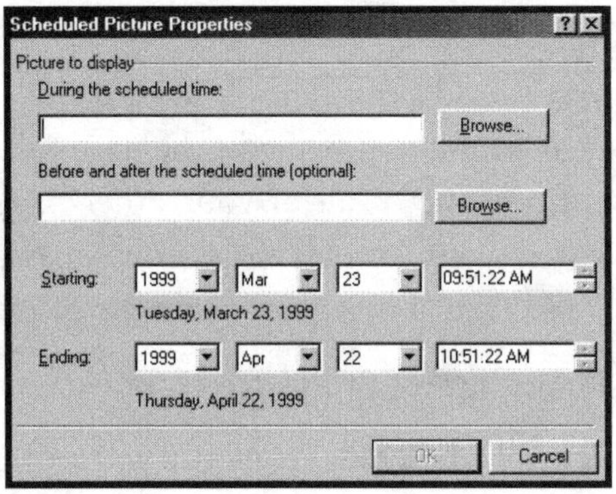

The only difference
between the
Scheduled Picture
and Scheduled
Include Page
Properties dialog
boxes is that you
specify pictures in
one and pages in
the other.

4. Optionally, you can type the file name (or relative URL) of a picture or include page you want to display before and after the scheduled time in the second text box. You can also use the Browse button to select a picture or include page.

5. Under Starting, choose when you want the schedule period for the picture or include page to start. (The default is the current year, month, day, and time.)

6. Under Ending, choose when you want the schedule period for the picture or include page to end. (The default is one month from the current year, month, day, and time.)

7. Click OK to insert the scheduled picture or include page.

Adding a Search Form

One of the handier features you can add to your Web site is a search form that allows visitors to do a keyword search of your site. It's easy! The only requirement is that your Web server has the FrontPage Server Extensions installed for your account. There are two ways to set up a search form for your Web site:

✿ Using the Search Page template

✿ Adding the Search Page component to another page

Using the Search Page Template

This is the easiest way to add a search form to your site. Create a new page, using the Search Page template. Then edit the page to add your own content and link to it from one or all of your other pages. You might, for instance, want to link to your "Search" page from a navigation bar inserted in a shared border. To create a new page using the Search Page template:

1. Select File, New, Page (or press Ctrl+N, or click the New Page icon).

2. Under the General tab, scroll down until you see the Search Page template (see Figure 5.17). Double-click it to open it (see Figure 5.18).

Edit the page to add your own heading, graphics, and other information. Edit the page properties to create your own title. Edit the author info at the bottom of the page or, if you want to, go ahead and add the include page (address.htm) that you created earlier. When satisfied, save your new file (as search.htm, for instance).

Adding the Search Form Component to Another Page

You may already have created a page to which you want to add a search form. It's easy using the Search Form component. For this example, if

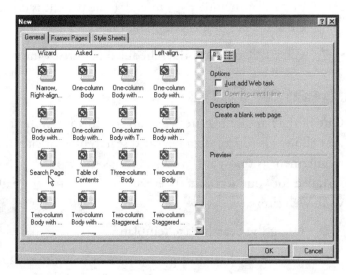

Figure 5.17

Select the Search Form template to create a new page with a ready-made search form.

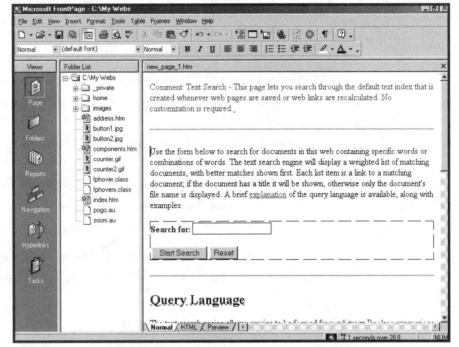

Figure 5.18

A new page with a
search form is
opened in
FrontPage.

component.htm is not displayed, double-click on component.htm in the
Folder List to bring it to the front. To add a search form to component.htm
(or any other page):

1. In Normal view, click where you want to insert the search form.
    Select Insert, Component, Search Form (see Figure 5.19).

Figure 5.19

The Search Form
Properties dialog
box lets you alter
the look and feel of
your search form.

2. Under the Search Form Properties tab, you can specify the input label, the character width of the input box, and the labels for the start and clear buttons. For this example, leave all the settings as they are.

3. Under the Search Results tab (see Figure 5.20), the Display options check boxes let you specify how you want the search results to be presented. If left clear, only file names will be listed. Check the appropriate box if you also want the match score, file date, or file size displayed. For this example, leave all the settings as they are. Click OK (see Figure 5.21).

4. To check out what your search form will look like when displayed in a browser, click the Preview tab. (See Figure 5.22.)

To actually test out your search form, you will need to publish it to a server with the FrontPage Server Extensions running. If you have installed a per-

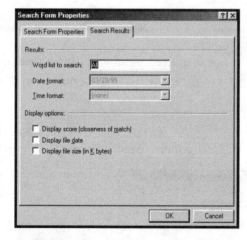

Figure 5.20

The Search Results tab lets you specify how you want search results to be presented.

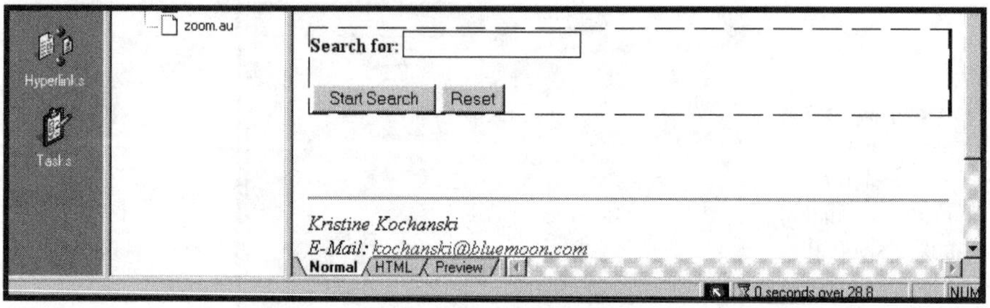

Figure 5.21

A search form is added to the page.

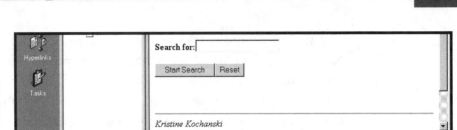

Figure 5.22

Use Preview
to show the
search form.

sonal web server (PWS) on your computer, you will be able to check out
your search form locally, before publishing your web to a FrontPage server
on the Web. (For instructions for installing PWS 4.0, see Appendix E,
"Implementing Special Features.") Here are some quick pointers on what
else you can do with the Search Form component:

- Double-click the Search Form component in Normal view to re-
  edit its properties. Change the input and button labels to give your
  search form a different look and feel (that way, it won't look like
  every other FrontPage search form on the Web).

- Under the Search Results tab, you should always leave **All** as the
  Word list to search unless you're creating a search form for a discussion group. (To limit the search for a discussion group, replace **All**
  with the name of the discussion group folder.)

- FrontPage 2000 automatically generates an index of the words included in your web. As you save new pages, new words are continually
  added to the index. However, when you delete a page, or remove
  material from a page, the index entries for those pages are not removed from the search index. To create a new search index, with
  outdated entries removed, click Tools and Recalculate Hyperlinks.
  (If you have a lot of pages in your web, this can take a couple of
  minutes, so be patient.)

Creating a Table of Contents

Another feature seen on many Web sites is a table of contents that provides
links to all of the pages in the site. Using FrontPage 2000's Table of Contents component makes adding a table of contents for your web a snap.

The Table of Contents component can create a table of contents of every page in your web, of all pages linked to from your default home page (index.htm or default.htm, for instance), or of only pages linked to from any other page you might specify. For this example, you will create a table of contents of all pages linked to from your default home page. Before creating a table of contents, you may need to do a little set-up work first:

○ Your default home page (index.htm or default.htm, for instance) should have hyperlinks from it to other pages in your web. If not, you'll need to edit your default home page to add some hyperlinks to it. (If the pages you're linking to don't exist yet, you should go ahead and create them first.)

○ Because page titles are used to create the table of contents entries, you should make sure that descriptive titles have been created for all the pages that will be listed in the table of contents. Right-click on any page, select Page Properties, and then type a descriptive title in the Title box.

○ To see how the Table of Contents component can present a hierarchical listing of all pages branching off from your default home page, you should have at least one page linked to from your default home page which links to another page.

As with the Search Form, there are two ways to create a table of contents:

○ Using the Table of Contents template

○ Adding the Table of Contents component to another page

Using the Table of Contents Template

If you've done the prep work detailed in the previous section, here's all you have to do to create a new page using the Table of Contents template:

1. Select File, New, Page (or press Ctrl+N, or click the New Page icon).

2. Under the General tab, scroll down until you see the Table of Contents template. Double-click it to open it (see Figure 5.23).

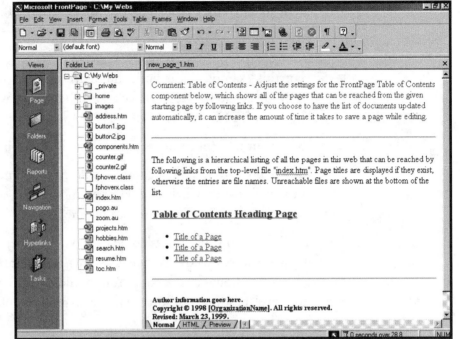

Figure 5.23

A new page created with the Table of Contents template.

3. To edit the properties of the Table of Contents component (under "Table of Contents Heading Page"), double-click it (see Figure 5.24).

4. The name of your default home page is automatically displayed in the box (Page URL for starting point of table) at the top of the dialog box. For this example, just leave this option as it is. If you

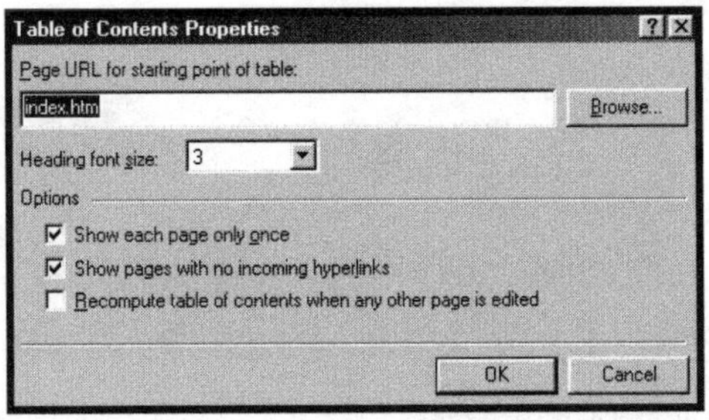

Figure 5.24

You determine what your table of contents will display by editing its properties.

wanted to create a table of contents branching off from a different page, you would type its file name or relative URL (or use the Browse button to select it).

5. For this example, clear both the first check box (Show each page only once) and the second check box (Show pages with no incoming hyperlinks). Click OK.

6. Save your table of contents page (as toc.htm, for instance).

7. To see how your table of contents will look, you need to preview it in your browser. Click File, Preview in Browser, and double-click the browser you want to use (see Figure 5.25).

Since the links from your default home page will be different, your table of contents won't look exactly like what's shown in Figure 5.25. The basic layout, however, should be the same. You should enhance the page by adding a top-level heading (Heading 1), a background color or image, or applying a theme before publishing.

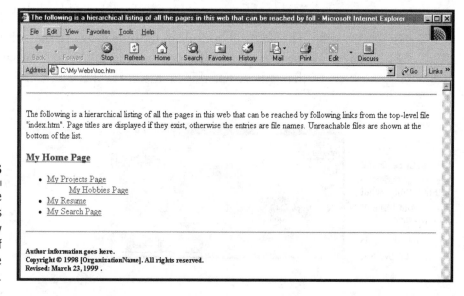

Figure 5.25

Preview of the table of contents page generated by the Table of Contents template in Internet Explorer.

TABLE OF CONTENTS CHECK BOX OPTIONS

In the Table of Contents Properties dialog box, you control what will be included in your table of contents by selecting or clearing any of the Options check boxes.

Selecting the first check box (Show each page only once) will include a linked page only the first time it appears in the table of contents.

Selecting the second check box (Show pages with no incoming hyperlinks) will include all pages in your web, regardless of whether they are linked to from any other pages.

Selecting the third check box (Recompute table of contents when any other page is edited) will create a dynamic table of contents that will change as your site changes.

Adding the Table of Contents Component to Another Page

You don't have to use the Table of Contents template to create a table of contents. You may prefer using the Table of Contents component to insert a table of contents into a page you've already created. Do the following:

1. Create or open a page into which you want to insert the table of contents. Position the cursor where you want to insert the table of contents, and then select Insert, Component, Table of Contents.

2. Make any changes you want to make in the Table of Contents Properties dialog box. I'd recommend clearing any of the check boxes that are checked. (See the sidebar, "Table of Contents Check Box Options," in the previous section for descriptions of the check box options.) Click OK.

3. Save your page and then preview it in your browser.

Using the Banner Ad Manager Component

The Banner Ad Manager component allows you to insert a revolving banner ad (or any other set of images) in your page. You can link your banner ad to any other page, or you can use it as a way of inserting slide shows into your page.

Before you start to use the Banner Ad Manager component, you should either create the images you are going to use or decide what images you already have that you want to use. The images, ideally, should all be the same dimensions (make a note of the width and height). To use the Banner Ad Manager:

1. Position the mouse cursor where you want to insert the banner ad. (Banner ads are usually displayed at the top of a page.) Select Insert, Component, Banner Ad Manager.

2. Type the dimensions of your banner ad images in the Width and Height boxes.

3. From the Transition effect list, you can select a transition. For this example, leave the Dissolve transition selected.

4. In the next text box, Show each picture for (seconds), type the number of seconds you want each image to be displayed. For this example, leave 5 as the number of seconds.

5. In the Link to box, type the URL of the page you want your banner ad to link to. For example, to link the banner ad to Microsoft's FrontPage site, type **http://www.microsoft.com/frontpage/**. To link to a file in the same folder, type the file name. You can also use the Browse button to select a file in your web to link to.

6. Click the Add button to add the first banner image. Select the banner image you want to add (if the image you want to use is outside of your web, click the second icon to the right of the URL box to select it).

7. Repeat Step 6 for each additional image you want to add (see Figure 5.26). Click OK when done.

8. Click the Center icon on the Formatting toolbar to center your banner ad, as shown in Figure 5.27. Save your page.

Before you will be able to actually test the banner ad, you'll need to publish it to a FrontPage server. To preview it locally, you need to have installed a

Figure 5.26

Two images are added to the Banner Ad Manager.

Figure 5.27

A banner ad is added to the top of the page.

Figure 5.28

You need to publish a banner ad to a FrontPage server before you can preview it in your browser.

personal web server. Figure 5.28 shows an example of a banner ad displayed in Internet Explorer.

Wrapping Up

If you've made it all the way through this session, you've covered a lot of ground. You should have at least a basic understanding of how to add comments, hit counters, hover buttons, include pages, scheduled pictures, scheduled include pages, timestamps, search forms, tables of contents, and banner ads to your FrontPage pages.

If you've got any time left this morning, feel free to experiment further with any of the components covered in this session.

There are also a few components that weren't covered in this session: the Office components (Spreadsheet, PivotTable, and Chart), the Marquee component, the Substitution component, and the Categories component. Feel free to come back later and experiment with these other components. For more information on using the Office Spreadsheet, Office PivotTable, and Office Chart components, click the Help icon within those components.

Take a break now for lunch. You've got lots more to do in the next session, so get something nourishing. If you feel like it, go for a short walk (don't be gone too long, though!). See you back here in an hour or so for the Sunday Afternoon session, "Finalizing Your Pages."

Finalizing Your Pages

- ✿ Saving and Previewing Your Web Site
- ✿ Organizing Files in Your Web Site
- ✿ Working with FrontPage Reports
- ✿ Making Changes to Multiple Pages
- ✿ Completing Web Tasks

Wow, look how far you've come in the last day and a half. You started with only basic knowledge about Web page design, and in less than 48 hours, you've graduated to top-notch Web designer. Now it's time to clean up all those "little things" you need to do before you actually publish your web online. In addition to the editing tools you've already learned, you'll find that FrontPage contains some very handy, well-designed tools to make cleanup fast and easy.

Saving and Previewing Your Web Site

When you were learning how to add hyperlinks to your Web site, you spent some time checking your links by viewing pages in Preview as well as perusing your pages in one or more browsers.

Before I get into the nitty gritty of site clean-up and management, take a few minutes now to check your entire site using the same methods you learned Saturday morning. Be on the lookout not just for broken links, but also for anything that might seem amiss: misaligned table text, figures that do not load properly, formatting problems—anything. Take careful notes on what to fix—or better yet, use the Tasks feature to create reminders for each problem. Also, remember these things about your Web site:

- ✿ Don't forget that your main home page must have a specific name—most likely index.html. Check with your WPP to find out for sure which you need. If you don't yet have a host for your Web site, go with index.html. You can fix this at the last minute if need be. Remember,

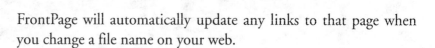

FrontPage will automatically update any links to that page when you change a file name on your web.

○ If you're using frames, the frames page itself must be the default index page.

○ Be sure that you've saved all the files. The fastest way to confirm this is to select File, Exit, and then click Yes or Yes to All when prompted to save your pages and/or graphics.

○ Sometimes I find it helpful to publish the web to another Web folder on my hard drive, or to the personal web server. I then open that web in my browser. This technique gives me the ability to see the site from a slightly new perspective. It also helps to identify some problematic links that might not otherwise be obvious—such as those that still point to a file URL that is on the hard drive rather than within the FrontPage Web site.

I found a big problem with my site's home page when I opened it in Netscape 4.5. I forgot that it doesn't support the graphic image background I added to my table, and the results produced in Netscape are illegible (see Figure 6.1). I need to fix that one right away!

Organizing Files in Your Web Site

Even if you're not the "detail type," you know it's important to keep files reasonably organized on your hard drive. For example, you most likely store your working Office documents in the My Documents folder, your applications are stored in the Program Files folder, system files in your Windows folder, and so on. You know that if you just store files any old place, you eventually end up with such a mess on your computer that it's almost impossible to find anything without extensive searches. (There's nothing more frustrating than the "now where the heck did I put that blasted thing??" syndrome.)

Along the same lines, it's good to keep your web files organized logically within the folder structure. By default, FrontPage creates a folder in your web called images, and stores any imported graphic files there unless you

Figure 6.1

This button bar looked fine in Internet Explorer, but Netscape Navigator doesn't support the table background image.

tell it otherwise. FrontPage also creates some folders for its own use. You'll recognize these easily; they have names like _private, _theme, or _fpclass (see Figure 6.2).

The more your web grows, the more important it will be to keep your files neat and tidy. If you have several topics within your web, and each site includes several pages, consider storing all those related pages in one folder. To create new folders in your web, follow these steps:

TIP The _private folder—and any other folder name that is preceded by an underscore (_)—is hidden to visitors, as are the files stored there. If you need to create more hidden folders or files, create them under the _private folder, or contact your WSP for help.

1. Click the Folders button on the Views bar to switch to Folders view.

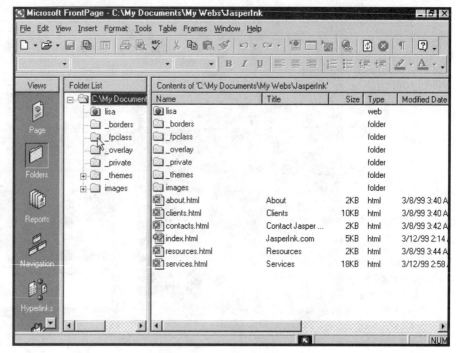

Figure 6.2

Any folder or file name that begins with an underscore (_) is invisible to visitors.

2. Select File, New, Folder. FrontPage will create a new folder. The default name, New_Folder, will be highlighted and ready for you to enter in a more logical name (see Figure 6.3).

3. Type the new name and press Enter. In the example, I'm adding a folder to sort out all the files that relate to this book.

FIND IT ON ▶ THE WEB

You can access the sample pages and files for this book at **www.prima-tech.com/ frontpage2000** or at my Web site, **www.jasperink.com/frontpage**.

4. After you've created the folders for your major categories, simply drag all the related files to the appropriate folders. Remember you can move or copy files and folders from one web to another by dragging them out of or into the site's Folders view.

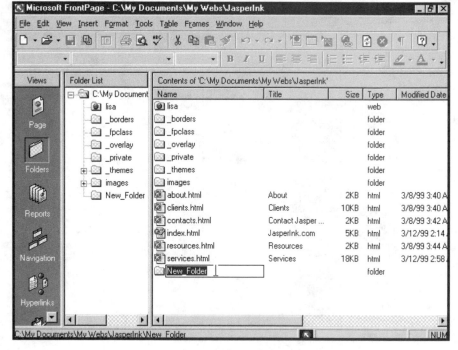

Figure 6.3

I'll keep the sample files for this book in a separate folder so I don't confuse them with my main pages.

Feel free to also create subfolders within those folders. In other words, use whatever organizational system best suits your needs, be it a handful of folders, or a detailed multilayer folder structure. See Figure 6.4 for an example.

While you're at it, make sure that all your files have names that make sense to you. When it's time to go back and edit one page of the dozens or hundreds of pages in your site, you'll appreciate this advice. Except for the home page, file names are not important to anyone other than you. The browser doesn't care what you name a file as long as you use the correct extension. Your visitors will rarely need to know a specific page's file name as long as the link works properly.

Take a Break!

Your Web site will be ready for posting shortly. Take a short break now before you head into the home stretch. When you come back, you'll tour the FrontPage reports, which help you keep your site up-to-date and efficient.

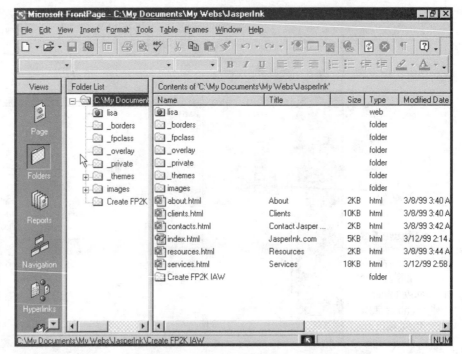

Figure 6.4

This web contains both subfolders and subwebs, making it much easier to manage files for a large—or even medium—web.

A WEB WITHIN A WEB WITHIN A WEB?

If you're hosting more than one Web site within your domain, you can actually publish each one as a *subweb* within your main FrontPage web.

For example, the Jasper Ink Web site also is home to my personal Web site. Other than links to each other and the fact that I maintain both of them, the two sites are unrelated. Thus, I treat them as separate Web sites, but keep the files for both sites under the **www.jasperink.com** umbrella site.

Each subweb has its own home page, and can use files with the same names as the other site without conflict or confusion.

As my business grows, I might decide to allow my employees to create their own personal Web sites and host them within the jasperink.com domain. Using FrontPage's security features, I can give each employee authoring and maintenance rights to his or her pages without compromising the security of the overall site. (See Appendix E, "Implementing Special Features," for more information on site security.)

By storing subwebs within a main web, you can conveniently publish updates to the entire domain in one fell swoop (perhaps as part of an automated maintenance procedure that runs overnight), or you can update and publish the subwebs individually.

Then you'll learn how to make changes to multiple pages in your web, and you'll complete the remaining items on your Task list. So off you go. . .come on back when you're ready to wrap things up.

Working with FrontPage Reports

After you're comfortable with your folder and file organization and naming schemes, you're ready to look at what FrontPage has to say about your web design and structure.

As you learned on Friday evening, the Reports view includes 15 different reports about your site. Some are informational only, others provide detailed views you can study. This allows you to streamline and improve the overall effectiveness of your site.

Generating a Site Summary

To begin working through the various reports, start by clicking the Reports button on the Views bar. If this is your first time working in the Reports view, the Site Summary report will appear first, as shown in Figure 6.5.

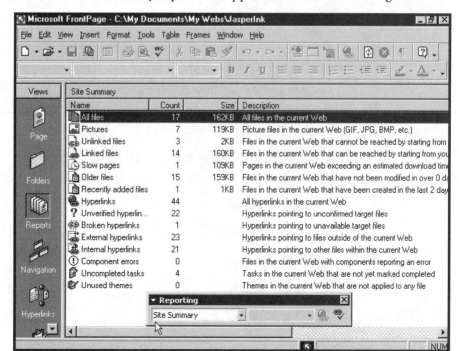

Figure 6.5.

The Site Summary is the at-a-glance view of the various FrontPage reports.

The site summary lists the overall results of each of the 15 reports at a glance, so you can quickly identify trouble spots.

NOTE If it doesn't appear by default, open the Reports toolbar while you're working in Reports view. Right-click anywhere on a FrontPage toolbar and click Reporting.

The Reporting toolbar gives you convenient access to the various FrontPage reports via a drop-down list—including some reports that are not available in the standard Site Summary. I won't cover those advanced reports here, but feel free to peruse them at your leisure.

The Reporting toolbar also lets you customize options and values for certain reports. For example, you can define what minimum load time is considered "slow" for the Slow Pages report. (You can also change these options by selecting Tools, Options, and then clicking the Reports View tab.)

NOTE Subsequent returns to the Reports view take you back to the last report you viewed onscreen. To reopen the Site Summary, select View, Reports, Site Summary.

Using the FrontPage Reports

To access any report, just double-click its listing in the Site Summary, or choose a specific report from the View, Reports submenu. The available reports include the following:

- *All Files.* Lists the number and collective size of every file in your web; double-click the report to see the details of each file:
    - Name
    - Title
    - Location
    - Size
    - Type

- Date
- Time it was last updated
- Who did the updating
- Any additional comments the page creator might have entered during the design process

NOTE In the Site Summary, the total number of files and their collective size will give you an idea of how much storage space your web will use on the Web server. Keep in mind, however, that by default the report does not include the size of any hidden or system files that FrontPage may have created automatically. To add hidden files to the report (and to make them appear in the Folders view), select Options, Web Settings. Then click the Advanced tab, and select the Show documents in hidden directories check box.

- **Pictures**. A subset of the All Files report. Lists the total number of graphics files (.gif, .jpg, and so on) in your Web site and their collective size. No detailed report is available for just the graphics files; however, you can get this information from the All Files report.

TIP In most of the detailed reports, you can click a field's column heading to sort the report's line items by that field. Thus, if you want to know the name, size, and type of only the graphic files in your web, open the All Files report. Click the Type column heading, and then scroll down the list to see all the files of a particular type.

- **Unlinked Files**. Lists any files in your web that cannot be reached by starting from your home page. You may have created a page and later changed your mind about using it, or you might have forgotten to add a link to it from another page. Double-click this report to pinpoint those files and either delete them or work them into the web structure. You can remove unwanted files directly from this report by selecting them and pressing Delete.

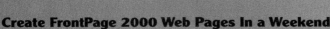

- **Linked Files**. The counterpart to the Unlinked Files report, this report lists the total number of files that *can* be reached via hyperlinks within the web. No detailed view is available.

- **Slow Pages**. Visitors don't like sitting around waiting for pages to load before they can go on. Double-click the Slow Pages report to see the full list, and then open each page one by one to see what you might do to speed up this page. Most often, you'll find that pages with lots of graphics, or even one large graphic, will quickly increase the load time for a page. To avoid this problem, keep the size of your graphics files as small as possible.

TIP You can see the estimated load time of a page while you're editing it. Just check the status bar while you're in Edit view. Near the right end of the status bar, you'll see a small hourglass icon followed by the number of estimated seconds and the default connection (modem) speed to assume. Right-click the connection speed to select a new speed from the shortcut menu.

- **Older Files**. This report lists the number and collective size of the pages in your web that have not been updated for 30 days. Use this report to keep track of pages that will occasionally need a quick refreshing. (It's a safe bet that a page called "Today's News" that has not been updated for 89 days doesn't really contain today's news—unless of course you're Bill Murray in the movie *Groundhog Day.*) Double-click the report to see the details of each file. You can change the number of days since the update via the Reports View tab of the Options dialog box.

- **Recently Added Files**. The counterpart to the Older Files report, this report lists any files that have been added to your site within the last several days (2 by default). If you recently created a file and now can't remember what you called it, here's a good place to start looking.

- **Hyperlinks**. This report shows a summary of the total number of hyperlinks in your site, including internal and external. No detailed

view of this report is available. Instead, double-clicking this report opens the Broken Hyperlinks report, which you worked with on Saturday afternoon. Check the individual External Hyperlinks and Internal Hyperlinks reports to see the breakdown.

- **Unverified Hyperlinks**. A subset of the Hyperlinks report, this view shows only links that have not been checked for accuracy (they may or may not be broken). Double-clicking the report opens the Broken Links report, so you can find out for sure.

- **Broken Hyperlinks**. A subset of the Hyperlinks report, you can use this helpful tool to find errors in your links. Flip back to "Testing Your Work" in Saturday afternoon's session for a detailed explanation of using the Broken Hyperlinks report.

- **External Hyperlinks**. A subset of the Hyperlinks report, this is the total number of links that point to other Web sites. No detailed view is available. Click the Hyperlinks button on the View bar to check out your hyperlink structure.

- **Internal Hyperlinks**. A subset of the Hyperlinks report, this is the total number of links to pages and bookmarks within your own Web site. No detailed view is available. Click the Hyperlinks button on the View bar to check out your hyperlink structure.

- **Component Errors**. This report lists the total number of files in your web containing FrontPage components that are not working properly. Double-click the report to list and open specific files.

- **Uncompleted Tasks**. This report gives you a quick peek at the status of your Tasks list. Double-click the report to switch to the Tasks view. (Later in this session you'll diligently work on completing those annoying leftover tasks.)

- **Unused Themes**. You may have changed course mid-stream in your design process and decided to use a different theme. If so, there may still be files related to the old theme in various folders. Double-click the report to eliminate all of them immediately. To see the individual files, open the All Files report and click the In Folder column

header to sort the files by that field. Then scroll down to the group of files listed under the _themes folder.

NOTE As I discussed, you must have the Show Hidden Files option from the All Files report enabled to see hidden files (any file in a folder that begins with _).

As you work your way through each of these reports, fix as many problems as you can. If there's anything you can't or don't want to deal with right away, add it to your Tasks list.

To refresh the Site Summary after you've done some cleanup, press F5. FrontPage will recalculate the reports and show you the updated summary, as shown in Figure 6.6.

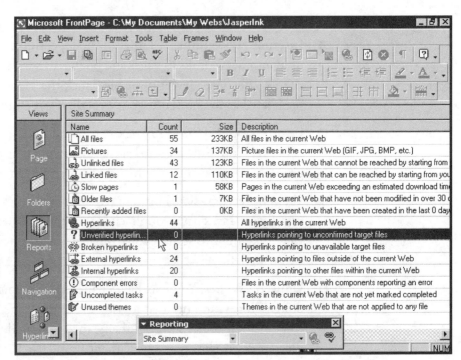

Figure 6.6

Refresh the Site Summary report to get an up-to-date view of your site information.

Making Changes to Multiple Pages

Mark my words, there *will* be a time when you need to make the same change to all or many of the files in your web. What if your company's name changes or you've misspelled a word that the Spelling Checker doesn't recognize? Imagine opening all those pages individually to search for each occurrence of the text that needs to be changed. Eeek! I shudder at the very thought. Thank goodness for FrontPage's *global* Find/Replace feature! To make changes to multiple pages, follow these steps:

▼ ▼

The term *global* generally refers to something that applies to the entire web. For example:

⚙ A theme is applied *globally* to all pages in your site unless you specify otherwise

⚙ A change you make to shared border settings or the information within it is applied *globally* to all the pages that share that border

▲ ▲

1. Switch to Folders view, and then select Edit, Replace. The Replace dialog box will open (see Figure 6.7).

2. Click in the Find what text box and enter the word or phrase that needs to be changed.

3. Press the Tab key and enter the new word or phrase in the Replace with text box.

4. Under Find where, select All pages to search the entire site.

Figure 6.7

FrontPage's global Find and Replace sure beats searching one page at a time.

5. Choose any of the following options as necessary:

  ✿ **Match case**. By default, if you enter "office," FrontPage will find both "office" and "Office." Select Match case to find text that matches exactly as you enter it.

  ✿ **Find whole word only**. By default, FrontPage will find all occurrences of the text in the Find what box. If you enter "ham," FrontPage will return "ham," "champion," "New Hampshire," and "Birmingham." Select Find whole word only to limit the search to only the word "ham."

  ✿ **Find in HTML**. By default, FrontPage searches only text that appears in Normal view. Select Find in HTML to search the HTML code behind the pages (such as changing all occurrences of heading 1 to heading 2) or to change text found on hidden pages.

6. Select Find in Web. FrontPage will run the search and return a list of occurrences it found, as shown in Figure 6.8.

7. Double-click the first occurrence to make the changes on that page now. FrontPage will open the page and highlight the first occurrence of the word on that page, as shown in Figure 6.9.

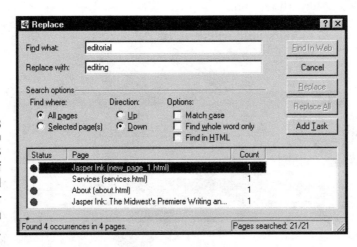

Figure 6.8

FrontPage finds every instance of the word and creates a task for each page you need to edit.

Figure 6.9

This part of the procedure works just like Word's Replace feature.

Figure 6.10

FrontPage will prompt you to go on to the next page of replacements.

8. Select Replace to change only that occurrence, Replace All to change all occurrences on that page, or Find Next to skip this occurrence and find the next one. When FrontPage can find no more occurrences, it prompts you to open the next page that contains occurrences of your search (see Figure 6.10).

9. Select Next Document to go on, or Cancel to stop the search. Eventually, you'll end up back at the Replace dialog box.

10. Select an item on the occurrence list and select Add Task to make a note of the change and fix it later (coming up next, in fact).

11. After you've handled each of the occurrences found (or scheduled them for later), click Cancel to close the Replace dialog box and end the search.

Completing Web Tasks

You're just about finished. You've got the heaviest design work done, tested links, dumped unwanted files, and you're ready to put the finishing touches on your web. Just whip through the Tasks list, get your ISP and WPP information in order (see Appendix A), and you're ready to launch the site.

Depending on your working style, you may reach this point and have very few to-do items on your task list, and you can get them all squared away in a few minutes. If you're like me, however, there may still be several hours of work yet to do. Either way, ya gotta do what ya gotta do. To open the Tasks list and see how scary it looks, follow these steps:

1. Click the Tasks button on the View bar. FrontPage will reveal the list of tasks remaining to complete (see Figure 6.11). Quickly review the list. If there's a lot there, go ahead and take a break before you proceed. If you're willing to hang in there just a bit longer, go on to step 2.

2. Double-click the first item on the list. The Task Details dialog box will appear, as shown in Figure 6.12.

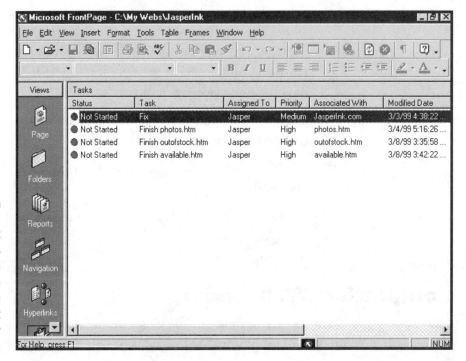

Figure 6.11

For me, adding an item to the Tasks list is the same as choosing the Procrastinate option. I like software that supports my bad habits.

Task Details

Task name: Finish available.htm

Priority
- High
- Medium
- Low

Assigned to: Jasper

Associated with: available.htm

Completed: No

Modified by: (Has not been modified)

Created by: Jasper on 3/8/99 at 3:42:22 PM

Description:
Added by the FrontPage New Page dialog.

Start Task   OK   Cancel

Figure 6.12

Tasks include brief notes to remind you of the task details.

---

3. The information in the dialog box will serve as a reminder for what this task involves. To get to work, click Start Task. FrontPage will set up whatever you need to finish the task, such as opening a page to edit.

4. After you complete the job, click Save. When FrontPage prompts you to mark the task as completed, click Yes (see Figure 6.13).

5. Return to the Tasks view. Notice that the status of the first task now reads Completed (see Figure 6.14). By default, all completed items will remain on the Tasks list until you close the web or you refresh the Tasks list by pressing F5.

Figure 6.13

You better believe I want you to mark it completed. Now stop pestering me!

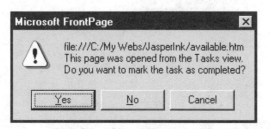

Microsoft FrontPage

file:///C:/My Webs/JasperInk/available.htm
This page was opened from the Tasks view.
Do you want to mark the task as completed?

Yes   No   Cancel

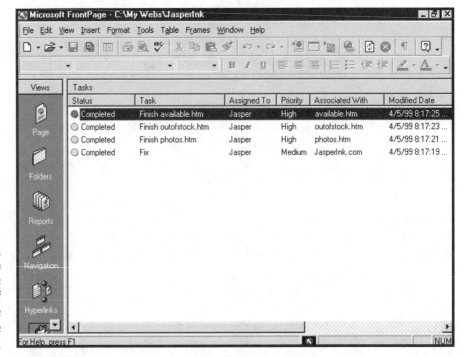

Figure 6.14

You'll get some satisfaction out of completing all the items on the task list.

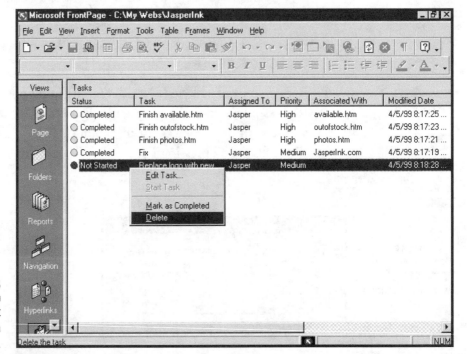

Figure 6.15

Use the shortcut menu to make a quick decision.

6. Right-click a task item to view its shortcut menu, as shown in Figure 6.15. From here you can mark the item as completed (no cheating), or you can choose to start, edit, or delete the task altogether.

Work your way through the tasks one at a time until you've resolved all the outstanding issues. When that's done, switch back to the Site Summary and press F5 to refresh the report. Check for anything you might have missed on the first pass. When you're satisfied everything is correct, save all your files, close the web, and exit FrontPage.

FIND IT ON ▶
THE CD

The CD that accompanies this book includes several excellent third-party programs and utilities that can help you manage your site more efficiently.

FastStats gives you vital information about your Web site, such as which search engines and keywords are used to access your Web site.

Coast *WebMaster* is site analysis and management software that simplifies and automates daily site maintenance tasks.

WS-FTP Pro and *CuteFTP* are equally outstanding file transfer utilities for posting your Web pages if your WPP does not support publishing directly from FrontPage.

See Appendix F, "What's on the CD-ROM?" for more information on these and other programs.

What's Next?

All finished? Great! Now stand up, fold one arm over your stomach and one behind your back, bend forward from the waist, and take a bow. Congratulations! Your web is complete. All that's left to do (for now, anyway) is to post your pages online. It might take you a few days to work out the details of selecting your Internet Service Provider (ISP) and Web Presence Provider (WPP), so I haven't counted it as part of your work this weekend. Rest assured—everything you need to know is covered in Appendix A, "Publishing Your FrontPage Web Pages." In the remaining appendixes, you'll also find tons of helpful information on things you can do to improve and enhance your web. You'll learn how to add sound and video, build forms for visitor feedback, how to promote your site and attract visitors, and much, much more.

As a reward for your hard work, I saved something fun for Sunday night. It's another optional session, but I know you'll want to check it out. Web sites are a great deal more interesting and attractive if your graphics are original, creative, and well done. In our last session together, "Creating Web Art Special Effects," you'll get a chance to play with two FrontPage-friendly graphics programs, Image Composer and PhotoDraw, and learn how to create, modify, and manipulate graphics for use in your Web site. If you'd rather take the night off and rest up for the upcoming week, that's cool, but be sure to come back to this session some other time.

SUNDAY EVENING

Bonus Section: Creating Web Art Special Effects

⚙ Creating Text Effects with Image Composer

⚙ Creating Transparent Drop Shadow Effects

⚙ Creating Custom Color Palettes

⚙ Using Image Composer's Button Wizard

⚙ Creating 3-D Effects with PhotoDraw 2000

T he clip art that is included with FrontPage 2000 enables you to enhance your FrontPage pages. If you want to give your Web site a special look to set it apart, you may want to consider creating your own personalized Web art images. You don't need to be a graphics professional to create attractive and effective Web art for your Web pages. You just need to know how to apply the right tools to get the results you want.

There are two image editing software programs covered in this session: Microsoft Image Composer 1.5 and Microsoft PhotoDraw 2000. Image Composer 1.5 is included with the stand-alone version of FrontPage 2000, while PhotoDraw 2000 is included along with FrontPage 2000 as part of Office 2000 Premium Edition. Image Composer 1.5 is not included with Office 2000 Premium Edition.

● ●
NOTE   While PhotoDraw 2000 is available as a separate retail product, Image Composer 1.5 is only available as part of the stand-alone versions of FrontPage 98 or FrontPage 2000.
● ●

While many of the methods covered in this session will relate to any image editing software, you may want to read only those sections that apply to the software you have. I'll cover many of the basic techniques and methods for creating effective Web art images in this session, including:

● Text special effects, including using gradient fills and drop shadows. I'll use both Image Composer and PhotoDraw 2000 to illustrate these techniques.

- ✪ Fancy Web buttons, using Image Composer's Button Wizard.
- ✪ Eye-catching 3-D Web images, using PhotoDraw 2000.

NOTE Because this session covers a number of different software programs, I won't explain what every single option means, but I will cover the steps you need to complete the examples. To learn more about the programs utilized in these examples, feel free to come back later and experiment further.

Creating Text Effects Using Image Composer

Using an image editor to apply special effects to text is one of the best and easiest ways to add pizzazz to your FrontPage 2000 Web pages. In this section, I'll show you how to use Image Composer 1.5 to create a text banner using a gradient fill and a drop shadow. I'll also show you how to create a custom palette, so you can get optimum results when saving your image as a transparent GIF image.

Starting Image Composer

If you've installed Image Composer 1.5 on your computer, just follow these steps to start Image Composer:

1. Click the Start button, and then point to Programs and Microsoft Image Composer.

2. Click Image Composer 1.5 to start the program (see Figure 7.1).

TIP You can also start Image Composer from within FrontPage 2000 by double-clicking on any JPEG or GIF image inserted in a FrontPage Web page. For this to work, Image Composer must be defined as its default image editor. It is the default if you installed the stand-alone release of FrontPage 2000, but may not be the case for other FrontPage 2000 releases. To check or modify which image editor is defined for FrontPage 2000, click Tools and Options, and then click the Configure Editors tab.

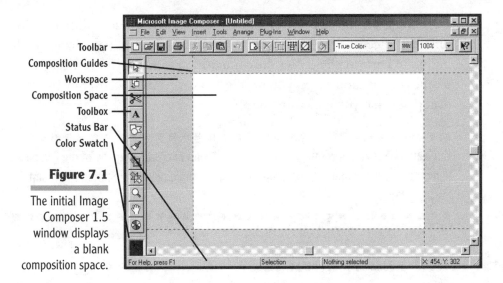

Toolbar
Composition Guides
Workspace
Composition Space
Toolbox
Status Bar
Color Swatch

Figure 7.1

The initial Image
Composer 1.5
window displays
a blank
composition space.

Resizing the Composition Space

The composition space defines the size and dimensions of your image. You can resize the composition space at any time, although you may want to start out with a specific size for your image. To resize the composition space to 500 pixels wide and 150 pixels high:

1. Right-click inside of the composition space, and then select Composition Setup.

2. Type **500** for the Width and **150** for the Height. Leave the Composition space color white (see Figure 7.2). Click OK.

Figure 7.2

The Composition
Setup dialog box
lets you specify the
width, height, and
background color of
your image (the
composition space).

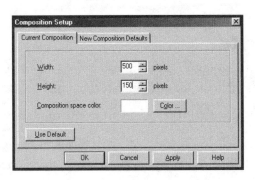

Depending on the size of your Image Composer window (different for different screen resolutions), you may want to use the right-hand scroll button to horizontally center the composition space. If you vertically center the composition space, you may risk having it covered over by the Text dialog box that you'll be using next.

TIP You can also resize the composition space by clicking and dragging any of the composition guides or the corners of the composition space (hold down the Shift key to maintain the aspect ratio).

A Quick Word about Sprites

Sprites are objects created or inserted into Image Composer's workspace, such as text, images, and shapes. An image is created in Image Composer by creating and manipulating the sprites that compose it. You can move, size, and dimension Sprites independently. Sprites overlap each other relative to the order in which you create them. The Arrange option on the menu bar allows you to easily re-order them to change whether sprites display in front of or behind other sprites. You can also store sprites in the workspace outside of the composition space. They won't be included in your image unless you place them inside of the composition space.

BUZZ WORD A *sprite* is an image object with shape and transparency.

Creating a Text Sprite

For starters, you're going to create a text sprite (a sprite composed of text) that you'll use as the basis for creating a text banner. To create the text sprite:

1. Click the Text tool (the "A" icon) in the toolbox.

2. In the Text dialog box, select Arial Black as the Font, Bold as the Style, and 48 as the Size. Check the Smoothing checkbox. Leave the other settings as they are (see Figure 7.3).

Figure 7.3

A 48-point, bold, Arial Black font is selected for the text sprite.

NOTE "To smooth or not to smooth, that is the question." Generally, it is a good idea to turn smoothing on for your larger fonts (16 to 18 points or bigger). The optimum point-size for starting to apply smoothing will vary somewhat from font to font. For smaller size fonts, you should leave smoothing turned off, since turning it on can give them a blurry or fuzzy look.

4. If most of the composition space is visible, just leave the Text dialog box open (or you can move it out of the way), and then click inside of the composition space. This allows you to see how your text will look, while easily making any changes you want to your text's font, style, size, and so on.

5. For your text, type **My Banner.** After typing the "B," just grab and pull either the left or the right border to resize the sprite. Next, place the insertion point after the "B," click, and type the remainder of the text (see Figure 7.4).

6. Go ahead and close the Text dialog box now. Click the Selection tool (the "Arrow" icon) in the toolbox. Click inside of your text sprite and drag it to the center of the composition space. Since you're going to be adding a drop shadow positioned down and to the right from the text sprite, you may want to position your text sprite just a bit up and to left in the composition space (see Figure 7.5).

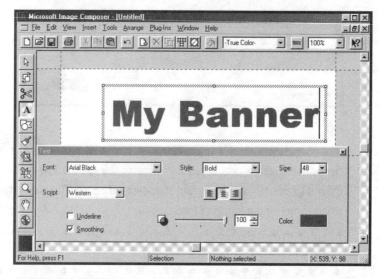

Figure 7.4

The text "My Banner" is typed into the composition space.

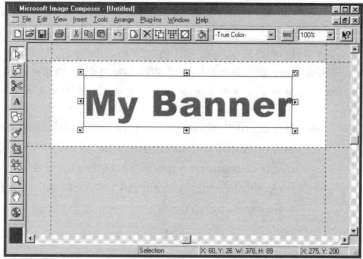

Figure 7.5

Insert and position the text sprite "My Banner" in the center of the composition space.

Applying a Gradient Fill

Using a gradient fill is a good way to give your text banner that special look that will set it apart from the crowd. To apply a gradient fill to your text sprite:

1. Click the Effects tool (the seventh tool from the top) in the toolbox.

2. Select Gradient as the Category, and then click the Details tab (see Figure 7.6).

Figure 7.6

Use the Details tab to control the colors and opacity of a gradient fill, as well as save any gradient you create so you can use it later.

For this example, you'll be creating a vertical gradient fill using two colors. The gradient will blend from the top to the bottom. To specify the top color for the vertical gradient fill:

1. Click the upper-left color square to display the Color Picker dialog box. If it isn't already selected, click the True Color tab (see Figure 7.7).

2. To narrow down the number of color choices, click the Custom Palette tab (see Figure 7.8).

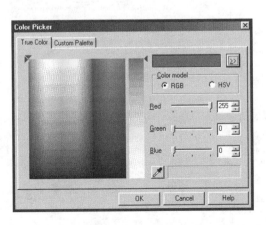

Figure 7.7

In the Color Picker's True Color tab, you can pick a color from the color matrix. Specify RGB or HSV color values, or use the eyedropper to pick up and drop a color.

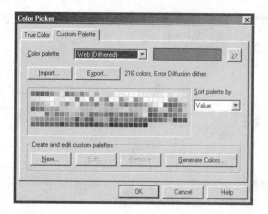

Figure 7.8

In the Color Picker's Custom Palette tab, you can pick from the 216 colors that are included in the Web (Dithered) palette.

3. Click one of the darker colors (your pick). Don't worry about understanding the other options right now, you'll be coming back to this later. Just click OK.

4. Click the upper-right color square, and then repeat steps 2 and 3 above, selecting the same color you selected for the upper-left color square.

5. Repeat for the lower two color squares, but choose a lighter color than you chose for the upper two squares. Feel free to experiment, trying different color combinations, until you get one that looks good to you. To see what the gradient fill will look like when applied to your text, just click the Apply button (see Figure 7.9). When you get a combination you like, close the Effects dialog box.

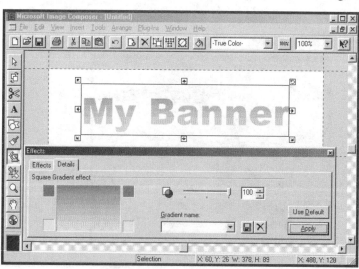

Figure 7.9

Two different colors, one darker and the other lighter, are selected in the upper and lower color squares to create a vertical gradient fill.

Applying a Drop Shadow Effect

A great way to give your text banner a 3-D look is to apply a drop shadow. To apply a drop shadow to your text sprite:

1. Click the Effects tool on the toolbar and select Outlines as the Category.

2. The Drop Shadow effect should already be selected. Just click the Details tab.

3. On the Details tab, select the Distance, Angle, Opacity, and Softness settings you want to use. Click the Color rectangle to select a color for your drop shadow. Feel free to experiment, trying out different combinations. You can always return to square one by clicking the Use Default button.

4. Click Apply to apply the drop shadow effect. For some example settings, see Figure 7.10.

5. Close the Effects dialog box when you get a result you like.

Creating a Custom Palette

Images that use blend effects, like the gradient and drop shadow effects you've just applied, should look fine if you save them as *JPEG* (Joint Photographic Experts Group) images. The only problem with JPEG images, however, is

Figure 7.10

You can set the distance, angle, opacity, softness, and color for a drop shadow effect.

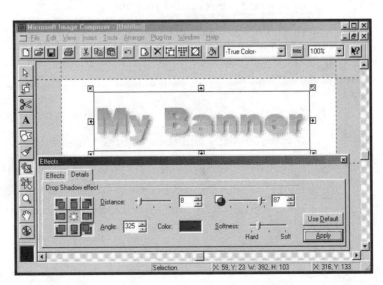

that you can't save them with a transparent background. They also tend to be just a little fuzzier than *GIF* (Graphics Interchange Format) images.

▼ ▼

JPEG images are true-color images that select colors from a palette of up to 16.7 million colors. They are ideal for displaying color photographic images, for instance. *GIF* images, on the other hand, are limited to selecting from a palette of up to 256 colors, but have the added advantage of allowing both interlacing and transparency.

▲ ▲

To have your image display transparently against a Web page's background color or background image, you've got to save it as a GIF image. GIF images can only choose from a palette of up to 256 colors whereas JPEG images have a palette of 16.7 million colors. By default, Image Composer saves GIF images using its Web (Dithered) palette. It applies the same stock 216 color palette to render all GIF images. Some images won't suffer much, but others will have their quality degraded considerably.

◆ ◆

The only way to insure that you will get optimum results when saving GIF files is to save them with a custom palette.

◆ ◆

A custom palette is essential if your image includes any blend effects, such as gradient fills or softened drop shadows. A custom palette chooses only from the colors included in your image (or selection) and thus can include many more tonal variations of your image's colors. To create a custom palette for your image, do the following:

1. Click the Color Swatch (lower-left corner, underneath the toolbox).

2. If it isn't already selected, click the Custom Palette tab.

3. Click the New button. In the New Color Palette dialog box, type a name for your custom palette (**My Palette**, for instance). Leave the other settings (256 and Error Diffusion) as they are. Click OK.

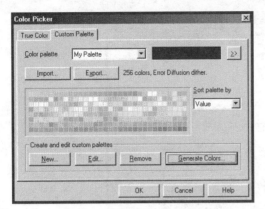

Figure 7.11

Create a custom palette, *My Palette*, composed of only colors included in the image.

4. Click the Generate Colors button. In the Generate Colors dialog box, select 256 as the Number of colors, and select Composition for the Generate from option.

5. Click Add, and then click Close (see Figure 7.11). Click OK.

Saving Your Image as a Transparent GIF Image

If you want your image to be transparent, you have to save it as a GIF image. To save your image as a transparent GIF:

1. Select File, Save As.

2. In the Save in text box, click where you want to save your image.

3. Type a File name for your image (**MyBanner.gif**, for instance).

4. In the Save as type box, select CompuServe GIF (*.gif).

5. In the Color format box, select My Palette.

6. The Transparent color check box should be checked. The color box should match the color of your composition background, in this case, white. If this color is not white, you'll need to click the box and select white as the color (to make sure the color you select is *really* white, double-click it—true white will have an RGB value of 255/255/255).

7. Change the Threshold slider value to 8 (see Figure 7.12). Click Save.

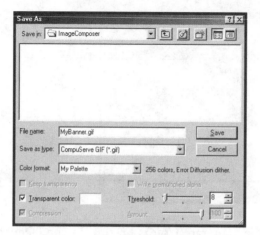

Figure 7.12

When you save a GIF image, you can specify that it be saved with a custom palette.

NOTE The transparency threshold number determines the range of shades in a particular color that will be rendered transparent when you save the image. The higher the threshold, the wider the range of shades that will be included. Setting a higher transparency level, for instance, can be handy if the background you want to render transparent contains several close shades of the same color. Set too high of a transparency level, however, and you're liable to have color shades rendered transparent that you want to show up as is. This can be especially true when using a drop shadow effect that blends into the background. If you set too high a transparency threshold, shades that you want to display as part of the blend effect will be turned transparent along with the rest of the background.

To limit transparency to only the specific color shade you've selected, select 1 as the transparency threshold value.

Displaying Drop Shadows against a Non-White Background

The transparent GIF image you just created will only look good when displayed in a browser against a nearly white background color or a background image in which the predominant color is white. If you try to display it against a dark background color (or dark background image), you'll see a very noticeable halo effect surrounding your drop shadow. See Figure 7.13

Figure 7.13

If the composition space color and a Web page's background color do not match closely, softened drop shadow effects will display a halo effect.

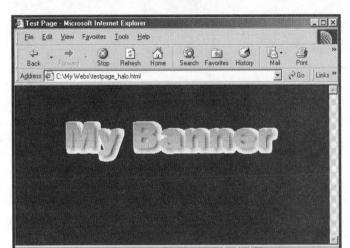

for an example of what a halo effect looks like in Internet Explorer. To avoid the halo effect, you need to follow these steps:

1. Before applying the drop shadow effect to your text sprite, you should set the color of the composition space to a color that is close to the background color (or background image's predominant color) you'll be using in the Web page where the image will be displayed. This doesn't have to be exact, but the closer the better.

2. Apply the drop shadow effect to your text sprite, choosing one of the lighter colors (rather than darker colors).

3. Generate a custom palette for your image. (See "Creating a Custom Palette" earlier in this section.)

4. Save your image as a GIF image. Click the Color format box and select the name of the custom palette you just created. Click the Transparent color box and select the same color you chose for the composition space color. Make sure a low Threshold value is set (less than 10). Don't make it too low, in case your composition space color and your transparent color are not exactly the same.

See Figure 7.14 for an example of a drop shadow displayed against a dark background color, without the halo effect.

Figure 7.14

If the composition space color and a Web page's background color match closely, softened drop shadow effects will display seamlessly without a halo effect.

Take a Break!

If you don't have both Image Composer 1.5 and PhotoDraw 2000, you might want to take a break now. Get up and stretch your bones (it's been a long weekend!). If you need a picker-upper, try brewing a cup of tea or go grab a soda. I'll see you in five or ten minutes when you'll learn how to create 3-D buttons using Image Composer's Button Wizard.

Using Image Composer's Button Wizard

Image Composer 1.5 includes a very handy Button Wizard that makes creating eye-catching buttons and logos a breeze. You will create a Home button that you can use as an image link to link back from any of your Web pages to your home page. You can use the Button Wizard to create a single button or several buttons at the same time that share the same design and dimensions. (This comes in handy when creating Home, Back, and Next buttons.) To use the Button Wizard to create the example Home button:

NOTE If you exited Image Composer at the end of the last section, you'll need to run it again.

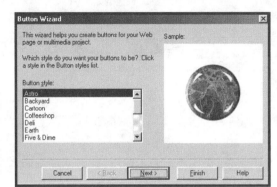

Figure 7.15

In the Button Wizard, you can select from a list of different button styles.

1. Select File and New to start a new image. (If you experimented further with the previous example, without resaving it, you'll be prompted to save your unsaved changes.)

2. To run the Button Wizard, click Insert and Button (see Figure 7.15).

3. At the Button Wizard dialog box, select a Button style. For this example, click Operation (see Figure 7.16). Click Next.

4. For this example, leave 1 as the number of buttons. Click Next.

5. Leave "Home" as the label for the first button. Leave the Image check box cleared. Click Next.

6. For this example, leave the first radio button (Exact fit for each button) checked. Click Next, and then click Finish.

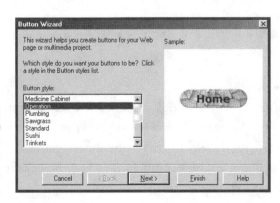

Figure 7.16

Select the Operation button style in the Button Wizard.

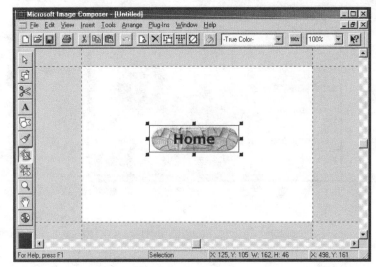

7. Click and drag the button into the composition space as shown in Figure 7.17.

NOTE You didn't include an image on your button in Step 4 above. If you decide to include an image, and want the image to display centered on the button, leave the box for the label text blank. If you include both label text and an image, they will be displayed side-by-side on the button (although you can superimpose them later in the Button Editor, if you want).

Using an image, rather than a text label, is a good way to add fancier text to your button. For instance, you might create a text sprite, apply special effects to it, save it as a transparent GIF file, and then display it on your button. You are limited to a file no larger than 320 pixels high and 240 pixels wide.

Using the Button Editor

You may be happy with the look of the basic button created by the Button Wizard. There's no need, however, to just stop with whatever result the Button Wizard produces. There's a lot more you can do to refine your button by editing it in the Button Editor. Use the Button Editor to make further changes to your button:

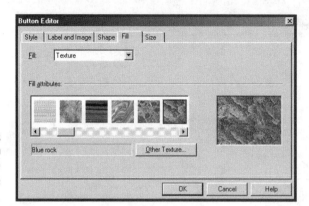

Figure 7.18

It is a good idea to select the fill before you select the label.

1. Double-click the button to edit it. Click the Fill tab (it is a good idea to set your fill before you decide on a color for your label's font).

2. For this example, leave Texture set as the Fill (you can also select to use a Gradient or a Color fill). From the textures displayed in the Fill attributes box, select one of the darker textures (see Figure 7.18). You could also click the Other Texture button here to select a texture from anywhere else on your hard drive.

3. Click the Label and Image tab, and then click the Font button to edit the font for your label. For the Font, try selecting Verdana. For the Style, click Bold, Italic. For the Size, select 24. Leave the other settings as they are (Smoothing checked, Opacity set to 100).

4. Click the Color box and select a color for your label (try to pick one that will complement the texture you picked). Click OK (see Figure 7.19).

5. Click OK to return to the Label and Image tab.

Figure 7.19

You can select the font, style, size, color, and other characteristics for your button's label.

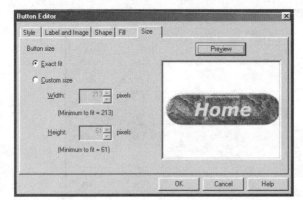

Figure 7.20

You can preview
what your button's
going to look like
on the Button
Editor's Size tab.

6. Click the Size tab. You can change the size of your button here, but
   for now leave it as it is. Click the Preview button to see what your
   button's going to look like (see Figure 7.20). If you like it, just click
   OK. If not, feel free to change the settings under the different tabs
   to come up with a different look.

When you exit the Button Editor, the new characteristics are applied to
your button in the composition space, as shown in Figure 7.21.

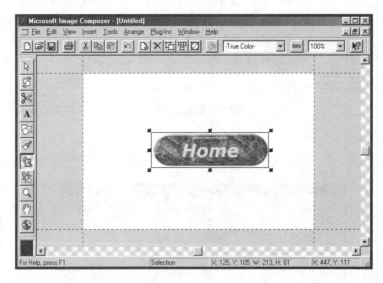

Figure 7.21

Changing the
characteristics of
your button is easy.

If you want your button to have a transparent background, you should first generate a custom palette (see directions for doing this in "Creating a Custom Palette" from the "Creating Text Effects Using Image Composer" section), and then save it as a GIF image using the custom palette. Make sure the Transparent color box matches the composition space color (white, in this case).

If the button does not need a transparent background, you should save it as a JPEG file. The only thing you need concern yourself with (other than the location where you want to save your image and your image's file name), is the compression amount. Try setting a compression amount between 15 and 20. The higher the compression level, the smaller the resulting file. Some images can take higher compression amounts and still give you good results, while others may require a lower compression amount.

Take a Break!

If you have both Image Composer 1.5 and PhotoDraw 2000, I've added a third section to this session that focuses specifically on using PhotoDraw 2000. However, if the clock is creeping toward midnight and you're thinking about having to get up early in the morning to go to work, feel free to come back and do the rest of this session at another time. In the Image Composer sections of this session, you've already learned a lot about creating attractive and effective Web art images.

However, if the night is still young, or you're up for burning the midnight oil, take a short break right now. Get up and shake your arms to get some circulation back in them. If you're hungry, go raid the fridge (you deserve it!). I'll see you in five or ten minutes when you'll learn how to create eye-catching 3-D Web art images in PhotoDraw 2000.

Creating 3-D Effects with PhotoDraw 2000

PhotoDraw 2000 is available as a stand-alone product or as part of the Microsoft Office 2000 Premium Edition suite. If you have the stand-alone version of FrontPage 2000, you can download a 30-day trial version of PhotoDraw 2000 from Microsoft's Web site at **www.microsoft.com/Office/PhotoDraw/**.

FIND IT ON ▶
THE WEB

Using PhotoDraw 2000, you can create many of the same kinds of effects that can be created with Image Composer 1.5. You can also use PhotoDraw 2000 to easily create 3-D effects, something that Image Composer 1.5 can't do. In this section, you'll learn how to create many of the same, or similar, text effects covered in the first section of this session. Then you'll learn how to apply special 3-D effects to your text using PhotoDraw 2000.

Starting PhotoDraw 2000

With PhotoDraw 2000 installed on your computer, you should be ready to go. To start PhotoDraw 2000, just follow these steps:

1. Click the Start button, point to Programs, and then click Microsoft PhotoDraw.

2. Leave the Blank picture radio button selected. Click OK.

3. Leave Default Picture selected. Click OK (see Figure 7.22).

Resizing the Picture Area

The picture area defines the size and dimensions of your image. You can resize the picture area at any time, although you may want to start out with a specific size for your image. To resize the picture area to 600 pixels wide and 200 pixels high:

1. Right-click inside of the picture area, and then click Picture Setup.

2. Change the Units measurement from Inches to Pixels.

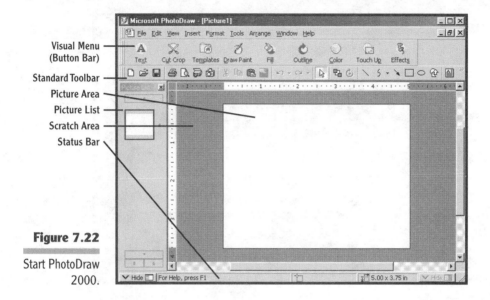

Visual Menu
(Button Bar)

Standard Toolbar

Picture Area

Picture List

Scratch Area

Status Bar

Figure 7.22

Start PhotoDraw
2000.

TIP

PhotoDraw 2000 creates images for many different media, not just for the Web. However, if you plan to primarily use the program for creating Web images, I recommend that you also change the Units measurement from Inches to Pixels under the New Picture Defaults tab.

3. Type **600** for the Width and **200** for the Height. Leave all the other settings as they are (see Figure 7.23). Click OK.

Figure 7.23

The Picture
Setup dialog box
lets you specify the
width, height,
measurement
units, and
background color of
your image (the
composition space).

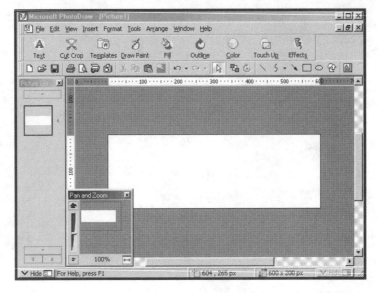

Figure 7.24

The zoom factor for the picture area has been increased to 100%.

Zooming the Picture Area to 100%

Right now the picture area doesn't take up very much of the workspace. To increase the zoom factor to 100%:

1. Click View, and then Pan and Zoom.

2. Click the button at the top of the slider (or slide the slider button upwards) until 100% is displayed as the zoom factor (see Figure 7.24).

3. Click View, and then Pan and Zoom to turn off the Pan and Zoom window.

Creating a Text Object

For this example, you're going to start by creating a text banner, similar to the one in the first Image Composer section. You'll specify the font, select a fill, and add a shadow effect behind the text. After that, you'll use the text *object* that you created as the base for trying out some of the 3-D effects that are available with PhotoDraw 2000. Begin by creating your text object:

In Microsoft PhotoDraw, an ***object*** is any selectable item inserted in the picture or scratch areas, such as text, bitmap or vector graphics, shapes or lines, and so on. A picture can be composed of a single or multiple objects.

1. Click the Text button on the button bar, and then click Insert Text.

2. In place of "Your text here," type **My Banner** as your text.

3. In place of Times New Roman, select Verdana as the font.

4. Select 40.0 pt as the Size and Bold Italic as the Style (see Figure 7.25).

5. Click the Text Flow listing. Leave the Smoothing check box selected. (You only need to clear this for fonts smaller than 16 points or so.) Leave the other settings as they are as well. Close the Text *workpane* (click the "x" button).

BUZZ WORD

In Microsoft PhotoDraw, a **workpane** is the expandable vertical pane from which you select the tools, effects, textures, colors, and styles you want to use in creating your image.

Figure 7.25

A text object, "My Banner," is specified in a 40-point, bold italic, Verdana font.

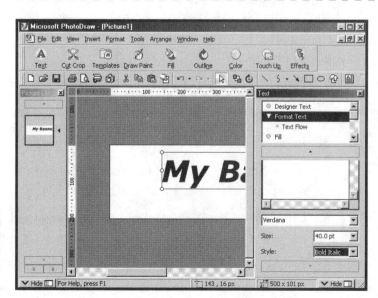

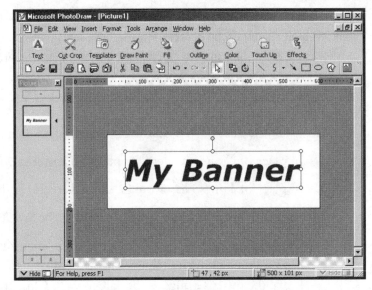

Figure 7.26

Create and position
the text object
"My Banner" at
the center of the
picture area.

6. Click and drag your new text object to position it in the center of
the picture area as shown in Figure 7.26.

Defining Your Text Object's Fill Characteristics

Actually, you didn't have to close the Text workpane before defining the fill
characteristics for your text object, but I wanted you to be able to position
the text object before going further. To define the fill characteristics for
your text object:

1. Double-click the "My Banner" text object.

2. Click the Fill listing.

3. In place of Solid Color, select Two-Color Gradient.

4. In the Start section, click the Start group button on the right, and
then point to Active Pallet (see Figure 7.27).

5. Click one of the darker colors (try the darker red, fifth color from
the left in the first row). Leave Transparency set at 0%.

6. Repeat for the End section, selecting one of the brighter colors (try
the golden yellow, third color from the right in the first row). Leave
Transparency set at 0%.

Figure 7.27

To define the colors
for a gradient fill,
you can select your
colors from the
Active Palette.

7. Depending on the dimensions of your PhotoDraw window, you may
   need to use the scroll button at the bottom to see the rest of the Text
   workpane. Click the button on the left of the Shape gallery box to
   display the gradient fill options (see Figure 7.28). Select one of the
   gradient fill options (try the second gradient option from the right).

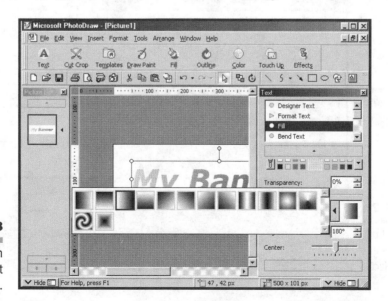

Figure 7.28

You can select from
a variety of different
gradient fill options.

8. Leave Angle and Center settings as they are. You could adjust the Angle setting to have the gradient fill slant in one direction or the other. By adjusting the Center setting, you could give more emphasis to either the start or end color of the gradient fill.

9. Close the Text workpane.

Adding a Shadow Effect

Adding a shadow effect behind your text object is a great way to set it off from the background and give it a 3-D look. To add a shadow effect behind your text object, just follow these steps:

1. Click the Effects button on the button bar, and then click Shadow.

2. Select one of the shadow effects (try the "Drop, Down Right" option).

3. Click the Color list button at the right of the Color box, point to Active Palette, and then select a color for your shadow effect. Select one of the lighter colors (try the twelfth color over from the left in the sixth row).

4. Set the Transparency to 25 (see Figure 7.29).

Figure 7.29

You can select from a variety of different shadow effects.

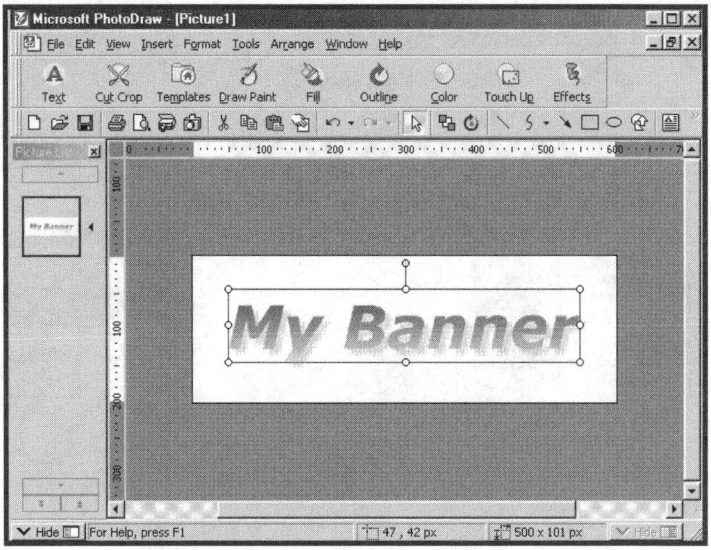

Figure 7.30

Add a shadow effect behind the text object.

TIP To get a lighter shadow effect with PhotoDraw 2000, you should always select a lighter color, rather than simply increase the Transparency level. If you increase the Transparency level over 40, your shadow effect will tend to drop out if you save your image as a transparent GIF image.

5. Depending on the dimensions of your PhotoDraw window, you may need to use the scroll button at the bottom to see the rest of the Shadow workpane. To create a soft edge around your shadow effect, change the Soften level to 100. Close the Shadow workpane (see Figure 7.30).

Adding a Bend Effect

You can bend and distort your text in a number of different ways. For this example, you'll be bending your text into a semi-circle. To bend your text object:

1. Double-click your text object, scroll down in the Text workpane's top window, and click the Bend Text listing.

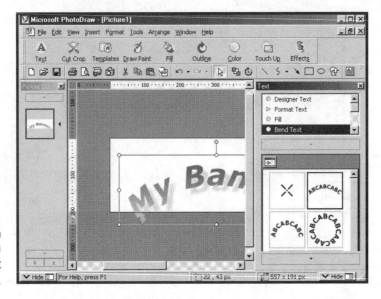

Figure 7.31

You can select from a variety of different Bend Text effects.

2. Click the upper-right option "Quarter circle down" (see Figure 7.31).

3. If you can't see the bottom of the Text workpane, use the scroll button at the bottom to move to the bottom of the workpane. Adjust the Amount slider (sliding it slightly to the left), to decrease the amount of the bend (see Figure 7.32).

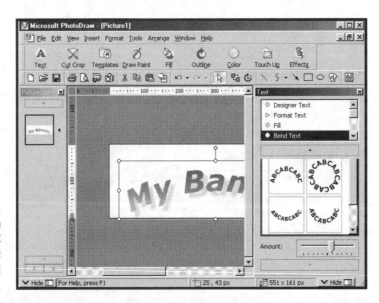

Figure 7.32

You can adjust the amount of the bend in the Bend Text effect.

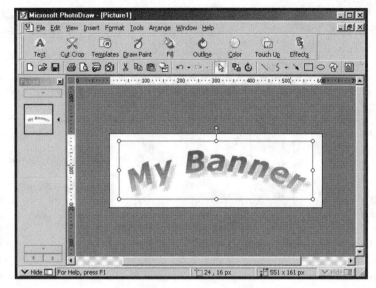

Figure 7.33

A Bend effect has been added to the text object.

4. Close the Text workpane. Click and drag your text object to reposition it vertically in the picture area (see Figure 7.33).

Adding 3-D Effects

So far, all the effects you've used have been 2-D effects, but that was just to lead up to adding the finishing 3-D touches to your image. By adding a 3-D effect to your text object, you can radically transform its appearance. To add a 3-D effect to your text object:

1. Click the Effects button on the button bar, and then click 3-D (see Figure 7.34).

2. Use the scroll bar (and the top and bottom scroll buttons, if you can't see all of the workpane) to view the 3-D options. Click any of the 3-D options to see the result in your text object. You'll be able to adjust the tilt and rotation angles, so don't worry about that aspect.

3. For right now, click the 3-D effect at the top-right ("Designer 3-D 1"), as shown in Figure 7.35.

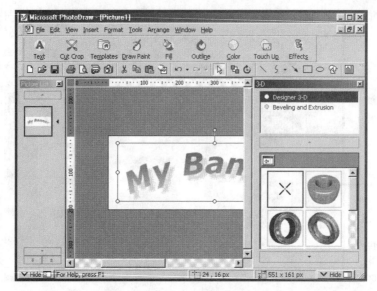

Figure 7.34

There are a variety of 3-D effects you can apply to an object.

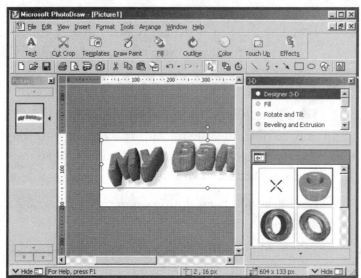

Figure 7.35

Selecting the top-right 3-D effect applies a "wood grain" 3-D effect to the text object.

Rotating and Tilting

When you apply a 3-D effect to an object, you can control the amount of rotation and tilt within the picture space. To access these settings:

1. In the 3-D workpane's top window, click the Rotate and Tilt listing.

2. Leave the top two settings (Rotation and Tilt left and right) as they are. Change the Tilt up and down setting to 25.0 (see Figure 7.36).

TIP   The rotation and tilt controls are great for creating the frames for a GIF animation. Just create an image using a 3-D object, and make multiple copies of the image. Then edit the Rotate and Tilt settings for each image. Change the relative position in each so that when shown in sequence, the object would appear to move within the picture space. When finished, save all of the images as GIF images, and then import them into a GIF animation editor to create the GIF animation. (Use GIF Animator, for instance, which is included with the stand-alone version of FrontPage 2000.)

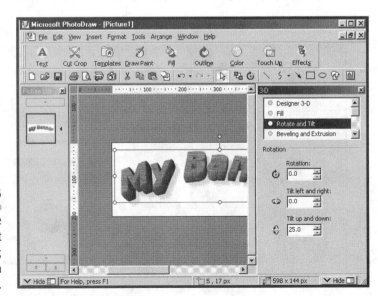

Figure 7.36

You can control the rotation and tilt (left and right; up and down) of a 3-D object.

Controlling 3-D Lighting Sources

PhotoDraw has quite a few options you can select to control the lighting sources of a 3-D object. To change the lighting of your 3-D object:

1. Click the Lighting listing. Try some of the different Lighting options to see the results. (Use the scroll bar and scroll buttons to see all of the options, if you have to.) For this example, select the fourth Lighting option in the first column (the slate blue ring).

2. Click the Settings listing (under Lighting) in the workpane's top window (see Figure 7.37).

3. If you want to try a different Lighting effect, click the button on the left of the selected Lighting style. Select the lighting style you want to use from the gallery of available lighting styles (see Figure 7.38). (Just reselect the currently selected Lighting effect, unless you want to change it.)

4. You can change four different light sources: one indirect light source and three direct light sources. (The indirect light source is the button with a sun on it, while the direct light sources are the buttons

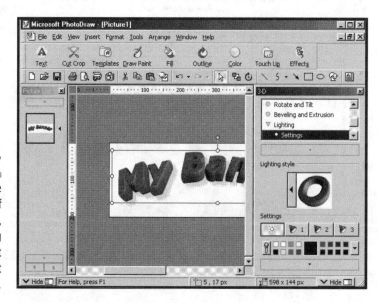

Figure 7.37

You can change the lighting settings of the 3-D effect, including setting the ambient light and three different direct lights.

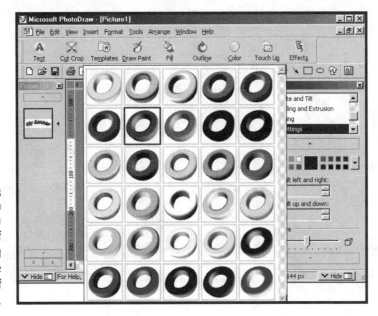

Figure 7.38

You can select from
a gallery of
available lighting
styles that can be
applied to any of
the lighting sources.

with the lamps on them.) If you pass the mouse over their buttons, you'll see them labeled as "Indirect Light," "Direct Light 1," "Direct Light 2," and "Direct Light 3." Click the different light sources to see the colors assigned to them. You can select a color for any of the light sources (black means that the light is turned off).

5. Click the first direct light source ("Direct Light 1"). Click the yellow color from the primary color squares. If you need to, use the scroll button to scroll down and display the two tilt controls for the light source. The first tilt control (Tilt left and right) will tilt the light to the left or right. The second tilt control (Tilt up and down) will tilt the light up or down. Try changing the first tilt control (left and right) to -30.0, and the second tilt control (up and down) to 25.0. Feel free to experiment with the other light sources, defining different colors and tilt amounts.

6. At the very bottom of the workpane is the Perspective slider (you may need to use the scroll button to see it). You can use it to control

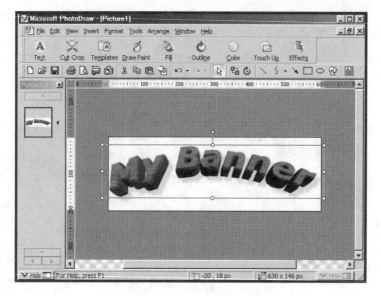

the object's degree of perspective. Move it a little to the right to see the effect.

7. Close the 3-D workpane. Click and drag your text object to center it again in the picture area, if you need to (see Figure 7.39).

Creating a Custom Palette

If you save your image as a JPEG image, it should look great, because a JPEG image can pick from a palette of 16.7 million colors. However, if you want your image to be transparent, you'll need to save your image as a GIF image. GIF images can only choose from a palette of up to 256 colors. By default, PhotoDraw 2000 saves GIF images using its Web (Dithered) palette, which applies the same stock 256-color palette to render all GIF images. Sometimes this will work fine, and other times it won't, depending on the particular image. To get optimum results for every GIF image that you save, you should always first create a custom palette, and then select that palette when saving your image as a GIF image. A custom palette selects from the actual colors included in your image to create a 256-color palette. The Web (Dithered) palette, on the other hand, includes many colors that are not included in your image. You can create a custom palette from any color picker within PhotoDraw. To create a custom palette for your image:

1. Right-click your image and select Picture Setup. Click the button to the right of the Color box and click More Colors.

2. Click the Custom Palette tab if it isn't already selected.

3. Click the New button. In the New Color Palette dialog box, type a name for your custom palette (**My Palette**, for instance). Leave the other settings (256 and Error Diffusion) as they are. Click OK.

4. Click the Generate Colors button. In the Generate Colors dialog box, for the Number of colors, select 256. For the Generate from option, select Picture. Click Add, and then click Close. Click OK. Click OK again.

Saving Your Image as a Transparent GIF Image

If you want your image to be transparent, you have to save it as a GIF image. To save your image as a transparent GIF:

1. Click File and Save As.

2. In the Save in box, select where you want to save your image.

3. Type a File name for your image (**MyBanner** for instance).

4. In the Save as type box, select Graphics Interchange Format (*.gif)

NOTE Ignore the little pop-up box you get here, suggesting you use the Save for Use In wizard. The Save for Use In wizard will not allow you to save your image with a custom palette, locking you into using the Web (Dithered) palette, instead. I recommend you avoid using the Save for Use In wizard for this reason.

5. Click the Options button and select My Palette, instead of Web (Dithered), as the Palette. Click OK. Click Yes at the "flattening" message.

Displaying Drop Shadows against a Non-White Background

If you save an image with a softened shadow effect, for instance, as a transparent GIF image, it may display a halo effect if displayed against a Web page background that is very different from the color of your images picture area. If you know that you want to use a specific background color in your Web page, you should try to match the color (it doesn't have to be exact) in the picture area for your image. The same holds for displaying an image against a Web page's background image. You should select a color for your picture area that is close to one of the more predominant colors in the background image.

For a more detailed discussion of this issue, see "Displaying Drop Shadows against a Non-White Background" in the "Creating Text Effects Using Image Composer" section at the start of this session.

Wrapping Up

Finishing this session won't turn you into a graphics pro, but you should at least know some of the key tricks the pros actually use to create effective and appealing Web art images. To become really proficient takes much longer than a single evening. I hope that what you've learned tonight will be a good start. After doing this session, you should be familiar with how to:

○ Create eye-catching text banners in Image Composer or PhotoDraw 2000.

○ Apply gradient fills and drop shadows in Image Composer or PhotoDraw 2000.

○ Use Image Composer's Button Wizard to quickly and easily create 3-D buttons for your Web pages.

○ Use PhotoDraw 2000's 3-D effects to create 3-D text banners. Then rotate and tilt them at any angle.

○ Create a custom color palette for your images in Image Composer or PhotoDraw 2000 that will insure optimum image quality when saving your images as transparent GIF images.

- Create transparent GIF images that will display against a Web page's background color or background image without a noticeable halo effect.

This is the end of the weekend! If you made it through everything, then you're simply incredible. If you are human, however, you probably skipped some of the optional bonus examples or sessions along the way. Feel free to come back next weekend to cover any areas that you skipped. Look in the appendixes for the following additional material:

- Find a FrontPage 2000 Web server and publish your FrontPage pages onto a FrontPage web.

- Add interactive forms to your FrontPage pages.

- Add multimedia effects—sound, animation, and more—to your FrontPage pages.

- Learn how to set up your Web pages to snag search engines and how to promote your Web site.

- Implement special features, such as controlling access to your Web site or folders, displaying database query results, and inserting Java applets and ActiveX controls.

If you've completed most of the activities in this book, you should have a solid footing in FrontPage 2000. Using that knowledge, you should be able to go on and learn more as time goes by. You learned enough this weekend to be able to create a very credible and attractive FrontPage Web site. With more time and effort, you'll be absolutely blowing their socks off! Remember though, that the key to creating an effective Web site is the content, not the trappings. One of the virtues of FrontPage 2000 is that it allows you to focus on the content and organization of your Web site, while it takes care of the HTML and the different formatting intricacies that are involved. In addition, the more you use and experiment with it, the more proficient you'll become.

Publishing Your FrontPage 2000 Web Pages

O nce you've finished fine-tuning your FrontPage 2000 Web pages and spent some time learning how to create your own personalized Web art images, you're going to want to publish your Web pages onto the Internet. Even if you haven't finished your site yet, you may want to experiment with publishing your Web pages anyway.

What You'll Need

Before you can start publishing your FrontPage 2000 Web pages onto the Web, you need the following:

- A dial-up account or other connection to the Internet. This can be a local ISP or it can be a national ISP, such as the Microsoft Network, America Online, or CompuServe.

- A Web presence account, preferably with either the FrontPage 2000 or FrontPage 98 server extensions installed for your account. While you can also publish to a server without the FrontPage server extensions installed, you won't be able to include any of the features in your pages that require them.

Getting on the Internet

Most of you already have a dial-up account or other connection to the Internet. For those of you who do not, you'll need to get connected to the Internet in order to publish your FrontPage 2000 Web pages onto the Internet.

One thing you may want to look for when shopping for an ISP is whether they provide free Web space with the FrontPage 2000 or FrontPage 98 server extensions enabled. If so, that may save you from having to find a separate FrontPage Web presence provider.

Finding a FrontPage Web Presence Provider

Many ISPs these days offer anywhere from two to ten or more megabytes of free Web space along with your dial-up account. While most ISPs do not offer the FrontPage 2000 or 98 server extensions, you may be lucky enough to find one that does. Check with your Internet provider to see if they can enable the server extensions for your account.

If your ISP doesn't support the FrontPage server extensions, check to see if any ISPs in your area include the FrontPage server extensions in your free Web space allotment. Keep in mind that changing your ISP would also mean changing your e-mail address. To take advantage of FrontPage features that require the server extensions, you'll need to find a separate FrontPage Web presence provider.

Finding a Free FrontPage Web Presence Provider

Yes, there is a free lunch! There are Web presence providers who provide free Web space in exchange for being able to sell pop-up or banner advertising that displays when visitors surf your Web pages. Some free Web presence providers also include the FrontPage server extensions at no extra cost. If you want to experiment with the different FrontPage 2000 features that require the server extensions, this can be a great option. Here's a brief listing of some free FrontPage Web presence providers:

FIND IT ON ▶
THE WEB

- ✪ HyperMart at **www.hypermart.net**
- ✪ Web Provider at **www.webprovider.com**
- ✪ Tripod at **www.tripod.com/planet/membership/signup/**
- ✪ Tripod-UK at **www.tripod.co.uk**

- The DJ Café at **www.members.djcafe.com/**

- Freenation at **www.freenation.com**

- Tony-Net at **www.tony-net.net**

TIP When starting out you may want to use one of the free FrontPage servers to experiment and play around with FrontPage 2000. If so, you need to keep the search engines from indexing your site until you're ready for the prime time. You may also decide later that you want to publish your site to a for-pay FrontPage server. For information on how to keep search engines from indexing your site until you're ready to lift the curtain, see Appendix D, "Web Site Promotion Tips and Tricks."

Finding a For-Pay FrontPage Web Presence Provider

If you're planning on putting up a business site, getting a domain name hosted, requiring more services, or desiring larger space and traffic allowances, you'll want to consider finding a for-pay, rather than free, FrontPage Web presence provider. To search Microsoft's database of registered Web presence providers, see Microsoft's Web Presence Providers page at **microsoft.saltmine.com/frontpage/wpp/list/** (FrontPage 98) or **www.microsoft.com/frontpage/wpp/list.htm** (FrontPage 2000).

FIND IT ON ▶
THE WEB

TIP You can use Microsoft's list of registered FrontPage presence providers to look for a dial-up ISP in your local area that also supports the FrontPage server extensions. Just select your state or province (U.S. or Canada) from the View by State/Province list and then click Go. Check any companies listed that are located within your local calling area to see if they also offer dial-up accounts.

Publishing to a FrontPage Web Server

This section tells you how to publish your Web pages to a Web server with either the FrontPage 2000 or FrontPage 98 server extensions installed. In most cases, you only need to know the following to publish your FrontPage Web site to your folders on a FrontPage Web server:

✿ **The URL**. This is provided by your FrontPage Web presence provider, and is where you will publish your Web pages. This might be something like http://username.servername.net or http://www.servername.net/username/. Be sure you use the exact URL specified by your provider.

✿ **Your username and password**. Your FrontPage Web presence provider will provide these to you, usually in an e-mail message. They are case sensitive, so when using them, be sure to type them exactly as they appear.

• •
After you get an account on a Web server that provides the FrontPage 98 or FrontPage 2000 server extensions, you may need to request that the server extensions be installed for your account. If you're not sure if the FrontPage 98 or 2000 server extensions have been installed for your account, check first with your provider before trying to publish your site.
• •

Publishing Your FrontPage 2000 Pages

Do you have an account on a Web server with either the FrontPage 98 or FrontPage 2000 server extensions? Have the server extensions been enabled for your account? If so, you should already have everything you need to start publishing your FrontPage 2000 Web pages. To publish your Web pages to a FrontPage Web server, just follow these steps:

1. Select File, Publish Web.

2. Type the URL for the FrontPage Web you're publishing to (see Figure A.1). When publishing to a FrontPage server, always use an HTTP (Hypertext Transfer Protocol) URL (http://username.servername.net/ or http://www.servername.net/username/, for instance).

Figure A.1

In the Publish Web dialog box, you specify the URL for the location where you want to publish your FrontPage Web pages.

3. To change any of the publish options, select the Options button (see Figure A.2).

4. To publish your Web pages, click the Publish button. If you're not connected to the Internet, when prompted just click Connect.

5. Type your username and password. (Usernames and passwords are case sensitive.) Click OK (see Figure A.3).

Figure A.2

Publish changed pages only is the default option selection. Other available options are: Publish all pages, Include subwebs, and Secure connection required (SSL).

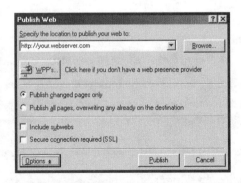

Figure A.3

You can view the progress of the publishing process.

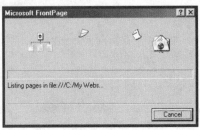

Figure A.4

You can click a link
to view your
published Web site
after successfully
publishing it.

NOTE   If you've previously published your Web site, you may be prompted to overwrite files that have been changed or to delete files that are no longer part of your FrontPage web.

6. When prompted that your Web site was published successfully, you can choose to view your published site (yes do!). Just click the provided link. Otherwise, click the Done button (see Figure A.4).

Maintaining Your Site on a FrontPage Web Server

After publishing your Web site to your FrontPage Web server, you can open it directly in FrontPage 2000 if you wish. You can add folders, edit or

---

PUBLISHING TO A FRONTPAGE 98 WEB SERVER

FrontPage 2000 works just fine publishing to a Web server with the FrontPage 98 server extensions. There are a few things, however, you can do in FrontPage 2000 that won't work if you publish to a server with the FrontPage 98 server extensions enabled. These include:

- Subwebs nested within other subwebs (subwebs nested within the root web are okay)

- Database query results (Database Results Wizard)

- Sending form responses to a database

If your current Web presence provider doesn't support either the FrontPage 98 or FrontPage 2000 server extensions and you're not planning on finding a provider that does, see the section, "Publishing to an FTP Server," in this appendix.

delete files, and so on. To open your remote FrontPage Web site within FrontPage 2000, do the following:

1. Select File, Open Web.

2. In the Folder name box, type the URL for your FrontPage Web server folder (your FrontPage Web presence provider will tell you what you need to type here). Click Open. (You can also click the pull-down handle to the right of the Folder name box to select from a list of FrontPage webs you've opened previously.)

3. At the Enter Network Password dialog box, enter your username and your password (your FrontPage Web presence provider will tell you what your username and password are). Check the check box (Save the password in your password list), if you don't want to have to enter these every time. Click OK.

4. When your folders in your remote FrontPage Web site appear, click Open to open the web in FrontPage 2000.

That's it. You can now do anything in your remote FrontPage web that you can do in your local FrontPage web (C:\My Webs, for instance). One of the advantages of opening your remote FrontPage Web site in FrontPage 2000 is that you can easily maneuver and browse within your site to test it out. To preview an open page, just select File, Preview in Browser.

PUBLISHING LOCALLY TO A PERSONAL WEB SERVER

Unlike FrontPage 98, FrontPage 2000 does not include a personal web server that you can install on your local hard drive. While most FrontPage 2000 features can be tested out on your local disk-based web (C:\My Webs, for instance), some features won't work until you actually publish your site to a server with the FrontPage 98 or FrontPage 2000 server extensions installed. For information on installing Microsoft Personal Web Server 4.0 and the FrontPage 2000 server extensions so you can preview these features on your local hard drive, see "Installing the Microsoft Personal Web Server" and "Installing the FrontPage 2000 Server Extensions on Your PWS" in Appendix E, "Implementing Special Features."

TIP Some people create their Web site entirely on their remote FrontPage Web server. However, if your server crashes, or suddenly goes out of business, you might lose everything on your site. For that reason, it is a good idea to make all changes to your FrontPage web on your local computer, and then publish them to your remote FrontPage server. That way you only need to republish your site if anything happens to your remote FrontPage server.

Publishing to an FTP Server

If the FrontPage 98 or 2000 server extensions are not available or haven't been installed for your Web presence account, FrontPage 2000's web publishing wizard will transfer your files to your server using FTP. If your web includes any FrontPage features not supported by an FTP server, you'll be notified when you publish your files.

CAUTION If the FrontPage server extensions are available for your Web presence account, but have not been installed, do not try to publish your site using FTP. Ask your Web presence provider to install the FrontPage server extensions for your account, and then follow the steps given previously to publish your site using HTTP. You should only use FTP to publish your site if the FrontPage server extensions are not available for your account.

You should *never* publish to a server that has the FrontPage server extensions installed using FTP ("ftp://..."). You should *always* use HTTP ("http://..."). Always make sure that "http://" is at the start of your server's URL when publishing to a FrontPage server.

If you do use FTP to publish to a FrontPage server, the server extensions may be corrupt and you may need to have them reinstalled for your account.

Publishing your files to an FTP server is pretty much the same as publishing to a FrontPage server. The only difference is you publish using the File Transfer Protocol ("ftp://...") instead of the Hypertext Transfer Protocol ("http://..."). To publish your Web pages to an FTP server, follow these steps:

1. Select File, Publish Web.

2. Type the *full* "ftp://" URL for the folder to which you want to publish your pages.

NOTE For the full URL of the location to which you want to publish your pages, you should include: 1) the server name or your domain name, 2) the path on your server to your own folder, and 3) the specific folder (or folder path) that you want to publish to (if you're not publishing to your root folder). For instance, if your FTP server name is server1.myprovider.net and your personal folder on that server is located at /users/yourname, and the specific subfolder you want to publish to is /yoursub, then the URL (the location where you want to publish your pages) would need to be ftp://server1.myprovider.net/users/yourname/yoursub/.

3. To change any of the publish options, select the Options button.

4. To publish your Web pages, click the Publish button. If you're not connected to the Internet, when prompted just click Connect.

5. Type your username and password. (Usernames and passwords are case sensitive.) Click OK.

NOTE If you've previously published your Web site, you may be prompted to overwrite files that have been changed or delete files that are no longer part of your FrontPage web.

6. Click the provided link to view your published site, or click the Done button.

FrontPage 2000 will remember the last URL you used to publish to an FTP server, so the next time you publish to an FTP server (as long as you don't publish to another location), you won't have to retype the full URL. You will have to type your username and password each time you publish, however.

FIND IT ON ▶
THE CD

Many FrontPage users prefer to use a regular FTP program, such as WS_FTP or CuteFTP, for instance, when publishing their Web pages to an FTP server. You can also download WS_FTP Pro or WS_FTP LE (free to qualified non-commercial users) at **www.ipswitch.com**. You can download CuteFTP at **www.cuteftp.com**. Both WS_FTP Pro and CuteFTP are included on this book's CD-ROM.

Maintaining Your Site on an FTP Server

You can use FrontPage 2000 to add new folders on an FTP server. This can be handy if you want to publish your FrontPage web into a subfolder that hasn't been created yet on your FTP server. Doing this for the first time is a two-step process. First you need to add the URL for your FTP server to FrontPage's list of FTP locations, and then you need to open that URL in FrontPage 2000.

Adding Your FTP Location

To add your FTP server to FrontPage 2000's list of FTP locations, just do the following:

1. Select File, Publish Web.

2. Click the Browse button, and then click the pull-down handle for the Look in box. Select the Add/Modify FTP Locations option (see Figure A.5).

Figure A.5

You can add your FTP location to FrontPage 2000's list of FTP locations, so you won't have to remember the URL, username, and password each time.

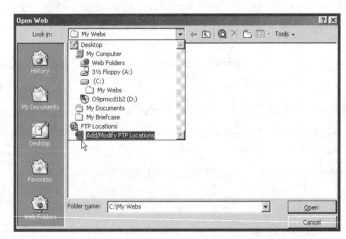

3. In the Add/Modify FTP Locations window, first type the name of your FTP (for instance, ftp://servernumber.providername.net).

4. Select the User radio button, then type your username. Type your Password. Click the Add button. Click OK.

You only need to do this once. After you've done this the first time, you won't need to do it again to open your FTP location. Follow the steps in the next section to open your FTP location.

Opening Your FTP Location

To open your FTP server in FrontPage 2000, do the following:

1. Select File, Open Web.

2. Click the pull-down handle for the Look in box, then click on the URL for your FTP server (under FTP Locations).

3. You'll need to know which folders lead to your personal folder. Just double-click on the folders that form the path to your personal folder. Once you're inside your personal folder, you can add a new folder by clicking the Create New Folder icon.

What You Can't Publish to an FTP Server

When you publish your Web pages to an FTP server using FrontPage 2000, you won't be able to include a number of features or components that require the FrontPage server extensions. If your Web pages include any of these features, you'll get a message when you try to publish your Web pages. Here are the main features and components that can't be published to an FTP server (I haven't included *everything* here, just the features or components you are most likely to use):

- Hit counter
- Form handler
- Discussion group form
- Search form
- Subwebs or virtual servers

- Database Results Wizard
- Cascading style sheets
- Custom themes
- Dynamic HTML
- Shared borders

Getting Visitor Feedback with Forms

J ust about any Web site you visit has an area dedicated to user feedback. It may be an informal guest book, a product registration area, customer service inquiries, discussion groups, or online sales catalogs. You name it, it's out there. Even if it's just a personal Web site, hearing from your visitors is important. Why should yours be any different?

Forms give your visitors the opportunity to talk to you. Just as with paper forms, you can ask a user to fill in blanks, check boxes, choose options, and even write lengthy descriptions.

▼ ▼

A *form* is a grouping of data-entry fields, check boxes, radio buttons, and so on, that can be filled out by a visitor to a Web site. The data can be collected by the site manager in a variety of ways: as a text or HTML file, as a database record, in an e-mail, or to a custom-built application.

▲ ▲

● ●

Forms created in FrontPage require that the site be published to a server that has the FrontPage server extensions installed.

● ●

The type of form you build depends on what kind of information you want to get back, and how you want that information communicated to you. In this appendix, you will:

✪ Recognize the different types of form fields

277

- Create new forms using a FrontPage template and the Form Page Wizard

- Set field defaults and data limits

- Determine a way to retrieve the form results

- Create a confirmation page for visitors

Planning a Form

Before you jump in with both feet, take a few minutes to think about the purpose of your form and what kinds of information you want to gather from your visitors:

- Do you need contact information such as names, addresses, or e-mail addresses?

- Are they registering a product or purchase requiring serial numbers, model numbers, and the like?

- Do you want demographic information such as age or physical characteristics?

You get the idea. Make a list of everything you want to know. You might want to surf the net a bit and gather ideas from other forms you find. Remember that forms don't have to be boring. After you design the basics, you can format and edit a form page just like you would any other Web page, including adding graphics and backgrounds.

After you've decided on your questions, consider the layout of the form. Should the layout be in paragraphs, a table, or bulleted lists? The Form Page Wizard will use a combination of all these elements to design a form that best suits your needs. If you don't like the suggested layout, you can always modify it later.

Finally, consider how you want to save the form results, or the data that is generated. You can save the results as a Web page, a text file, an e-mail, or as data that can be dumped to a database. You can even devise custom scripts to handle the results.

Understanding Form Fields

For each question or data set you want to collect, you need a *form field*. You will recognize most form fields from your every-day use of application dialog boxes. Forms can incorporate check boxes, option buttons, menus and drop-down lists, push buttons, and a variety of other field types. You'll find these types of fields in any of the forms you generate using the built-in templates or the Form Page wizard. You can add others as needed. Here's a list of common form fields (see Figure B.1):

▼▼▼▼▼▼▼▼▼▼▼▼▼▼▼▼▼▼▼▼▼▼▼▼▼▼▼▼▼▼▼▼▼▼

A ***form field*** is a data entry field on an HTML form. The user makes selections or adds text to a form field, depending on the field type. Common form field types include check boxes, option buttons, text boxes, and drop-down lists.

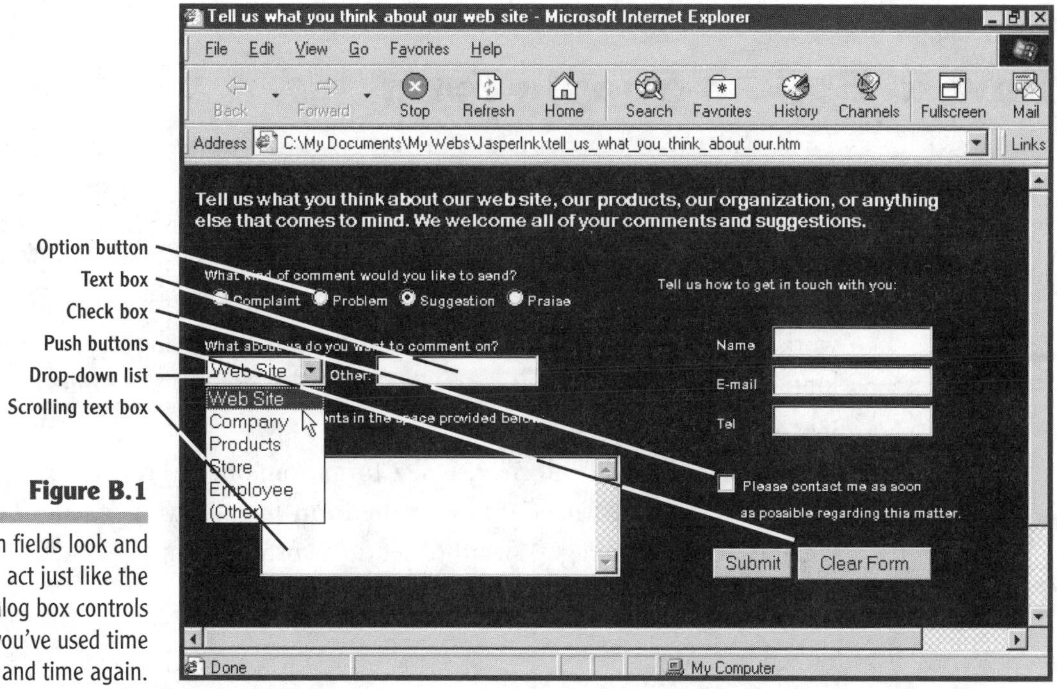

▲▲▲▲▲▲▲▲▲▲▲▲▲▲▲▲▲▲▲▲▲▲▲▲▲▲▲▲▲▲▲▲▲▲

Figure B.1

Form fields look and act just like the dialog box controls you've used time and time again.

Option button
Text box
Check box
Push buttons
Drop-down list
Scrolling text box

✪ **Option buttons (also called radio buttons)**. Use to present an "either/or" choice to the visitor. There can be many options in one group, but only one can be selected at a time.

✪ **Check boxes**. Use for multiple optional selections, such as what topics are of interest to the visitor. The visitor clicks each desired item to place a check mark in the box.

✪ **Drop-down menus**. Use to present a list of choices. The visitor chooses by clicking the desired item on the list. Same effect as a group of option buttons, but saves space on the page.

✪ **Text boxes**. Use a text box for a small amount of text, such as a name or address.

✪ **Scrolling text boxes**. Use to accommodate a larger amount of text, such as a comment or description.

✪ **Push buttons**. Use to let the visitor submit or clear the form, or to run custom scripts, such as calculating totals on an order form.

How to Build a Simple Form

There will always be purists out there who teach you how to build everything from scratch, so you'll learn the rules before you can learn how to break them. While there's certainly merit to that philosophy—and occasional times when it really might be necessary—why go to all that trouble if you don't have to? FrontPage's Form Page Wizard can save you hours of work, and it has several form templates. I don't know about you, but as long as I don't end up creating more work for myself in the long run, I'll take a shortcut any day.

In this appendix, you will create a new form from one of FrontPage's built-in templates and learn how to edit the form to meet your needs. Then you'll use the Form Page Wizard to set up a custom form.

Creating a Form from a FrontPage Template

FrontPage includes common form styles you're likely to use. You can add one to your Web site with just a few steps:

1. Switch to Page view, and then select File, New, Page. The New dialog box will appear, as shown in Figure B.2.

2. Review the list of available templates on the General tab and choose one of the available forms, such as Feedback Form. Click the form you want, then click OK. FrontPage will open a new page with the skeleton form already prepared for you (see Figure B.3). Scroll down the page to see the types of questions and fields included in the form.

3. From Normal view, edit the headings, text, and background of the form using regular page editing procedures. (You'll learn how to edit the properties of the fields themselves in a moment.)

4. Add a new field to the form by selecting Insert, Form, and selecting the desired field from the submenu, as shown in Figure B.4.

Figure B.2

You can save a lot of form-building time by starting with a form template, such as Confirmation Form or Guest Book.

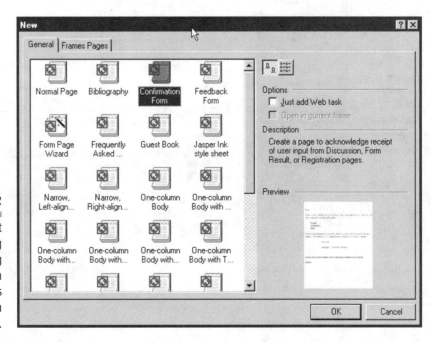

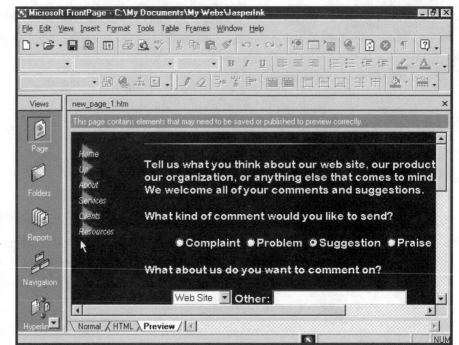

Figure B.3

FrontPage does most of the work for you. It lays out the basic form, and even includes default themes and shared borders settings.

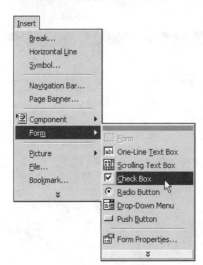

Figure B.4

If the template doesn't have everything you want, you can add your own questions and fields.

Creating a Form using the Form Page Wizard

If the available templates don't have exactly what you're looking for, you can ask FrontPage to help you design something more specific to your needs. To run the Form Page Wizard, follow these steps:

1. Switch to Page view, and then select File, New, Page. The New dialog box will appear.

2. Click Form Page Wizard, and then click OK. The wizard will open with a welcome message explaining the procedure you're about to perform. Read the message, and then click Next. The wizard opens to a blank list that you will use to add questions to your form (see Figure B.5).

3. Click Add to create the first group of questions. The wizard will present a list of question types. Click on a question type to see a description of the questions that are included in the group. For example, the contact information group will ask users for their name, company affiliation, address, and phone numbers.

4. Click in the text box if you want to edit the text of the question. You might, for example, change "Please provide the following contact information:" to "Please tell us a little about yourself:" You can be as creative or straightforward as you wish. Click Next when you're finished.

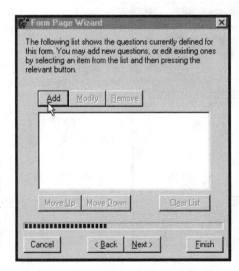

Figure B.5

Build a list of questions for your custom form using the Form Page Wizard.

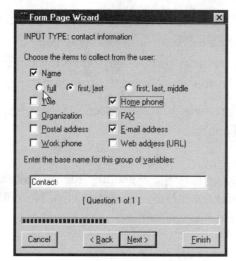

Figure B.6

Some people might not want to give you a lot of information unless they have to.

5. On the next page, the wizard will ask you to specify exactly what information you want to include and in what format, such as name, address, e-mail, phone and fax numbers, and so on (see Figure B.6). Check the boxes and options you prefer.

6. Click Next when you've made your selections. Your completed question will appear on the question list, as shown in Figure B.7.

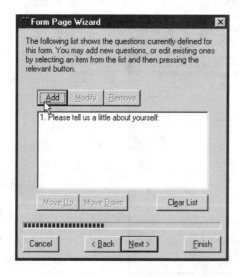

Figure B.7

Add to or edit the list of questions for your form.

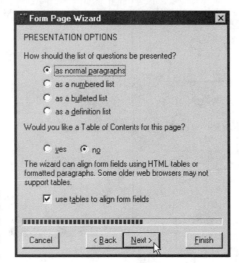

Now choose how
you want your form
to be designed.

7. Click Add to add more questions. Repeat steps 4 and 5 for each new question in your form. When you've finished building the list of questions, click Next. The wizard's Presentation Options page will appear (see Figure B.8).

8. Click one of the style options to tell the wizard how you want to present the questions.

9. If your form is rather long, you might want to consider adding an automatic Table of Contents at the top. If so, click Yes. FrontPage will include a Table of Contents at the top of your form, with bookmarks that point to each question on your list.

10. If it's OK for FrontPage to format your form using tables, check the Use tables to align form fields box. Click Next when you're done.

 TIP Click Back to make changes to your selections before generating the form.

11. Tell FrontPage what you want it to do with the results that are generated when the visitor submits the form. Give the resulting file a

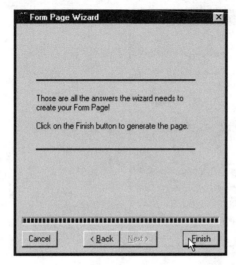

Figure B.9

Click Finish, then sit back and let the wizard work its magic.

name if prompted. (See "So What Happens to the Results?" later in this session for details on handling form results.)

12. Click Finish when you reach the last page of the wizard (see Figure B.9). FrontPage will generate the form and open it in Normal view for editing.

13. Edit the headings, text, and background of the form using regular page editing procedures. (You'll learn how to set the properties for the form fields themselves in a moment.)

14. Add a new field to the form by selecting Insert, Form, and selecting the desired field from the submenu.

Editing Form Field Properties

No matter if you used a template or the Form Page wizard, you've gotten a jump-start on your form. The text is edited and formatted, but you still need to customize the form fields so they look and work as you want them to. To edit the form properties for any field, follow these steps:

1. Right-click the field and select Form Field Properties from the short-cut menu. The Properties dialog box will appear.

The available controls and options will vary depending on which type of field you're editing. In the example, I'm editing the properties of a drop-down menu (see Figure B.10). In this particular instance, I can add, remove, or modify the items that appear in the menu and control the order in which they appear. I can also tell FrontPage how many items to initially show on the menu (the "height" of the list), whether or not the user can select more than one item, and where in the tab order this field should fall.

TIP *Tab order:* When filling in forms, it's often more expedient for the user to move between fields by pressing the Tab key rather than moving from keyboard to mouse to click in or on the next field. By default, a form's tab order (the order in which the fields are selected as the visitor presses the Tab key) is set according to the order in which the fields were created. (For pages generated by wizards or templates, this usually means the order in which they appear on the page.) To make adjustments, enter a specific number for each field in its Tab Order box.

TIP You can test a form's tab order by previewing the page. Click in the first field, then press the Tab key to move from field to field.

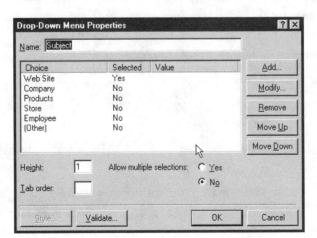

Figure B.10

You can control the look and function of form fields via their Properties settings.

2. Edit the properties as desired. It's beyond the scope of this book to explain every nuance of each field type, but most are self-explanatory. If you need help with a particular item or option, click What's This? (next to the Close button on the title bar of the dialog box), and then click the item you're asking about. FrontPage will display a pop-up help balloon that describes the item in question.

3. Click OK to save the changes and close the dialog box.

4. Switch to Preview view to check the functionality and appearance of your form and its fields.

Don't forget to include a push button (make the label read whatever you want—the default is Submit) so that visitors can submit their form.

WHAT IS FIELD VALIDATION?

You've probably already noticed a few things about fields:

- Form fields sometimes include a default answer, so the visitor can skip that question if the answer is already correct.

- Some fields only allow you to add a specific number of characters (like a ten-digit phone number) or numbers in a specific format (such as mm-dd-yyyy for a date field).

- A drop-down text box might include a question or prompt as the first list item, such as "Choose your type of operating system." When you click that item, the text box's drop-down list appears. You can't select the first item (the one that asks the question), but you can select any of the actual items on the list.

All of these types of controls are called *field validations*. The options vary depending on the field type. To set the validations for a field, select Validate in the field's Properties dialog box. The available options for that field will appear in the Validation dialog box.

You can experiment with each of these settings to learn what they do and how they control the function and appearance of a field. For detailed instructions, click What's This? or press F1 to open FrontPage Help.

(Just in case you're curious, the validation that controls the drop-down menu discussed above is called Disallow First Item. You'll see it in the Validation dialog box for a drop-down menu.)

So What Happens to the Results?

All these lovely forms are great, but without a way for FrontPage to deliver the results, you're just spinning your wheels, and your visitor's.

The type of form you use will most likely dictate how the results should be handled. If you're creating a guest book, for example, you'll probably want FrontPage to save all visitors' submissions to a Web page that other visitors can view. You might want customer service inquiries sent as an e-mail to your help desk coordinator. Orders from your online customers could be integrated into your order entry system. On the other hand, you might want FrontPage to save a text file for you so you can use it for some other purpose. To set or change the form handling options, follow these steps:

1. Right-click anywhere in the form and select Form Properties from the shortcut menu that appears. The Form Properties dialog box appears.

2. Click Options. The Options for Saving the Results of Form dialog box appears with the File Results tab in front, as shown in Figure B.11. Form handling options include the following:

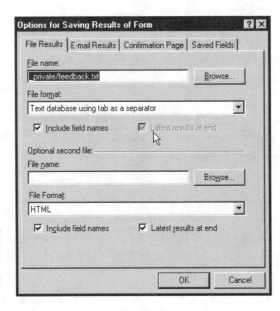

Figure B.11

How do you want to get the information back from your visitors?

- **Save to HTML or text file**. Each submission is added (or *appended*) to the end of an existing file. If you choose HTML file, you can make that file available for viewing on your Web site. Then visitors can read what other people had to say, and add their own comments. Note that by default, the results file is stored in the _private folder, which makes it invisible to visitors. If you want the page to be seen, move it to another location within your Web folder structure. If it's going to be visible, don't forget to format it to match the rest of your Web site (add shared borders, apply a theme, etc.).

NOTE   Your Web server must be running the FrontPage 2000 Extensions to use this option.

- **Save results to a database**. Each submission will be converted to a table and saved as a record in the database on your Web server. FrontPage directly supports Microsoft Access databases, but you can work with any database that accepts data from comma-, tab-, or space-delimited files—including Microsoft Excel.

NOTE   Your Web server must be running the FrontPage 2000 Extensions to use this option.

- **Save results using a custom form handler**. For more complex operations, such as commercial shopping sites, you can create custom scripts, or programs, that run when a form is submitted. The good news is that you don't need the FrontPage Extensions for this option. The bad news is that you need to know at least a little about Internet programming languages such as Perl. Talk to your network administrator or the tech support folks at your WPP for help.

You can find some very helpful ready-made scripts available for downloading (some free, some not) from a variety of Web sites that offer Web-building tools. For starters, try these:

FIND IT ON
THE WEB

- ✿ The Complete Resource for All Web Builders: **www.reallybig.com**
- ✿ HTML Directory: **www.htmldirectory.com**
- ✿ Weblunatic's Webmaster Zone: **www.biginfo.net**
- ✿ Click the E-mail Results tab and enter the requested information to have FrontPage compose and send you (or whomever you specify) an e-mail containing the form results. As your traffic grows, so will the volume of mail coming to your Inbox.

NOTE Your Web server must be running the FrontPage 2000 Extensions to use this option.

3. After you've set all the necessary options in the dialog boxes, click OK to save your changes and return to page-editing mode.

4. Save the page(s). Then test your form by clicking Preview in Browser, and go through the entire submission process.

TIP Dealing with form results can be a complex matter, especially if you're working with databases. You can use the FrontPage Help system to look up the specifics for the handling option you want to implement.

Sending Visitors a Confirmation

When the visitor submits a form, it's good (and sometimes critical) to acknowledge that their form was successfully submitted, as shown in Figure B.12.

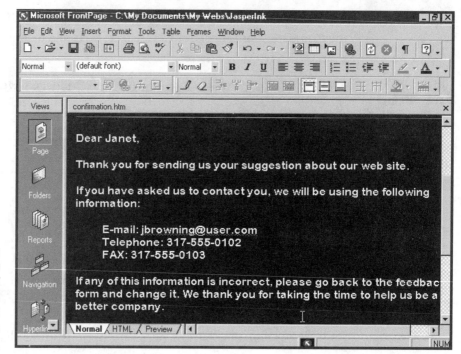

Figure B.12

Let your visitor
know you've
received their input
by including a
confirmation page.

By default (unless you're using a custom script), FrontPage creates a simple confirmation page, but you'll probably want to customize it a little. You might want a simple "thanks for your feedback" message, or a more sophisticated reply. For example, if you request the site visitor's name in your form, you can confirm the submission with a friendly greeting like, "Dear Janet, thanks for taking the time to check out our Web site. We appreciate your feedback and we will address any questions you might have as quickly as possible." You can also display the form results back to the visitor so they can double-check their entries and correct entries if necessary.

TIP

For complete details on creating and customizing confirmation pages, look up "Create a confirmation page and assign it to a form" in FrontPage Help.

Adding Multimedia

dding the right mix of multimedia effects into your FrontPage 2000 Web pages can not only make them more visually and aurally appealing, but more effective as well. Because of the versatility of HTML and the Web, you are not limited merely to static text and images as the content for your Web pages. Many other forms of electronic media can be either linked to or displayed inline. These can include:

○ GIF animations

○ Background and other sounds

○ Inline video

○ Streaming media (audio, video, and animation)

○ Microsoft Liquid Motion animations

The following sections cover these different multimedia options. This appendix does not provide exhaustive coverage of these topics. It does, however, include some examples, a few tips here and there, and some pointers for finding further tools and resources on the Internet.

Using GIF Animations

There are many GIF animations available to download from the Internet. A discretely placed GIF animation, in the form of an animated image link, for instance, can be a great way to add just a dash of dynamism to your page. You insert a GIF animation into your Web page the same way that you insert a regular GIF image. The differences are purely internal. GIF images can include either a single image frame or multiple image frames.

CAUTION There are many GIF animations available to download from the Internet. The copyright status of many of these GIF animations is not clear. If you use a GIF animation that you don't have permission from the author to use, or that has not been expressly made available by the author for free use by all without restrictions, you could be courting a lawsuit, especially if you are putting up a commercial or business Web site. The safe bet, and the ethically purer route, is to use only GIF animations that you have permission to use or that have been made available by their authors for free use by all without restrictions.

There are a few image viewers and editors that will play a GIF animation, but generally, you have to display a GIF animation in your browser (or FrontPage 2000's Preview window) for it to be played. Most regular image viewers and editors will only display the first frame.

Creating GIF Animations with Microsoft GIF Animator

If you have purchased the standalone version of FrontPage 2000 or FrontPage 98, Microsoft has included a GIF animation program, GIF Animator, along with Image Composer 1.5.

NOTE Microsoft GIF Animator is not included as part of the Office 2000 Premium Edition suite, nor is it available elsewhere. If you want to get Microsoft GIF Animator, one option is to purchase the upgrade version of FrontPage 2000 or FrontPage 98, which includes copies of both Image Composer 1.5 and GIF Animator. There are also numerous GIF animation programs available on the Internet. One of my favorites is GIF Construction Set. You can

FIND IT ON
THE WEB download it at **www.mindworkshop.com/alchemy/alchemy.html**. Check Tucows at **www.tucows.com** to find a listing of many more GIF animators that you can download.

If you installed Image Composer 1.5, then Microsoft GIF Animator is automatically installed at the same time. To run GIF Animator, click the Start button, point to Programs and Microsoft Image Composer, and then select Microsoft GIF Animator. Here are some brief pointers on how to use GIF Animator:

✦ On the toolbar, use the Open tool to insert the first image, then use the Insert tool to insert any following images. Images are inserted in reverse order (the last image you insert will be Frame #1), although you can change the order after inserting them (see Figure C.1).

✦ You can only insert GIF (*.gif) format image files. JPEG (*.jpg) format image files need to be converted to GIF format before they can be inserted.

✦ You can also drag and drop images from Image Composer 1.5 into the GIF Animator window, or paste images from the Clipboard.

✦ If you get less than desirable results using the Browser Palette (poor image quality) or the Optimal Palette (too big of a file), use the Load ("...") button to load a customized palette created in Image Composer that has been optimized for all of the images you want to use.

Figure C.1

Three images are inserted in GIF Animator to be the frames of the GIF animation.

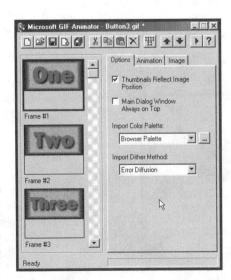

NOTE To create a customized palette that can be applied to all your animation frames in GIF Animator, first use Image Composer to insert and select all of the images you want to use in your animation into the workspace. Then create and save a customized palette that is optimal for all of the images. Select Selection when generating the new palette. (See the "Creating Text Effects Using Image Composer" section in the Sunday Evening session for more detailed instructions on how to create and save a customized palette in Image Composer.)

In GIF Animator, open and insert (or drag and drop) the images, then use the Load ("...") button to specify the customized palette you created and saved in Image Composer.

○ Selecting Error Diffusion as the Import Dither Method generally produces the best results, although it creates a somewhat larger file. If your images are composed of solid colors, select Solid.

○ To cause your animation to loop forever, under the Animation tab, select Looping, and then select Repeat Forever (see Figure C.2).

○ The Image tab controls the settings for the individual frames, including position, frame duration, undraw method, and transparency.

○ To define image settings for all of the frames, click the Select All tool from the toolbar (or press Ctrl+L).

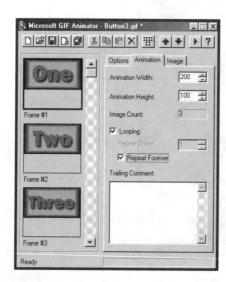

Figure C.2

Select Looping and Repeat Forever under the Animation tab to have the animation loop forever.

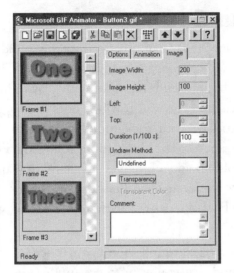

○ If the images are of unequal size (not the case in the figures), you can reset the Left and Top values to adjust the position of an image in its frame.

○ Always reset the Duration, which defaults to 0 (1/100 seconds). Try a value between 25 and 100. For an example, see Figure C.3, where the Duration is shown set to 100 (100 1/100s of a second, or one second).

○ The Undraw Method lets you control how one frame transitions to the next.

○ Transparency and Transparent Color let you specify a color in the frame as transparent.

○ Click the Preview tool on the toolbar to preview your animation (see Figure C.4).

Adding Background Sounds

You can use FrontPage 2000 to automatically play a sound file in the background when your Web page is loaded into a browser. The only problem with this is that the background sound will only play in Internet Explorer. It won't play in Netscape Navigator, which does not support Microsoft's BGSOUND tag. To have your background sound also play in Netscape Navigator, use Netscape's EMBED tag. In the following, I'll show you how to use FrontPage 2000 to add a background sound to your Web page that will play in Internet Explorer. Then I'll show you what codes you need to insert into your HTML file so the background sound will also play in Netscape Navigator.

Before you can add a background sound, you'll need to choose or create the background sound that you want to use. WAV (*.wav) sound files are pretty easy to find. You can probably find quite a few in different locations on your hard drive. Just click the Start button, point to Find, and select Files or Folders. In the Named box, type ***.wav** and click New Search. MIDI (*.mid) sound files aren't nearly as common as WAV sound files, but they can provide better audio quality, especially for music files, while taking up fewer bytes. To search for MIDI files on your hard drive, type ***.mid** in the Named text box.

Adding Background Sounds for Internet Explorer

The steps in FrontPage 2000 for adding background sound to your Web page will work with Internet Explorer, but not with Netscape Navigator. In the next section, "Adding Background Sounds for Netscape Navigator," I'll show you how to edit your FrontPage Web's HTML code to add the codes for playing a background sound file in Navigator. To use FrontPage 2000 to add background sound to your Web page that will play in Internet Explorer:

1. Choose the WAV (*.wav) or MIDI (*.mid) file you want to use as your background sound.

2. Open the Web page in FrontPage 2000 to which you want to add the background sound. Right-click the mouse anywhere inside of your Web page, and then select Page Properties.

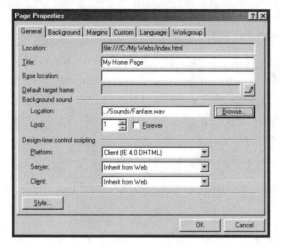

Figure C.5

The background
sound file is set to
play only once.

3. Click the Browse button in the General tab to locate and select the WAV or MIDI sound file you want to use. To look for a sound file on your hard drive that is outside of your FrontPage Web folder (C:\My Webs), click the second icon ("Select a file on your computer") to the right of the URL box (go to the folder where the sound file is and double-click it to open it).

4. Background sounds are set to play forever by default. I recommend that you always clear the Forever check box (background sounds that play forever are obnoxious). To have your background sound file play once, select 1 as the Loop value. (Select 2 to play it twice, 3 to play it three times, and so on; see Figure C.5.) Click OK.

5. To preview your background sound, click the Preview tab.

6. If you selected a sound file from outside of your FrontPage Web folder, you'll be prompted to save the sound file inside of your FrontPage web (File, Save). Just click OK to save the file within your FrontPage Web's root folder.

Adding Background Sounds for Netscape Navigator

Netscape Navigator does not support the BGSOUND tag that FrontPage 2000 uses to add background sound to a FrontPage Web page. If you want your background sound to also play in Navigator, you have to use an entirely different HTML tag, the EMBED tag.

For this example, it is assumed that you have already added a background sound for Internet Explorer in the previous section. You'll be using the same sound file in this section. Otherwise, you'll need to first copy the sound file you want to use into the root folder of your FrontPage web (C:\My Webs). In the following steps, substitute the actual sound file you'll be using for *yoursound.wav*.

1. Choose the WAV (*.wav) or MIDI (*.mid) file you want to use as your background sound.

NOTE While MIDI sound files offer better audio quality and are smaller than WAV sound files, Navigator users are less likely to have a plug-in player installed for MIDI files than for WAV files. For that reason, you may want to stick to using WAV sound files when adding background sounds for Navigator.

2. In FrontPage 2000, open the Web page to which you want to add the background sound, click the HTML tab to edit the HTML codes.

3. Scroll down to the bottom of your Web page's code and click the mouse just above the </body> code. Type the following code:

```
<noembed>

<embed src="yoursound.wav" height=2 width=2 autostart="true">

</noembed>
```

NOTE If you don't include the **<noembed>** and **</noembed>** tags, Internet Explorer will play both the BGSOUND background sound and the EMBED background sound at the same time. Although I don't recommend doing it, if you want the background sound to loop indefinitely, include a **loop="true"** attribute to the EMBED tag. I recommend that you not include a **hidden="true"** attribute to the EMBED tag to hide the plug-in player. Some plug-in players will not play the sound file at all. Instead, stick to setting "2" as the value for both the height and width attributes to make the display of the plug-in player as inconspicuous as possible (using a value of "1" here can have the same undesirable effect that setting hidden="true" can have—no sound at all). Positioning the EMBED tag at the end of the Web page, instead of at the beginning, keeps it from affecting your page's formatting.

● ●

4. To preview your background sounds in Netscape Navigator, first save your Web page (File, Save), and then run Navigator and open your Web page (in Navigator 4.5, select File, Open Page, and Choose File).

Adding Inline Video

You can use FrontPage 2000 to add inline video to your Web page. You can play the following formats: Video for Windows (*.avi), Windows Media (*.asf), and RealMedia (*.ra and *.ram).

● ●

NOTE   Inline video will only play in Internet Explorer; it won't play in Netscape Navigator.

● ●

You can use the Find utility option, (discussed earlier in the section on adding background sounds), to search for any Video for Windows (*.avi) files that might be on your hard drive. If you don't have any on your hard drive, you can find one on the Internet and download it. Then you can experiment with adding inline video clips to your Web pages. To add a Video for Windows (*.avi) video file to your FrontPage Web page:

1. In FrontPage 2000, open the page to which you want to add the inline video and click the mouse in the page where you want the video to play.

2. Select Insert, Picture, and Video.

3. To choose a Video for Windows (*.avi) file on your hard drive that is outside of your FrontPage Web folder (C:\My Webs, for instance), click the second icon ("Select a file on your computer") to the right of the URL box, and then go to the folder where the video file is and double-click it to open it.

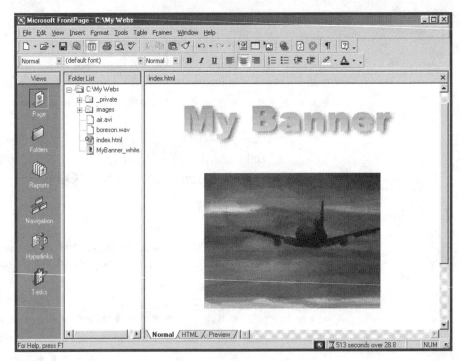

Figure C.6

You can insert and
center an inline
video on a page.

4. To center the inline video window, click the Center tool on the Formatting toolbar (see Figure C.6).

5. To preview the inline video, click the Preview tab.

Other Ways to Add Video and Sound

You can create hypertext links to video files. To include video clips that will
play in both Internet Explorer and Netscape Navigator:

1. Click the mouse where you want to create the hypertext link. Type
the text you want to use for the link, and then click and drag to
select the text. (Or, select any text already on your page that you
want to use as the link.)

2. Select Insert, Hyperlink.

3. You can select a video file from within your FrontPage web, or you can
click the second icon ("Make a hyperlink to a file on your computer")

on the right of the URL box to select a video file from anywhere on your hard drive. Double-click on the video file to select it.

4. To check out the link, click the Preview tab, and then click the link. You should see the video played by the Windows Media Player in a separate window.

● ●

You can create hypertext links to many different video and sound formats. The most common formats you are likely to run across are:

○ Video files (*.avi, *.mov, *.qt)

○ Audio files (*.wav, *.mid, *.rmi, *.snd, *.au, *.aif)

○ NetShow (Active Streaming Format) audio and video files (*.asf)

○ MPEG audio and video files (*.mpeg, *.mpg, *.mpe, *.mp2)

○ MPEG 3 audio files (*.mp3)

○ RealMedia files (*.ra, *.ram)

Most of these file formats should play in Internet Explorer without any trouble, but some may require extra plug-in support to play in Netscape Navigator.

● ●

Adding Streaming Media

Streaming media, like RealAudio and RealVideo (*.ra, *.ram), speeds up the process of downloading and playing an audio or video clip by starting to play it (or "streaming" it) before it has been entirely downloaded. RealAudio and RealVideo are not the only forms of streaming media available over the Internet, but they are the most common.

You can use FrontPage 2000 to display RealAudio or RealVideo either inline or through a hypertext link. The methods for doing this are the same as described previously for displaying inline video and for creating hypertext links to audio or video files.

Your server needs to have licensed and installed RealServer software in order to be able to stream RealMedia (RealAudio and RealVideo) files from your

Web site. If your server does not support streaming of RealMedia files, you can still offer them. Visitors to your site won't be able to see or hear them start playing until they've been completely downloaded from the Internet.

If you want to create your own RealMedia clips, RealNetworks (**www.real.com**) offers a free tool, Real Producer, that you can use for authoring your own RealMedia. You can download it from **www.real.com/ products/tools/producer/.** There are also a number of shareware sound editors available that can convert sound files from other formats to RealMedia (*.ra) files. Two of these are Cool Edit 96 (found on this book's CD or at **www.syntrillium.com**) and WaveConvert Pro PC (**www.waves.com**).

Using Other Streaming Media Types

RealMedia audio and video are not the only forms of streaming media you can add to your Web site. Here is a brief listing of some of the other options that are available:

- ✿ **TrueSpeech**. A streaming audio format that can be created using the Windows Sound Recorder and played by the Windows Media Player. A free TrueSpeech Player is available at **www.dspg.com**.

- ✿ **Shockwave**. A streaming media format available from Macromedia (**www.macromedia.com**), including audio, video, and animation. The production software and a free player can be downloaded.

- ✿ **Audioactive** (**www.audioactive.com**) also has a free player available that will stream Shockwave files.

- ✿ **Microsoft NetShow.** NetShow's Active Streaming Format (*.asf) combines both streaming audio and video, which are streamed by the Windows Media Player. Check out Microsoft's Web site for free downloads of content-creation tools at **www.microsoft.com/netshow/**.

Using Microsoft Liquid Motion Animations

Microsoft Liquid Motion is a great way to add interactive animated content to your FrontPage 2000 Web pages. You can easily create animated banners, logos, buttons, menus, and other Web page elements that will come to life, jumping, spinning, changing colors, shrinking, growing, emitting sounds, and more, when the mouse is passed over, clicked on, or passed off of the animation or any of the actors in the animation. All you have to do is create the animation in Liquid Motion, and then publish it to a folder in your FrontPage 2000 web (C:\My Webs).

FIND IT ON ▶ THE WEB A 45-day trial version of Liquid Motion is available for download at **www.microsoft.com/liquidmotion/**.

To find out more about Liquid Motion, see Prima Tech's *Create Web Animations with Microsoft Liquid Motion In a Weekend* by Steve Callihan. This book tells you everything you need to know to start creating your own dazzling Liquid Motion Web animations right away. See Prima Tech's Web page for the book at **www.prima-tech.com/book.asp?ID=76151822** or Steve Callihan's Web site for the book at **www.callihan.com/liquidmotion/**.

Publishing a Liquid Motion Animation to a Folder in Your FrontPage Web

To publish a Liquid Motion animation to a folder within your FrontPage 2000 web, just follow these steps:

1. In Liquid Motion, click the Publish tool on the toolbar.

2. At the Publish Wizard, leave the Local Disk radio button selected. Click Next.

3. Click Browse to select the folder where you want to publish your animation. From the Browse for Folder tree, select the folder for your FrontPage web (C:\My Webs, for instance). Click OK.

4. In the text box ("Save published files in"), at the end of the publish path, add the name for a folder where you want to publish your animation files. Liquid Motion will create the folder for you, so it doesn't already have to exist. For instance, if your FrontPage web is C:\My Webs\, and you want to publish your animation to a MyAnimation folder in your FrontPage web, then the text box ("Save published files in") should read: **C:\My Webs\MyAnimation**. Click Next.

5. At this dialog box, you can specify a different file name for your animation's HTML file, and you can choose a background color for your animation and its HTML file. Click Next to go to the next dialog box.

6. At this dialog box, you can specify the name of a splash image that will display in Internet Explorer 4.0+ while the animation is downloading. You can also specify whether other animated elements will be included on the page. Click Finish to finish publishing your animation.

7. Open your web in FrontPage 2000. Open the publish folder for your Liquid Motion animation (MyAnimation, for instance), and then double-click your animation's HTML file to open it in FrontPage 2000 (see Figure C.7).

8. To preview your animation, click the Preview tab (see Figure C.8). If you have any interactive elements in your animation, you can test them by passing the mouse over the animation, clicking on it, and so on.

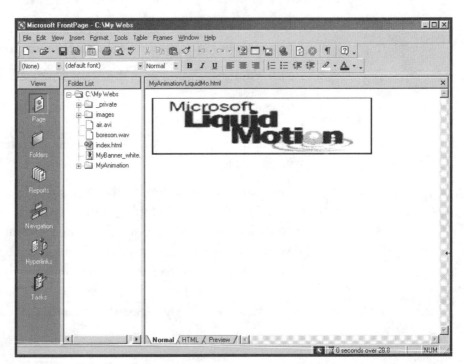

Figure C.7

A Liquid Motion animation's HTML file is opened in FrontPage 2000.

Figure C.8

You can preview a
Liquid Motion
animation in
FrontPage 2000.

Inserting a Liquid Motion Animation into a FrontPage 2000 Web Page

You may want to insert a Liquid Motion animation into a Web page you've already created in FrontPage 2000, rather than simply edit the HTML file created by Liquid Motion in FrontPage 2000. To insert a Liquid Motion animation into a Web page created in FrontPage 2000, just follow these steps:

1. Publish your Liquid Motion animation to the same folder as the Web page into which you want to insert it.

2. Open your animation's HTML file in FrontPage 2000, click the HTML tab, and copy (to the Clipboard) (Ctrl+C) everything starting with `<!--WEBBOT bot="lmwebbot"`... and ending with `<!--WEBBOT bot="lmwebbot" endspan -->`.

3. Open the HTML file (in the same folder) into which you want to paste the animation code and click the HTML tab. Position the mouse cursor where you want to paste the code. Be sure it is after the `<body>` code, but before the `</body>` code. (Also make sure you

don't position the cursor inside of any codes, which are marked by < and > characters.) Press Ctrl+V to paste the animation code.

4. Click the Preview tab to see the inserted animation.

Quick Tips for Using Liquid Motion Animations with FrontPage 2000

Here are some quick tips you should keep in mind when using Liquid Motion animations with FrontPage 2000:

○ If you want to move or copy a Liquid Motion animation from a FrontPage 2000 Web folder, move or copy all of the files and folders that were published with the animation, not just the *.html or *.jcz file.

○ If you want to insert the codes for the same animation more than once into a FrontPage Web page, you *must* publish separate animations (MyAnimation1, MyAnimation2, and so on). Then insert them separately into your FrontPage Web page.

○ If you want your Liquid Motion animations to play in both Internet Explorer and Netscape Navigator, you should be aware that these effects will display only in Internet Explorer 4.0+: spinning images/ text (spinning 2-D shapes are okay), 3-D shapes, filters/transitions, audio formats other than *.au format (8-bit, mono, mu-Law, 8000 Hz) audio files, audio panning, transparent backgrounds, and external triggers/script triggers.

○ To put your Liquid Motion animations on a diet (so they won't get too fat), either go easy on using, or don't include, external media in your animations, such as GIF or JPEG files, GIF animations, and audio files. Use Liquid Motion's own text and shape actors, rather than imported images.

○ When using FrontPage 2000 to republish a Liquid Motion animation to a FrontPage Web server, delete the *.jcz, *.x, and *.js files for that animation on the server, then republish the updated animation to the server. If you don't delete these files ahead of time, they won't be updated by FrontPage 2000, even if you've selected the "Published changed pages only" check box.

Web Site Promotion Tips and Tricks

There's little point in putting up your snazzy new FrontPage Web site if nobody is going to come to see it. Contrary to popular opinion, the world will not beat a path to your door, especially on the Internet. The fact of the matter is that with more and more people putting up their own Web sites, it is getting more and more difficult to get noticed. To make sure that your Web site is noticed, you need to know a few tips and tricks.

Snagging Search Engines

Some search engines have robots or spiders that crawl the Internet looking for new sites and pages, so you may not have to do anything to get your Web site indexed. For other search engines, indexes, and directories, you may have to first let them know that you exist before they'll index your site. (For more information on how to submit your Web site to the different search engines, see "Submitting Your Web Site" further on in this appendix.)

The trick is to prepare your Web pages so that you control how your site will be indexed. This helps insure that when surfers do relevant Internet searches, your Web page pops up to the top of the heap.

Using Keywords

You can increase the likelihood of your page showing up in an Internet search if your title, level-1 heading, and first paragraph contain *keywords* that searchers are likely to use when searching for the kind of content included in your Web site.

▼ ▼

When someone searches the Internet using a search form such as at AltaVista or Infoseek Guide, for instance, they type one or more **keywords** that they want to search for. The search index then responds with a listing of Web pages that contain the keyword or keywords.

▲ ▲

Including Keywords in Your Title

The title of your page is very important. Many search engines are much more likely to list your page in the first few pages of responses if the keyword or keywords being searched for are included in your title. Make your title both informative and descriptive, and don't be afraid to be a little verbose. A good way to do this is to first state the title of your site, and then follow it with a short description of your site, including as many relevant keywords that you can think of. To edit the title for your Web page:

1. Open your page in FrontPage 2000 and then right-click the mouse inside of the page and select Page Properties.

2. In the Title box, type a title and a description of your page (try to include keywords in both the title and the description). (See Figure D.01.) Click OK.

You should *always* include an informative title in your Web page. Getting listed by a search engine won't do you any good if Internet searchers pass by the link to your site because your title doesn't provide them any relevant information about your site.

■ ■

The closer a keyword is to the front of your page's title, the more weight a search engine will give to it. For instance, a title like "Yo-Yo Kingdom" would probably get somewhat better search engine results than "John's Incredibly Wonderful Yo-Yo Page" when a search is done on the keyword "yo-yo."

■ ■

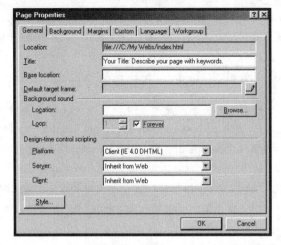

Figure D.1

You can edit your page properties to add a more descriptive title.

Including Keywords in Your Level-1 Heading

It is a good idea to start your Web page with a level-1 heading (the Heading 1 style in FrontPage). Many search engines give special weight to any level-1 heading that is included at the top of your page, so if you can sneak a few keywords into your level-1 heading, it will help to insure that Internet searchers will find your site. You should place your level-1 heading either at the very top of your Web page or immediately following any banner or logo graphic you've inserted at the top of your page. To include a level-1 heading at the top of your page:

1. Click the mouse at the top of your page and press the Enter key to add a line.

2. Click on the line you just created, and then select the Heading 1 style from the Style box.

3. Type the text for your level-1 heading (trying to include one or two keywords, if you can). To center your level-1 heading, click the Center tool on the Formatting toolbar.

Since search engines place special weight on *any* headings (Heading 1, Heading 2, and so on) that are in your Web page when indexing your site, you should avoid using these styles just to format your text in a bigger font.

Only use the heading styles to designate the order of precedence within your page's hierarchical structure, and not as formatting devices. If you want to increase the font size for a section of text in your page, first select the text, and then click the Font Size box and select a font size of 4, 5, or 6.

CAUTION A trick that sneaky Web authors used to use to get listed higher in Internet search response lists was to include one or more choice keywords repeated multiple times at the top of a Web page. These were all neatly concealed from public view inside comment tags. Search engines, however, would index the comment text and pop the page to the top of their response list for searches using the commented keyword or keywords. You should be aware, however, that search engines are aware of this trick. Now, if you try to do this, your page is liable to be demoted, if not eliminated, in a search engine's list of responses.

Including Keywords in Your First Paragraph

Many search engines will index the text at the start of your Web page, but ignore the rest. Others will weigh the first 30, 40, or more words higher than other words in your page when indexing your site. The more keywords you can strategically include in the first paragraph of your Web page, the more likely that Internet searchers will be able to find your page. Many search engines and directories will also display your page's initial 30 to 40 words when listing your site in a search response. Put special thought into composing the first couple of sentences on your page—the more informative you are, right off the bat, the better.

Don't just include keywords in your introductory paragraph, but include key phrases, as well. Many people will use a key phrase, like "real estate," "science education," "nuclear energy," "movie stars," and so on, when doing an Internet search. Try to anticipate the kinds of phrases someone might use when searching for a Web page like yours. Try to include those key phrases in your introductory paragraph.

NOTE There are some who recommend that you avoid using framed pages, because a "frameset" page doesn't actually contain any content, just links to the page frames that make up your framed page. Because it doesn't have any real content to be indexed, a framed page is less likely to get listed among the top responses to an Internet search. If you do want to use a framed page, be sure to include an informative title. You should also always include a META tag (user variable) description and list of keywords. See the next section for directions on how to include these in your Web page. Another trick is to go ahead and type a description of your site, including keywords and key phrases, in the "noframes" section of the framed page. The "noframes" section is the part of the framed page that will be displayed by a browser that doesn't support frames, but won't be displayed by a browser that supports frames. That doesn't mean, however, that a search engine won't index it.

Using User Variable Descriptions and Keywords

User variables are commonly referred to as "META tag variables," since the META tag in HTML is used to add this information to your Web page's head section. You can define user variables for your Web page that can include a description of your Web page or Web site and a list of keywords.

Some search engines will give special priority to META tag descriptions and keywords when indexing your site. Also, some search engines will display your META tag description, rather than the first paragraph of your page, when they list your site. Always include a META tag description and list of keywords in at least the front (index or default) Web page of your site.

Adding a META Tag Description

Adding a Meta tag description to your page is easy, so there's no reason not to do it. To add a META tag description to your Web page, do the following:

1. Right-click the mouse inside of your page and select Page Properties.

2. Click the Custom tab. Under User variables, select Add.

3. In the Name box, type **description**. In the Value box, type a concise description of your Web page. Try to include several keywords in

Figure D.2

You can add a META tag description to your page that some search engines will use when indexing your Web page.

your description that you think someone might use in trying to search for a page like yours (see Figure D.2). Click OK.

4. The "description" META tag variable is added to your page's list of user variables. Click OK.

Adding a META Tag List of Keywords

It is also a very good idea to add a Meta tag list of keywords to your Web page. It's easy! To add a META tag list of keywords to your Web page, do the following:

1. Right-click the mouse inside of your page and select Page Properties.

2. Click the Custom tab. Under User variables, select Add.

3. In the Name box, type **keywords**. In the Value box, type a list of keywords separated by commas (see Figure D.3 for an example). Click OK.

4. The "keywords" META tag variable is added to your page's list of user variables (see Figure D.4). Click OK.

Figure D.3

You can define a META tag list of keywords that some search engines will use when indexing your site.

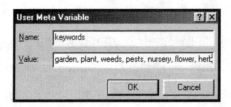

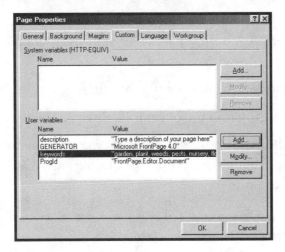

Figure D.4

The "keywords" META tag variable is added to your page's list of user variables.

TIP Another way to include words and phrases that might be indexed by a search engine is to include alternative text for any images on your page. The alternative text is displayed if visitors to your page have display of graphics turned off or are using a text-only browser. It can also be very helpful to visitors using a Braille browser. Most browsers also display alternative text when you pass the mouse over an image. To add alternative text to an image, right-click the image, select Picture Properties, and then click the General tab. In the Text box (under Alternative representations), type the alternative text that you want to attach to your image.

Blocking a Search Engine from Indexing Your Web Pages

Sometimes you don't want your Web page to be indexed. It might be under construction, or you might want to encourage visitors to come in at your front page, rather than at pages deeper into your Web site. Many search engines use robots to index Web sites on the Internet. It would be nice if you could tell them which pages you want indexed, and which ones you don't. Well, you can, in a way. That is, you can tell some robots where to go (primarily the AltaVista and Infoseek Guide robots, but there may be more). To have some control over which of your pages are indexed, and which aren't, follow these steps:

1. Right-click the mouse inside of your page and select Page Properties.

2. Click the Custom tab. Under User variables, click Add.

3. In the Name box, type **robots**. Type **noindex** in the Value box to tell a robot or spider not to index the page. Click OK. Then click OK again.

NOTE You can use other values with the "robots" variable:

- ✿ *index.* Index the current page.

- ✿ *follow.* Continue to any following pages.

- ✿ *nofollow.* Don't continue to any following pages.

You can also combine values. You might try one of these combinations:

- ✿ *noindex,follow.* Do not index the current page, but go on to any following pages.

- ✿ *noindex,nofollow.* Do not index the current page and do not index any following pages.

- ✿ *index,nofollow.* Index the current page, but do not go on to any following pages.

Announcing Your Web Site

Once you've put your Web site up, you're going to want to announce it to the world. This can be done a couple of different ways on the Internet:

FIND IT ON ▶
THE WEB

- ✿ Post an announcement on the newsgroup, **comp.infosystems.www.announce**

- ✿ Post announcements to appropriate online newsletter and mailing lists

Announcing Your Site to comp.infosystems.www.announce

FIND IT ON ▶
THE WEB

The newsgroup, **comp.infosystems.www.announce**, has been created specifically for posting announcements about what's new on the Internet. This newsgroup is limited to announcing *non-commercial* Web sites, so if you have a commercial Web site, you should not post to this newsgroup. It is considered poor etiquette to post new site announcements to other newsgroups, unless *on topic* announcements are allowed. Always check a newsgroup's FAQ or charter to see what kind of announcements are allowed before posting any announcements. To post to the **comp.infosystems. www.announce** newsgroup, you will need to have a newsreader configured and installed. This can be Netscape Messenger, Outlook Express, or Free Agent. You will need to subscribe to **comp.infosystems.www.announce**, so you can download messages from it and post your own announcement message. Be sure to read the newsgroup charter first at **www.sangfroid.com/ charter.html** before posting any announcements.

Announcing Your Site to E-Mail Newsletters and Mailing Lists

You can also announce your site to a number of e-mail newsletters and mailing lists. These include:

- ✿ Net Surfer Digest
- ✿ Internet Scout Project

Net Surfer Digest

FIND IT ON ▶
THE WEB

Net Surfer Digest is an e-mail newsletter that is a "guide to interesting news, places, and resources online." You can find out about it and how to subscribe to it at **www.netsurf.com/nsd/index.html**. Any announcement that you would like to have considered for inclusion should be e-mailed to **pressroom@netsurf.com**.

Figure D.5

Through the
Internet Scout
Project, you can
submit
announcements to
both the Scout
Report and
Net-Happenings.

Internet Scout Project

The National Science Foundation sponsors the Internet Scout Project to provide timely information to the education community about valuable Internet resources. It is composed of two services, Scout Report and Net-Happenings. Over 100,000 people receive the weekly Scout Report. Over 25,000 people receive Net-Happenings daily. Net-Happenings is also available as a newsgroup, **www.internet.net-happenings**.

To find out how to subscribe to Scout Report and Net-Happenings as well as to find out what their criteria is for accepting announcements, go to **www.scout.cs.wisc.edu/scout/** (see Figure D.5).

Submitting Your Web Site to Search Engines and Indexes

Some search engine robots and spiders roam freely around the Internet looking for new sites. However, the best way to get the most attention for your site in the shortest possible amount of time is to submit information about your Web site to the major search engines and index directories.

Getting Your Site Listed on Yahoo!

If you don't get your site listed anywhere else, you should try to get it listed at Yahoo! Getting listed at Yahoo! can make all the difference between whether you get a stream of new visitors each day, or just a trickle. Here are some pointers on getting your site listed at Yahoo!:

FIND IT ON ▶
THE WEB

- Be sure to thoroughly read the guidelines on how to suggest a new site to Yahoo! at **www.yahoo.com/info/suggest/**.

- Before actually starting, take the time to compose a description of your site in 30 words or less. Be sure to include as many appropriate keywords as you can in your description, but don't go overboard. The main thing is to have it accurately and informatively describe the content of your site. When you fill out Yahoo's site suggestion form, you can just paste in your description when asked for it. You should also save this description to use it when you submit your site to other search engines and index directories.

- When you suggest your site for a category at Yahoo!, the form asks you what other categories you think would be appropriate for your Web site. So, before suggesting your site for a category, look through Yahoo! for other appropriate categories. A good way to do this is to open Windows Notepad and make a list of appropriate categories. Then, when you suggest your site to the first category, you can also include the other Yahoo! categories that are appropriate for your site. That way, you only need to fill out Yahoo!'s site suggestion form once.

- Don't suggest your site to too many or to inappropriate Yahoo! categories. Suggest your site to only the three or four most appropriate categories for your site.

- Be patient! Yahoo! has actual human beings (not robots or spiders), visit your site and review its contents. Then, if they feel it is appropriate, they may recommend your site for inclusion in the category that you've requested. There is no guarantee that you will get listed in the categories that you request. Also, the amount of time that it takes to get listed in different categories can vary—anywhere from a week to a couple months. This is because some categories get a lot of suggestions to review, while other only get a few. Suggesting your site again won't help—it'll only bump you to the back of the queue. So, before suggesting your site to a category again, wait at least three months. Then, if you still don't get listed, try another category.

Manually Submitting Your Site to the Other Top Search Engines and Indexes

There are many places other than Yahoo! where you'll want to submit your site. I recommend that you individually and manually submit your Web site to each of these search engines and directory indexes, rather than try to use an automatic submission service. That's because you'll get better results if you can fine-tune your submission for each one. Later, you can use one of the automatic submission services to catch as many other submission sites as you can.

If you have already composed a description of your site (seeded with relevant keywords), you may want to open or paste it into Windows Notepad so you'll have it handy if you're asked to submit a description when you submit your site.

Here are the main search engines and index directories, along with their Web addresses to which you should submit your site:

FIND IT ON ▶
THE WEB

- **AltaVista** at **www.altavista.net**—click "Add a Page" link at bottom of page.

- **Infoseek** at **www.infoseek.go.com**—click "Add URL" link at bottom of page.

- **Excite** at **www.excite.com**—click "Add URL" link at bottom of page.

- **GoTo.com** at **www.goto.com**—click "Get Listed on GoTo" link.

- **WebCrawler** at **www.webcrawler.com**—click "Add Your URL" link at bottom of page.

- **Lycos** at **www.lycos.com**—click "Add Your Site to Lycos" link at bottom of page.

- **Snap** at **www.home.snap.com**—look for "Submit your site's URL here" at very bottom of page (in small print).

- **LookSmart** at **www.looksmart.com**—click "How to Add a Site" at bottom of left sidebar.

- **Netscape NetCenter** at **home.netscape.com**—click "Add Site" link at bottom of page.

- **HotBot** at **www.hotbot.com**—click "Add URL" link.

- **AOL NetFind** at **www.aol.com/netfind/home.html**—click "Add Your Site" link at bottom of page.

Using Free Site Submission Services

There are many other places on the Internet where you can get your site listed. It would take forever to do them all. However, after you've manually submitted your site to the main search engines and index directories listed in the previous section, try one of the free site submission services that are available on the Internet.

TIP
You might want to keep a log of where you've submitted your site and when. The free site submission services let you select or clear the sites you want to submit your site to, so having a log of where you've already submitted your site can help avoid submitting your site more than once to the same place. If you also include when you submitted your site to a particular service, then you can remind yourself to update your listing every six months or so. This will ensure that the listing accurately represents your current site.

Here are some of the free site submission services available on the Internet:

FIND IT ON
THE WEB

- **Submit It! Free Classic** at **siteowner.linkexchange.com/Free.cfm**—fill out a form to submit your site to 19 different places.

- **Signpost** at **signpost.merseyworld.com**—can automatically submit your site to over 90 different search engines and Web directories.

- **1 2 3 Add Masters Web Promotion Tool** at **www.netfit.net/123-add-masters**—you can submit to their top 30 search sites for free.

Promoting Your Web Site

There are many ways that you can promote your Web site. Here are just some of them:

- Getting reciprocal links
- Using banner exchange networks
- Joining Web rings
- Purchasing banner ads
- Using traditional promotional methods

Getting Reciprocal Links

A great way to boost your traffic over time is to trade reciprocal links. You should look for other sites that are related in some fashion to your own and offer to link to them if they will link to you. Someone else might also e-mail you that they want to link to you in return for your linking to them. Sometimes this takes a little negotiation, since where and how you link to someone else, or where and how they link to you, can make a difference. If someone just wants to link to you as one link among a hundred on their "links" page, then you probably wouldn't want to link back to them prominently on your front page, unless you think it represents a significant value to your visitors. On the other hand, you might want to create a "links" page of your own if anyone asks for a reciprocal link.

Another thing you can do is to put up a page of links that focuses on the general subject area of, or subject areas related to, your Web site. You may want to break your links up into different related areas. For instance, if your Web site is called "The Michigan Weather Page," you could put up a couple of link pages, "Michigan Resources" and "Weather Resources," then link to both prominently from your front page. That way, you won't just be sticking reciprocal links into a generic links page, and should be able to get a better link back in return. In other words, when you design your page, think of ways that you can work in opportunities for being able to offer quality reciprocal links. If you're using a navigation bar on your page, for instance, you might want to include links there to your "links" pages. Don't make it just an afterthought.

One key is to look for other sites with which you can form a relationship of synergy. The idea is that by prominently linking to each other, even swapping banner ads, for instance, both sites can generate more traffic by sharing traffic that is interested in both sites. Establish two or three of these synergic relationships, and you could see a significant boost to your traffic as a result.

Using Banner Exchange Networks

With a banner exchange network, you agree to display a banner ad on your page, in return for getting exposure through display of your banner ad on others' pages. Some banner exchange services allow you to restrict or focus the kinds of banner ads that will be displayed on your page. You can also suggest the type of pages on which your banner will be displayed. If your site is non-commercial, you may want to only display banner ads for other non-commercial Web sites.

The amount of exposure your banner ad will get on others' sites is determined by how many times the banner exchange's banner ad is displayed or clicked on in your own page or pages. The more traffic through your site, in other words, the more plays your banner ad will get on others' pages.

One trick here is to create an effective banner ad that will snag visitors for you. It doesn't do you any good to have your banner ad displayed on others' pages, if no one clicks on it. It pays to put some forethought into the kind of banner ad you want to create. If you have Image Composer 1.5 or PhotoDraw 2000 and have done the Sunday Evening session, "Creating Web Art Special Effects," you should be able to create a visually appealing banner ad. Of course, you can hire a graphics professional or advertising expert to create your banner ad for you, but that tends to be overkill for your basic "bootstrap" Web site.

Some banner exchange networks require a banner ad to be a specific dimension and not exceed a certain number of kilobytes in size (usually 10K or smaller). Transparent GIFs are usually discouraged or prohibited, since you can't anticipate what the background color, tone, or texture may be on pages where your ad will be displayed. (If transparent GIFs are allowed, don't use any shadow or blended edges, and turn smoothing off.) A few banner exchange networks will allow you to use a GIF animation for your banner ad, but most won't.

Many banner exchange networks' terms and conditions state that their banner be the only banner ad displayed on your page. They also want it displayed prominently toward the top of your page ("above the fold"). Members who stack exchange banners from different services, or who artificially inflate traffic to their site to earn extra credits, may have their memberships terminated.

You can usually view statistics on how many credits you've received, how many times your banner ad has been displayed, and how many times it's been clicked on.

Here are just some of the free banner exchange networks that you can use:

FIND IT ON ▶
THE WEB

- **LinkExchange** (formerly Internet Link Exchange) at **www.linkexchange.com**—this was the first free banner exchange network and is still probably the largest. You can specify that you want only non-commercial banner ads displayed on your pages.

- **123 Banners** at **www.123banners.com**—a fairly straightforward banner exchange network that doesn't allow you to specify which kinds of ads get displayed on your page.

- **Exchange-it!** at **www.exchange-it.com**—accepts ads only from Web sites with content suitable for children.

- **Ad-Xchange!** at **www.ad-xchange.com**—this banner exchange network doesn't require that you place its banner at the top of your page It only requires that it be placed somewhere on your Web site where it can be seen.

- **BannerWorks** at **www.bannerworks.com**—this is a "business-to-business" banner exchange network that allows you to target the audience for your ad. Animated banners are encouraged.

- ✿ **CyberLink Exchange** at **www.cyberlinkexchange.com**—lets you create banner ads with multiple click-points, so one banner ad can link to several Web pages.

For many links to other banner exchange networks, see Yahoo!'s Banner Exchanges category at **dir.yahoo.com/Computers_and_Internet/Internet/ World_Wide_Web/Announcement_Services/Banner_Exchanges/**. For instance, you might want to look in Yahoo!'s list for banner exchange networks that are focused for specific regions (United Kingdom, Australia, and so on) or subject areas (gardening, gaming, and so on).

Joining Web Rings

A Web ring is a way of joining together Web sites that share a common theme. When you join a Web ring, you insert the code and banner for the Web ring on your page. Then visitors to your page can visit other pages in the ring. Since you are part of the ring, others can visit your Web page from other pages participating in the ring. Web rings can be a great way of generating traffic that is targeted to your particular area of interest.

There are Web rings for just about any imaginable theme or subject. For links to lots and lots of Web rings, check out Yahoo!'s category for Web rings at **dir.yahoo.com/Computers_and_Internet/Internet/World_Wide_Web/ Searching_the_Web/Indices_to_Web_Documents/Rings/**.

FIND IT ON ▶
THE WEB

Purchasing Banner Ads

If you have a commercial site, you may want to consider advertising on other sites to get exposure. You could, for instance, pay for a banner ad on a Web site that has a lot of visitors who might also be interested in your Web site. Another option is to sponsor someone else's Web page. Sponsoring a Web page usually means that your banner ad will be displayed at the top of the page you're sponsoring.

Placing your own banner ad on others' Web sites doesn't necessarily have to cost a bundle. If you find a Web site with a good amount of traffic that you think would also be interested in your service or product, simply make an offer. There are really no rules of thumb for what the right price is. It is simply whatever you can agree upon. What's ten or twenty dollars a month, if it results in over $1,000 in sales? Of course, it might also result in no sales at all, in which case you can drop your ad. You could also offer to exchange banner ads, which wouldn't cost you anything.

Some Web sites are essentially in the business of selling advertising. It makes sense that a high-traffic site will charge more to place a banner ad than a lower-traffic site. If you want to advertise on Yahoo.com, for instance, expect to pay a bunch. Sites that are in the business of selling advertising usually also can provide daily or weekly statistical reports on how many times your banner ad has been displayed and how many click-throughs it has had.

Of course, once you start to attract enough traffic to your own site, you could start selling banner ads yourself.

Using Traditional Promotional Methods

Don't overlook using some of the traditional promotional methods. Not everything you do to promote your Web site needs to be Web-based. Here are just some of the traditional methods you can use to promote your Web site:

- Include your Web address (URL) on your letterhead and business cards.

- Include your Web address in any print or other advertising you might do. If you have an ad in the Yellow Pages, be sure to also include your Web address there.

- Send out press releases or press kits to local, regional, or national media outlets, as well as to any appropriate trade or professional media outlets.

- Get creative. Print your Web address on pens, notepads, buttons, t-shirts, and so on, and then include them in your press kits or pass them out to customers or potential customers.

Implementing Special Features

While a lot has been covered so far, covering absolutely everything you can do with FrontPage 2000 would take several weekends, at least. If you've done all of the optional sections, you may already be suffering from information overload.

This appendix covers some of the more advanced things you can do with FrontPage 2000. I won't be able to go into a lot of detail here, but hopefully I can get you started along the right path if you decide to make use of the following features:

- ✪ Setting up a password protected Web site
- ✪ Using the Database Results wizard
- ✪ Adding Java applets and ActiveX controls

Setting Up a Password Protected Web Site

With FrontPage 2000, you can set permissions and control user access to your FrontPage webs you create or edit on a Web server. The permissions that can be set by FrontPage 2000 are:

- ✪ **Browse.** A user can browse the files of a web.
- ✪ **Author.** A user can browse and edit files in a web.
- ✪ **Administrator.** A user can administer the web by adding and removing users.

You won't be able to test security restriction settings on your local web. First, you'll have to publish your site to your remote Web server. To set permissions and assign usernames and passwords, you'll need to have administrator rights for your Web folders. To test whether you have administrator rights, after you've published your site to your Web server, remotely open it in FrontPage 2000. If the Security option on the Tools menu is grayed-out, that means either you don't have administrator rights assigned to you or your Web server does not support setting security restrictions. If the option is grayed-out, request administrator rights for your Web site from your server administrator. If they aren't willing to do that, but you really need to set up security restrictions, you might want to consider finding another provider. As a last resort, you can request that the server administrator set the permissions and assign usernames and passwords for you. This is not a good solution, though, if you'll need to revise the security permissions on an ongoing basis, rather than just once.

In FrontPage 98, you could only set security permissions for your entire site. With FrontPage 2000, you can set separate security permissions for any subwebs you've created. This lets you assign different levels of permissions for different individuals (or lists of individuals, or workgroups) for different subwebs.

Setting Permissions

Once you've opened your remote web in FrontPage 2000, you can set permissions for your root web by doing the following:

1. Click the mouse on your root web folder ("http://...") to select it. Select Tools, Security (if not grayed-out), and then select Permissions (see Figure E.1).

2. To restrict access to registered users only, select the second radio button (Only registered users have browser access).

3. To add a user to the list of authorized users for your site, click the Add button.

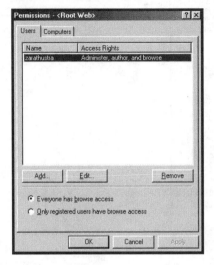

Figure E.1

The Permissions dialog box lets you assign usernames and access rights.

4. Just add a fictional user: in the Name box, type **Joe_Smith**. In the Password box, type a password (**blitzen205**, for instance). In the Confirm Password box, retype the password.

 NOTE Don't include any spaces in usernames or passwords. In usernames, substitute underscores (_) in place of spaces. You should also be aware that both usernames and passwords are case-sensitive. When you provide a username and password to a user, tell them to type the username and password exactly as shown.

5. For this example, leave the Browse the Web radio button selected (to allow Joe Smith to only browse your pages). The other radio buttons allow you to assign either author or administer rights to Joe Smith (see Figure E.2).

6. Click OK to add Joe Smith to the list of registered users for your site (see Figure E.3).

Figure E.2

A username,
password, and
browsing rights
have been
assigned.

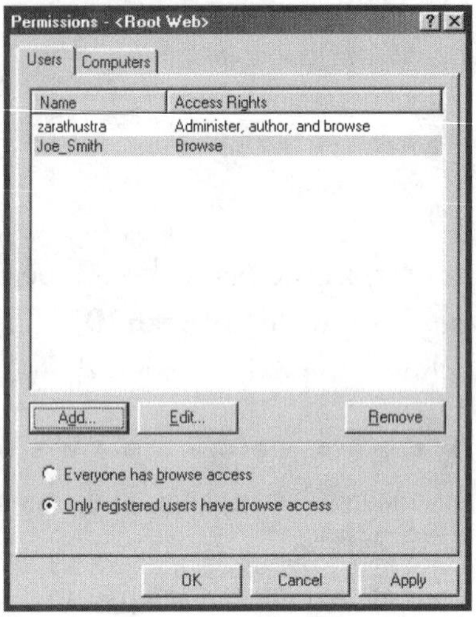

Figure E.3

A new user
has been added
to the list of
registered users.

7. Repeat these steps for as many other users that you want to add. To change the settings for any user, just highlight the username and select Edit. To remove a user, just highlight the username and select Remove. When done, just click the OK button to close the Permissions window.

Using the Database Results Wizard

Using the Database Results Wizard, you can easily display information from an online Access or Excel database on your pages. While operation of the Database Results Wizard is deceptively simple, getting the actual database results to work can be a little tricky.

Before You Start

Before you start trying to use the Database Results Wizard, you'll need to install the following:

- Microsoft Personal Web Server (Version 4.0)
- The FrontPage 2000 server extensions on your PWS
- A 32-bit ODBC driver (if not already installed)

Installing the Microsoft Personal Web Server

Unlike FrontPage 98, FrontPage 2000 does not require that a *personal web server* (PWS) be installed on your local computer. For that reason, a personal web server is not included with FrontPage 2000. Because the Database Results Wizard requires support for *Active Server Pages (ASP)*, you'll need to install a version of PWS that supports ASP, if you want to preview your database query results on your local computer.

▼ ▼

A *personal web server* is a web server you can install on your local computer, allowing you to publish and test out your pages locally first, before publishing them to your remote server.

Active Server Pages (or *ASP*) are a means for dynamically generating Web pages on a Web server running Microsoft Internet Information Server (ISS) version 3.0 or higher. Support for ASP is also built into Microsoft Personal Web Server 4.0.

▲ ▲

If you are using Windows 98, you can install Microsoft Personal Web Server 4.0, which has support for ASP built-in, from the Windows 98 CD-ROM. Just insert the Windows 98 disc in your CD-ROM drive and click the Start button, and then select Run. In the Open box, type **d:\add-ons\pws\setup.exe** (substitute the drive letter of your CD-ROM drive for *d:*) and click OK.

If you are using Windows 95 or Windows NT, you can download MS PWS 4.0 from Microsoft's web site at **www.microsoft.com/windows/**

FIND IT ON ▶
THE WEB

downloads/contents/wurecommended/s_wuservicepacks/nt4optpk/default.asp.

● ●

NOTE The personal web server software included on the FrontPage 98 CD-ROM, Version 2.0, does not have built-in support for ASP.

● ●

Installing the FrontPage 2000 Server Extensions on Your PWS

Microsoft PWS 4.0 comes with the FrontPage 98 Server Extensions already installed. Before you'll be able to publish your database to your personal web server, you first need to upgrade its server extensions to the FrontPage

2000 server extensions. To do this, you need to run the Server Extensions Administrator from the Start menu.

- For Windows 95/98, select Start, Programs, Microsoft Office Tools, and Server Extensions Administrator.

- For Windows NT Workstation, select Start, Programs, Administrative Tools, and Server Extensions Administrator.

- For Windows NT Server 4.0 (without Microsoft Information Server 4.0 installed), select Start, Programs, Administrative Tools, Server Extensions Administrator. For Windows NT Server 4.0 (with Microsoft Information Server 4.0 installed), select Start, Programs, Windows NT 4.0 Option Pack, Microsoft Internet Information Server, Internet Service Manager.

You can also run this using the Start menu's Run command: select Run, type **c:\program files\common files\microsoft shared\web server extensions\40\bin\fpmmc.msc**, and click OK.

With the Microsoft Management Console window open, do the following:

1. In the tree structure in the left-pane, click the "+" icon to the left of FrontPage Server Extensions to expand its contents (if it isn't already expanded). Then right-click the selection listed under FrontPage Server Extensions.

2. Select Task, and then select Upgrade Server Extensions.

NOTE   If Check Server Extensions is displayed as the Task option, that means that the FrontPage 2000 server extensions have already been installed.

Installing a 32-Bit ODBC Driver

Finally, you'll need a 32-bit ODBC (Online Database Connection) driver. Internet Explorer 4.0+ automatically installs a 32-bit ODBC drivers. 32-bit ODBC drivers are also included with Windows NT 4.0 SR Pack 2 (but not SR Pack 1).

To check that ODBC drivers have been installed, click the Start button and select Settings, Control Panel. Look for an icon labeled either as "ODBC" or "ODBC Data Sources (32bit)."

Only 32-bit ODBC applications are supported on Windows 95/98. Windows NT 4.0 supports both 16-bit and 32-bit ODBC applications, so if you're unable to get the Database Results Wizard to work, you may need to update your ODBC drivers.

If you don't already have 32-bit ODBC drivers installed, you can download and install the latest versions, included in Microsoft Data Access Components 2.1, from Microsoft's Web site at **www.microsoft.com/data/odbc/**.

FIND IT ON ▶
THE WEB

Creating a Database Connection

The first thing you need to do, of course, is to create the database you want to use and then connect it to your FrontPage web. FrontPage 2000 has included a sample Access 2000 database that you can use in testing out the Database Results Wizard. To locate the sample database file:

1. Click the Start button, point to Find, and select Files or Folders.

2. In the Named box, type **fpnwind.mdb** and click Find Now. (To find all Access database files, just type *.**mdb**.)

3. In the lists of results, right-click on fpnwind.mdb and select Copy.

Now, you need to add the database you just copied to your FrontPage web:

1. If FrontPage 2000 isn't open, run it and open your local web folder (C:\My Webs, for instance).

2. Inside of the left-pane for your web, right-click the mouse, and then select Paste (see Figure E.4).

3. Just leave Database1 as the name for the database connection. Click Yes.

4. At the dialog box recommending that you store your database in the fpdb folder, click Yes.

You'll notice now that a file, global.asa, and a folder, fpdb, have been added to the Folder List.

NOTE Microsoft recommends storing your database file in the fpdb folder, although this is not required. With the FrontPage 2000 server extensions installed on a server, FrontPage 2000 automatically marks this folder as not browsable, so that your database can be accessed only through Active Server Pages (ASP) created for that purpose.

Running the Database Results Wizard

Once you've created or selected the database file you're using and have made a database connection in FrontPage 2000, you're ready to run the Database Results Wizard to create a sample table of query results.

NOTE If you get an error that stops you from running the Database Results Wizard, it may be because a 32-bit ODBC driver has not been installed for your Microsoft Access database. You should download and install Microsoft Data Access Components (MDAC) 2.1 from

FIND IT ON ▶ Microsoft's site at **www.microsoft.com/data/odbc/**.
THE WEB

1. If a new blank page (new_page_1.htm) is not open in the right-pane, click the New Page icon on the toolbar.

2. Click File, Save As. In the File name box, type **mydata.asp**. Click Save.

3. Select Insert, Database, and Results (see Figure E.5).

4. Leave the second radio button (Use an existing database connection) selected. Database1 should already be selected. Click Next (see Figure E.6).

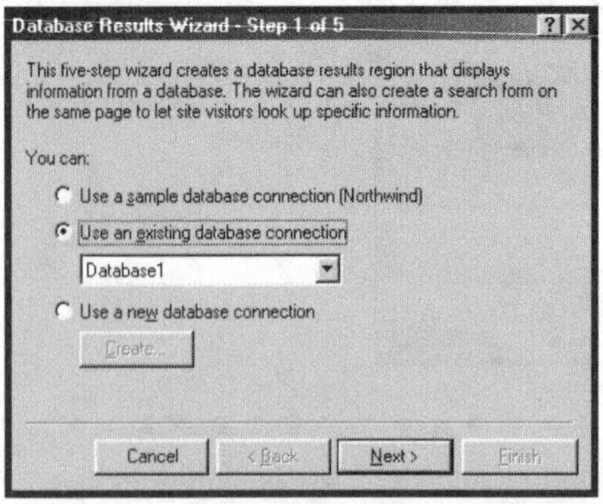

Figure E.5

In Step 1 of 5 of the Database Results Wizard, you can select to use a sample, existing, or new database connection.

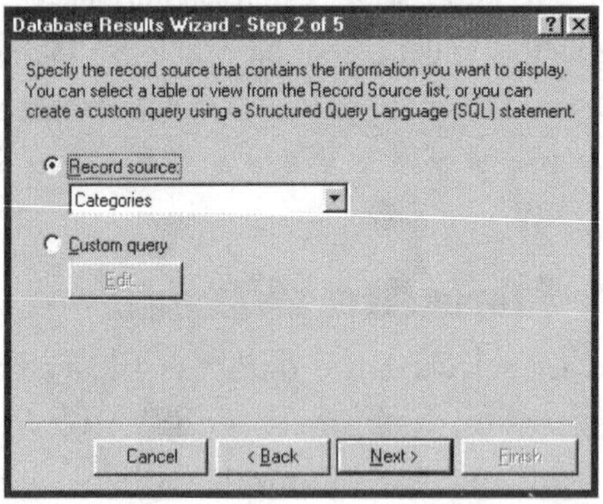

Figure E.6

In Step 2 of 5, you can select a record source from your database, or you can create a custom query.

5. Leave the first radio button (Record source) selected. Click the pull-down handle and select Products as the record source (see Figure E.7). Click Next (see Figure E.8).

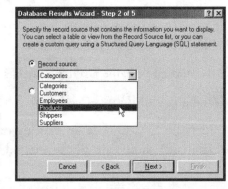

Figure E.7

The Products record source is being selected as the record source.

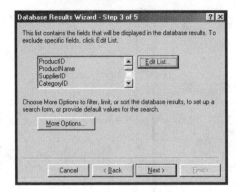

Figure E.8

You can edit the list of fields for your record source or set additional options.

NOTE Creating custom database queries is an advanced topic and should be attempted only by users who are experienced with working with online databases.

6. The Edit List button lets you remove, add, or reorder the data fields that will be displayed (see Figure E.9). You can set a number of additional options by clicking the More Options button (see Figure E.10). Feel free to play around with these two buttons later. For this example, just click the Next button (see Figure E.11).

7. Step 4 of 5 lets you specify the format of your query results. You can select to format your query results as a table or a list. For this example, leave all selections as they are. Click Next (see Figure E.12).

Figure E.9

You can remove, add, or reorder data fields that will be displayed.

Figure E.10

Clicking the More Options button lets you set filter criteria, specify the sort order for database result fields, limit the number of records returned, and specify a message for when no records are returned.

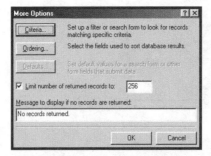

Figure E.11

You can specify how the results of your query will be formatted.

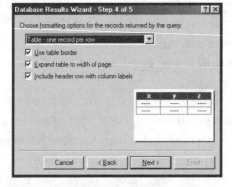

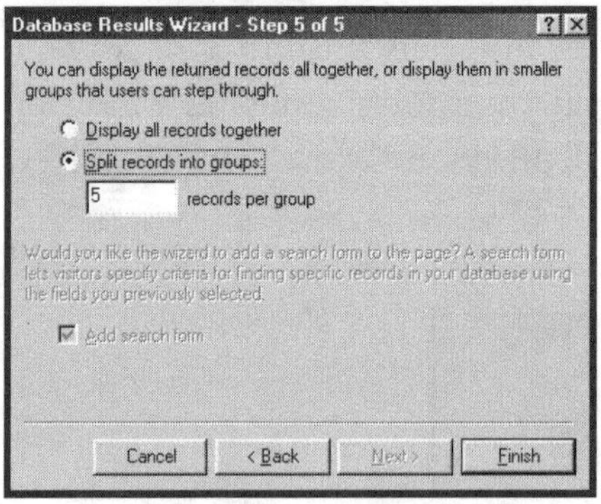

Figure E.12

You can display the records returned by your query as one long list or split up into groups.

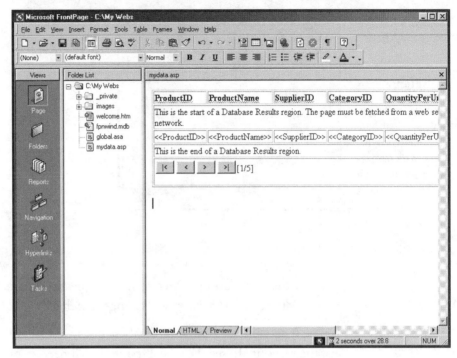

Figure E.13

A table in mydata.asp, shows how the database query results will be displayed.

8. The last dialog box lets you choose to display all of the records or to split the records into groups. For this example, just leave the second radio button (Split records into groups) selected. Leave the number of the records to be displayed in each group set at 5. Click Finish (see Figure E.13).

9. Click File, Save.

Verifying Your Database Connection

You can verify that your database connection has been made properly. Just do the following:

1. Select Tools, Web Settings. Click the Database tab.

2. Click the Database1 connection to select it and then click the Verify button.

Figure E.14

You can verify your database connection (the check mark replaces a question mark if the verification is successful).

3. If the verification is successful, the question mark to the left of the Database1 connection will change to a check mark (see Figure E.14).

You can't actually see how your database query results are going to look yet, just their layout. To see the actual results, you'll need to publish the database to your personal web server and then create a System DSN for your database.

Publishing Your Database

The next thing you need to do is publish your local web (c:\My Webs, for instance) to the personal web server that you installed on your local hard drive.

1. Select File, Publish Web.

2. Select the address for your personal web server. Leave the first radio button (Publish changed pages only) selected. Click Publish.

3. After you've successfully published your web, click the hyperlink ("Click here to view your published web site").

4. The default home page of your published web will be displayed in your browser. To preview your page with the database results, you'll need to add its path in the address box (http://*yourpws*/**mydata.asp**, for instance) and then press Enter (see Figure E.15).

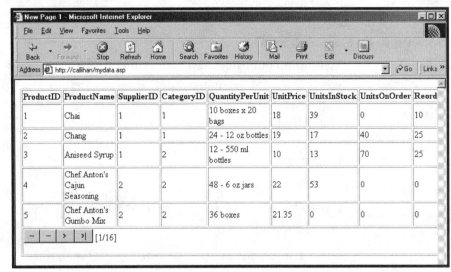

Figure E.15

Your database query results are displayed in your browser.

ProductID	ProductName	SupplierID	CategoryID	QuantityPerUnit	UnitPrice	UnitsInStock	UnitsOnOrder	Reord
1	Chai	1	1	10 boxes x 20 bags	18	39	0	10
2	Chang	1	1	24 - 12 oz bottles	19	17	40	25
3	Aniseed Syrup	1	2	12 - 550 ml bottles	10	13	70	25
4	Chef Anton's Cajun Seasoning	2	2	48 - 6 oz jars	22	53	0	0
5	Chef Anton's Gumbo Mix	2	2	36 boxes	21.35	0	0	0

| – | – | > | >| | [1/16] |

5. At the bottom of the table of results, click the > button to view the next group of records. The other buttons allow you to view the previous group of records (the < button), view the last group of records (the >| button), and view the first group of records again (the |< button).

NOTE

If you open your web on your personal web server (or your remote FrontPage 2000 Web server), you won't be able to see your database query results in the Preview view. Instead, open the page (mydata.asp, for instance) that has your database results, and then select File, Preview in Browser.

If this has all worked for you the first time through, feel free to get up from your computer, walk into another room, then jump up and down and scream a few times! If it hasn't worked for you, however, don't feel too bad. There are a lot of different pieces that need to fall into place. It took me several times through to figure out what the real deal is. Just go back over the steps detailed here and try to find out which step or steps didn't get done quite right.

Publishing Your Database to a FrontPage 2000 Server on the Web

You should publish your database only to a server with the FrontPage 2000 server extensions installed. Your server also has to support publishing ASP pages and have installed Microsoft Data Access Components (MDAC) 2.1, SP1. There is no need to have a System DSN assigned for your database connection, as long as your database does not reside outside of your FrontPage web.

If you are connecting to a database that is outside of your FrontPage web, you will need to have a System DSN assigned for your database connection. To specify the System DSN:

1. Publish your web to your server and then open your remote web in FrontPage 2000. Open the ASP page that contains your database results region. Right-click your database region and select Database Results Properties.

2. Select the third radio button (Use a new database connection), click the Create button, and then click the Add button.

3. Select the second radio button (System data source on web server). Type the name of the System DSN in the box to the left of the Browse button. (You can also click the Browse button to browse for a System DSN that lives on the server). Click OK.

4. Click Verify to verify the new connection. Click OK. Complete the following dialog boxes to finish editing the database results properties.

Finding Out More about Working with Online Databases and ASP Pages

In this section, you've barely touched the surface of working with online databases and ASP pages. Even using the Database Results Wizard, there's a good deal more that can be done than what's been covered here, such as publishing an Excel database or creating custom queries. Still, you will hopefully have learned enough in this section to begin using online databases and

ASP pages. To find more information and guidance for using these capabilities of FrontPage 2000, be sure to check out Microsoft's FrontPage Web site at **www.microsoft.com/frontpage/** for tips and tricks, FAQs, and white papers on online databases and ASP. For information on using ASP, check out these resources on the Web:

FIND IT ON ▶
THE WEB

FIND IT ON ▶
THE WEB

- ✿ activeserverpages.com at **www.activeserverpages.com**
- ✿ ASP Developers Network at **www.aspdeveloper.net**
- ✿ The ASP Developer's Site at **www.genusa.com/asp/**
- ✿ ASP-Help.com at **asp-help.com/**

NOTE   When checking out other sources on publishing online databases, you should realize that FrontPage 2000 uses a different method for making database connections than was used by FrontPage 98, so guides or tutorials on how to use FrontPage 98's Database Results Wizard may be misleading. Be sure that the information applies specifically to using FrontPage 2000.

Adding Java Applets and ActiveX Controls

A great way to add variety or interactivity to your FrontPage 2000 pages is to include Java applets or ActiveX controls. Java applets are created using the Java programming language, while ActiveX controls are created using Microsoft's ActiveX technology. You don't have to be a Java or ActiveX programmer, however, to includes these features in your FrontPage 2000 pages. There are many sources on the Web where you can find ready-made *Java applets* or *ActiveX controls* that you can easily include in your pages.

BUZZ WORD   A *Java applet* is a small program (thus the word "applet") created in the Java programming language that can be downloaded with a Web page and executed by any Java-enabled browser. All current Web browsers should support running Java applets.

▼▼▼▼▼▼▼▼▼▼▼▼▼▼▼▼▼▼▼▼▼▼▼▼▼▼▼▼▼▼

An **ActiveX control** is a component that can be added to a Web page to provide extended functionality in a Web page, such as animation sequences, transactions, calculations, and so on. ActiveX controls can be created using a variety programming languages. Currently, only Internet Explorer 4.0+, or browsers that use its engine (such as Neoplanet, for instance), support running ActiveX controls.

▲▲▲▲▲▲▲▲▲▲▲▲▲▲▲▲▲▲▲▲▲▲▲▲▲▲▲▲▲▲▲▲

Adding Java Applets

To add a Java applet to a FrontPage 2000 Web page, click Insert, Advanced, Java Applet (see Figure E.16). Here are some tips for adding a Java applet to your FrontPage Web page:

❖ In the Applet source box, type the name of your Java applet's *.class file. This is case-sensitive, so you should type the file name exactly as it appears: MyApplet.class, for example.

❖ As long as your applet files (*.class and *.jar) are in the same folder as the FrontPage Web page to which you are adding the applet, you should just leave the Applet base URL box blank.

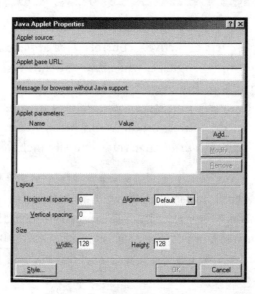

Figure E.16

You can fill out the Java Applet Properties dialog box to add a Java Applet to your FrontPage Web page.

Figure E.17

The AUTHOR parameter is defined, with a value of "Joe Java, http://www.joejava.com."

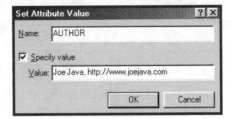

- The source for your Java applet should provide you with any parameters that need to be defined for the applet. To add a parameter, just click the Add button, and then type the parameter's name and value. (See Figure E.17 for an example.)

- Authors of Java applets will often require that you include COPYRIGHT and AUTHOR parameters that have to be typed exactly as specified. If not, the applet will not play.

- The source for your Java applet should also provide you with the width and height of the applet window. Type those values in the Width and Height boxes.

- The Layout options let you control how the applet window will be displayed on your page. The Horizontal spacing value lets you add space to the left and right of the applet window. The Vertical spacing value lets you add space above and below the applet window. The Alignment lets you specify a horizontal alignment (Left, Right, Center) or a vertical alignment (all of the remaining options).

- The Style button lets you format your Java applet using cascading style sheet properties.

- After you've added the Java applet, if you've entered everything correctly, you should be able to view the applet by clicking the Preview tab. (Figure E.18 shows an example Java applet playing in the Preview view.)

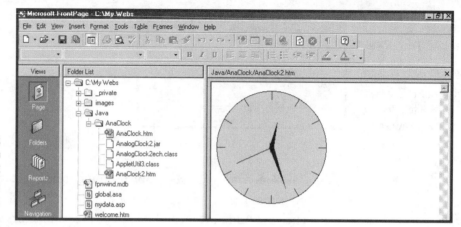

Figure E.18

A Java applet that displays an analog clock is playing in the Preview view.

Copying and Pasting Java Applet Codes

Filling out the Java Applet Properties window can take some time, especially if your Java applet has many parameters that need to be added. If the source for your Java applet has the applet displayed on their Web site, it may be a whole lot quicker to do the following instead:

1. View the applet's page source. In either Internet Explorer or Netscape Navigator, just right-click the applet's Web page, and then click View Source.

2. Click and drag the mouse to highlight the applet code, everything starting with <applet> and ending with </applet>. Then press Ctrl+C to copy the code.

3. Open the page in FrontPage to which you want to add the Java applet, click the HTML tab, position the cursor in the HTML where you want to place the applet. Then press Ctrl+V to paste in the code.

4. You may need to edit the code slightly. For instance, if you are placing all the Java applet files in the same folder as the applet's HTML file, then you should delete any "codebase" attribute value included in the "applet" tag.

5. To preview your Java applet, just click on the Preview tab.

Places Where You Can Get Java Applets

There are lots of places on the Web where you can find Java applets that you can download and use in your Web pages. Here are some places on the Web where you can find Java applets:

FIND IT ON ▶
THE WEB

- ✿ Applet Depot at **www.ericharshbarger.org/java/**

- ✿ Gamelan: The Official Directory for Java at **www.developer.com/ directories/pages/dir.java.html**

- ✿ The Java Boutique at **www.javaboutique.internet.com/**

Adding ActiveX Controls

Adding ActiveX controls is a good deal simpler than adding Java applets. The trade-off is that ActiveX controls will play only in Internet Explorer 4.0+, not in Netscape Navigator, while Java applets will play in both browsers. To add an ActiveX control to a FrontPage Web page, do the following:

1. Select Insert, Advanced, ActiveX Control (see Figure E.19).

2. Select one of the ActiveX controls from the list (try Calendar Control 9.0). Click OK.

3. Click the Preview tab to preview the control (see Figure E.20).

4. To edit its properties, in the Normal view, double-click on the ActiveX control (see Figure E.21).

Figure E.19

You can select from a list of all of the ActiveX controls installed on your computer.

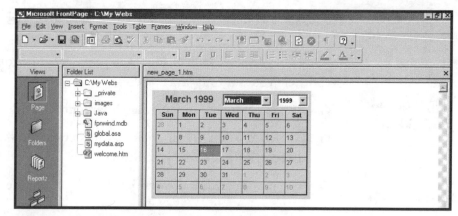

Figure E.20

The Calendar Control is displayed in the Preview window.

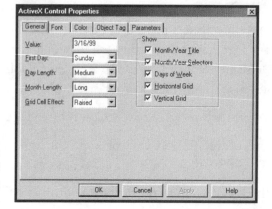

Figure E.21

You can edit the properties of the ActiveX Control.

Enabling or Disabling ActiveX Controls

ActiveX controls will only display in browsers that support ActiveX, which means right now in Internet Explorer 4.0+ only. You can enable or disable ActiveX controls for your web before publishing. You can also target your web to a specific browser or browsers, which will automatically enable or disable features (such as ActiveX controls) that will only work in one or some browsers. To do this:

1. Select Tools, Page Options, and then click the Compatibility tab (see Figure E.22).

2. To target your web to a specific browser or browsers, click the pull-down handle in the Browsers list (see Figure E.23).

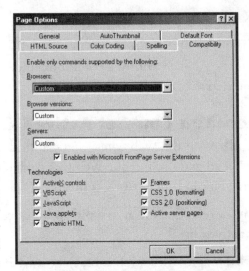

Figure E.22

You enable or disable ActiveX controls for your web by checking or clearing the ActiveX controls check box.

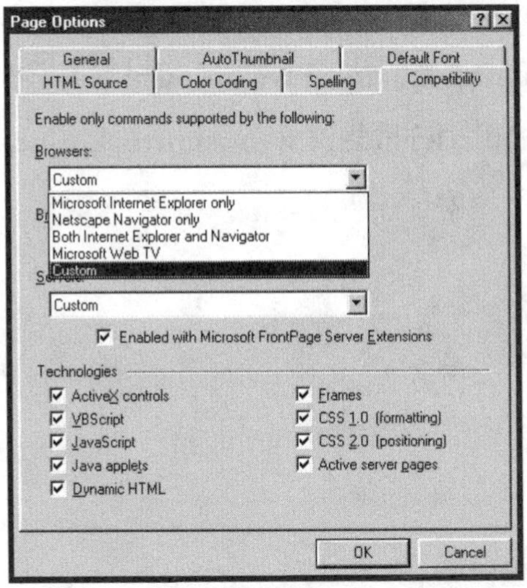

Figure E.23

You can target your web to a specific browser or browsers.

ActiveX controls will be disabled and not published to your web if you select any of these options from the Browsers list: Netscape Navigator only, Both Internet Explorer and Navigator, or Microsoft Web TV. To publish ActiveX controls to your web, select one of these two options: Internet Explorer only, or Custom.

ActiveX controls will also be disabled and not published to your web if you select this option from the Browser versions list: 3.0 browsers and later. To publish Active X controls to your web, select one of these options: 4.0 browsers and later, or Custom.

You can also clear the ActiveX controls check box under Technologies to disable publishing ActiveX controls to your web.

Places Where You Can Get ActiveX Controls

There are lots of places on the Web where you can find ActiveX controls that you can download and use in your Web pages. Here are some places on the Web where you can find ActiveX controls:

- ActiveX by developer.com at **www.developer.com/directories/ pages/dir.activex.html**

- Active Web Design—Resource Library at **awdsites.com/library/ index.htm**

- ActiveX Control Library at **www.download.com/PC/Activex/**

- ActiveX unofficial guide at **www.shorrock.u-net.com/index.html**

What's On
the CD-ROM?

The CD that accompanies this book contains shareware that will help you use the Internet more effectively.

Running the CD

To make the CD user-friendly and take up less of your disk space, no installation is required. This means that the only files transferred to your hard disk are the ones you choose to copy or install.

CAUTION This CD has been designed to run under Windows 95/98 and Windows NT 4. Neither the CD itself nor the programs on the CD will run under earlier versions of Windows.

Windows 95/98/NT4

Since there is no install routine, running the CD in Windows 95/98/NT4 is a breeze, especially if you have autorun enabled. Simply insert the CD in the CD-ROM Drive, close the tray, and wait for the CD to load.

If you have disabled autorun, place the CD in the CD-ROM drive and follow these steps:

1. From the Start menu, select Run.

2. Type **D:\CDInstaller.exe** (where D:\ is the CD-ROM drive).

3. Select OK.

The Prima License

The first window you will see is the Prima License Agreement. Take a moment to read the agreement, and click the "I Agree" button to accept the license and proceed to the user interface. If you do not agree with the license, click the "I Decline" button to close the user interface and end the session.

The Prima User Interface

Prima's user interface is designed to make viewing and using the CD contents quick and easy. The opening screen contains a two-panel window with three buttons across the bottom. The left panel contains the structure of the programs on the disc. The right panel displays a description page for the selected entry in the left panel. The three buttons across the bottom of the user interface make it possible to install programs, view the contents of the disc using Windows Explorer, and view the contents of a help file for the selected entry. If any of the buttons are "grayed out," it means that button is unavailable. For example, if the Help button is grayed out, it means that no Help file is available.

Resizing and Closing the User Interface

As with any window, you can resize the user interface. To do so, position the mouse over any edge or corner, hold down the left mouse button, and drag the edge or corner to a new position.

To close and exit the user interface, either double-click the small button in upper left corner of the window, or click the Close button (marked with a small "x") in the upper right corner of the window.

Using the Left Panel

The left panel of the Prima user interface works very much like Windows Explorer. To view the description of an entry in the left panel, simply click the entry.

Some items have subitems that are nested below them. Such parent items have a small plus (+) sign next to them. To view the nested subitems, simply click on the plus sign. When you do, the list expands and the subitems are listed below the parent item. In addition, the plus (+) sign becomes a minus (-) sign. To hide the subitems, click on the minus sign to collapse the listing.

● ●

NOTE You can control the positon of the line between the left and right panels. To change the position of the dividing line, move the mouse over the line, hold down the left mouse button (the mouse becomes a two-headed arrow) and drag the line to a new position.

● ●

Using the Right Panel

The right panel displays a page that describes the entry you chose in the left panel. Use the information provided to provide details about your selection—such as what functionality an installable program provides. In addition to a general description, the page may provide the following information:

○ **World Wide Web Site**. Many program providers have a Web site. If one is available, the description page provides the Web address. To navigate to the Web site using your browser, simply click on the Web address (you must be connected to the Internet). Alternatively, you can copy the Web address to the clipboard and paste it into the URL line at the top of your browser window.

○ **E-mail Address**. Many program providers are available via e-mail. If available, the description page provides the e-mail address. To use the e-mail address, click on it to open your e-mail program (to send e-mail, you must be connected to the Internet). Alternatively, copy the address to the clipboard and paste it into the address line of your e-mail program.

○ **Readme, License, and other text files.** Many programs have additional information available in files with such names as Readme, License, Order, etc. If such files exist, you can view the contents of the file in the right panel by clicking on the indicated hyperlink (such as the word "here" displayed in blue). When you are done viewing the text file, you can return to the description page by reclicking on the entry in the left panel.

Command Buttons

You'll find that the CD is easy to use. The following list provides a brief explanation of the buttons:

- **Install.** Use this button to install the program corresponding to your selection onto your hard drive.

- **Explore**. Use this button to view the contents of the CD using the Windows Explorer.

- **Help**. Click on this button to display the contents of the Help file provided with the program.

- **Read File**. The Install button turns into the Read File button when you make a selection that has an Adobe Acrobat file attached. Clicking on the Read File button launches Adobe Acrobat Reader and opens the selected file. You must have previously installed Adobe Acrobat Reader.

Pop-Up Menu Options

Use the pop-up menu options to do the following:

- **Install.** If the selected title contains an install routine, choosing this option begins the installation process.

- **Explore.** Selecting this option allows you to view the folder containing the program files using Windows Explorer.

- **View Help.** Use this menu item to display the contents of the Help file provided with the program.

The Software

This section gives you a brief description of the shareware and evaluation software you'll find on the CD.

NOTE The software included with this publication is provided for your evaluation. If you try this software and find it useful, you must register the software as discussed in its documentation. Prima Tech has not paid the registration fee for any shareware included on the disc.

⚙ **2002 Background Images & Sounds**. 2002 Background Images & Sounds (formerly 505 Backgrounds and then 1001 Backgrounds) is an ever-expanding gallery of backgrounds, watermarks, sounds, and now themes, which will add a professional finish to any Web site. It includes: 282 groups, 185 flags of the world, 185 background sounds, 45 themes with 28 images each, and 200 buttons.

⚙ **1st Theme Factory for FrontPage**. There are three different sets of themes for FrontPage: Series 1, Sports, and Entertainment. Each theme contains a ready-made package of background images, bullets, buttons, color schemes, images, and navigation bars. All themes are modeled for FrontPage, so they are easily swapped, added, or removed via the FrontPage command buttons. Series 1 includes 10 professionally designed themes in a variety of subjects. Sports includes ten sports-related themes, while the Entertainment theme set includes themes based on various entertainment genre, such as horror, comedy, and movies.

⚙ **Blounsker**. Running Blounkser from your Web server allows you to automatically change background or other GIF and JPEG image files on your site. You can predefine the sequence in which you wish them to rotate.

⚙ **Coast WebMaster**. Coast WebMaster is site analysis and management software intended for corporate administrators of large, dynamic Web sites. The purpose of the program is to simplify and automate daily site maintenance tasks. The program includes a smart HTML editor and requires no server-side extensions.

- **Cool Edit 96**. Cool Edit is a digital sound editor for Windows. Cool Edit enables you to create with sound: tones, pieces of songs and voices and miscellaneous noises, sine waves and sawtooth waves, noise, or silence. Cool Edit also gives you a wide variety of special effects to "touch up" your sounds: reverberation, noise reduction, echo and delay, flanging, filtering, and many others.

- **CuteFTP**. CuteFTP is a Windows-based File Transfer Protocol (FTP) client that allows users to utilize the capabilities of FTP without having to know all the details of the protocol itself. It includes URL parsing and clipboard monitoring, caching of entire directories on remote servers, queuing of transfers, resuming of uploading and downloading, directory comparison feature, macro record/playback scripting, and many more features.

- **Exploit Submission Wizard**. Submission Wizard offers Web users the ability to submit their sites automatically, and without hassle or complication, to the ever-increasing number of search engines on the Internet. Once the required data has been gathered, the program uses a standard Internet connection to submit a site to a host of major search engines and high-traffic sites, without requiring any further input.

- **FastStats**. FastStats's Log File Analysis gives you vital information about your Web site: how many hits per day you are getting, which search engines and keywords are used to access your Web site, what documents are missing (404 errors), and how well your Web server is performing (incomplete or "server busy" requests).

- **GifArt Clip Art Collection**. GifArt provides a wide range of clipart and other graphics. You can explore the site, viewing the graphics available there, as well as taking advantage of a multitude of links to other graphics Web sites. The latest collection of free graphics available at presstime is included on this disc. Simply use the Explore button to view the collection of graphics and either use them directly from the CD or copy them to your hard drive. The collection includes a wide range of bars, buttons, controls, backgrounds, icons, and animations.

- **MozillaTracker**. MozillaTracker is a small log analysis tool that tracks which browsers and operating systems Web page visitors have. You may save the gathered statistics as a report in text or HTML format, or print it directly.

- **My Creations Clip Art Collection**. My Creations provides a wide range of clip art graphics. You can explore the site, viewing a wide range of categories of clip art, much of it for free. The latest collection available at presstime is included on this disc. Simply use the Explore button to view the collection of graphics and either use them directly from the CD or copy them to your hard drive.

- **NetStudio**. NetStudio allows you to design graphics for your Web site without requiring you to draw the pictures by hand. The program offers one-click creation of text, buttons, navigation bars, banners, and other essential Web graphics components. You can also manipulate your image objects in a variety of ways. For example, you can adjust brightness and contrast, apply drop shadows, emboss items, incorporate washout and transparency effects, and so on. You can also insert more than one object onto a canvas to create a composite image and still retain the ability to edit each individual object.

- **Paint Shop Pro**. Paint Shop Pro is an image-editing tool that supports more than 30 image formats and a large palette of painting and drawing tools. The program is one of the easiest and most powerful you may ever use for image viewing, editing, and converting. Included are dockable toolbars, enhanced selection options, built-in special effects filters, RGB color separation, support for new image formats (Progressive JPEG, Mac PICT, and PNG with transparency), resampling, and masking options. Version 5.0 was a major update with new features such as multilevel undo functionality, complete layer support, "picture tube" brushes, CMYK separation, and pressure-sensitive tablet support. The program also included enhancements to Paint

Shop Pro's flexible painting and retouching brushes, adjustable cropping and selection tools, and images.

- **PickSee**. PickSee is a simple, pick-list format query tool for databases on the Web. It is designed to work with Access, Foxbase, xBase, Excel, Lotus, and other ODBC databases. Once you put PickSee on your Windows 95 or NT Web server, you can set up a new database table in just a few minutes. You use simple, fill-in-the-blank forms to select, sort, and output information to a browser, a download file, or as a static Web page. Put your database on the Web in five minutes without programming or scripting. Features enable you to password-protect, store, modify, and return query.

- **Signpost**. If you decide to move your Web site to a new server, you'll want to notify all those people who have bookmarked your old address. Signpost can change all your old Web pages into redirectors or pointers (signposts) to your new address.

- **Smart Site**. Smart Site allows a site administrator to find broken links, slow pages, spelling mistakes and HTML coding errors. In addition to these quality control features, Smart Site can also reveal what visitors to a Web site are looking at, when they are visiting, and what Web sites they are coming from. All of this information is available from one of several standard reports that Smart Site can generate, providing a complete solution for maintaining high quality, error-free Web sites.

- **TweakDUN**. TweakDUN is an easy-to-use utility that changes certain hidden default Registry settings in Windows 95 and NT 4.0. This process can reconfigure any software or hardware adapters, including Dial-Up Networking. It permits experimentation to find the optimal maximum transition unit and allows other important settings that will help to eliminate the fragmentation of data packets, one of the primary causes of slow data transfer rates on the Internet.

- **WebLog Manager Pro**. WebLog Manager Pro allows you to build a profile on search engine keywords, traffic, or Web hits; promote your site more effectively; understand whether a banner ad is working for you; and more. This Web site visitor tracking tool tells you where visitors come from, search engine keywords used to get to your site, browser type, visitor country, visitor ISP host, and how often a particular visitor visits your site.

- ✿ **WinZip**. The best way to handle compressed ("zipped") files, whether you get them from a friend or download them from the Internet. WinZip makes it painless to extract selected files or all the files from a zipped file, create your own compressed files (including self-extracting files that anyone can decompress—even if they don't own WinZip), and a wizard to walk you through the entire process.

- ✿ **WS_FTP Pro**. WS_FTP Pro is a Windows-based application for transferring files between your PC (the local system) and a remote system. Using WS_FTP Pro, you can connect to another system from your PC, browse directories and files on both systems, and transfer files between the systems. WS_FTP Pro comes with a number of preconfigured profiles for some of the popular FTP sites.

GLOSSARY

A

absolute URL. A complete path, or address, of a file on the Internet (such as *http://www.someserver.com/somedir/somepage.html*). Sometimes called a *complete URL*. See also *relative URL*.

Active Server Pages. See *ASP*.

ActiveX. Microsoft's set of programming technologies for creating interactive software components in a networked environment.

ActiveX controls. Software components incorporating ActiveX technology that can be used to add animation, pop-up menus, interactive forms, and other features to Web pages. ActiveX controls can be written in several languages, including C, C++, Visual Basic, and Java. They are currently only supported in Microsoft's Internet Explorer browser, Version 4.0 and greater.

address. The format style in FrontPage that is usually used for formatting signature blocks.

alias. An e-mail address that has no Inbox of its own, but instead works as a forwarding address.

anchor. See *bookmark*.

anti-aliasing. The blending of colors to smooth out the jagged stair-stepped edges ("jaggies") in fonts.

append. To add to the end of an existing file.

applet. A client-side program, such as a Java applet, that is downloaded from the Internet and executed in a Web browser. See also *Java*.

ASCII. The American Standard Code for Information Interchange, defining a standard minimum character set for computer text and data. ASCII files are sometimes called "DOS text" files, or "plain text" files.

ASP. Active Server Pages. A means for dynamically generating Web pages on a Web server running Microsoft Internet Information Server (ISS) version 3.0 or higher.

AU. A file format for audio files. Sound files used in FrontPage 2000's hover buttons must be 8-bit, mono, 8000Hz, mu-Law AU files.

AVI. Audio Video Interleaved, a multimedia format for sound and video that is common on the Windows platform.

B

background sound. A sound file that is played in the background when a Web page is displayed in a Web browser. Internet Explorer and Netscape Navigator use different methods for including background sounds in Web pages (see Appendix C, "Adding Multimedia").

bandwidth. The transmission capacity of a network, but also the amount of capacity consumed by a connection. A Web page containing many graphics will consume more bandwidth than one containing only text.

banner. Usually refers to an inline image displayed at the top of a Web page, often replacing the Heading 1 tag (H1).

Banner Ad Manager. A component in FrontPage that allows the timed display of sequential images, with transition effects definable between the image frames. Can be linked to a Web address or just used as a slide show.

bookmark. In FrontPage, a named location in a Web page that serves as the target of a hyperlink. In Netscape Navigator, a saved URL, performing the same function as what is called a *favorite* in Internet Explorer.

browser. See *Web browser*.

Bulleted List. The style used in FrontPage 2000 to create a bulleted list. See also *unordered list*.

C

cascading style sheets. Means for applying custom formatting characteristics to HTML elements in a Web page using the STYLE tag. A style sheet can either reside inside of the HTML file or in a separate file downloaded along with the HTML file. Current versions are Cascading Style Sheets, level 1 (CSS1), and Cascading Style Sheets, level 2 (CSS2). You can find out more about cascading style sheets at the World Wide Web Consortium's site at **www.w3.org/Style/.**

CGI. The Common Gateway Interface, an interface to a gateway through which a Web server can run programs and scripts in response to requests from a Web browser.

CGI script. A server-side script or program that is executed on a Web server in response to a request from a Web browser. A common use of CGI scripts is the processing of form responses. CGI scripts are often written in the Perl programming language.

client. A computer on a network that makes a request to a server.

client-side image map. An image map that utilizes the Web browser, rather than a server script, to execute hotspot hyperlinks. Not supported by some older browsers.

client-side program. A program that is downloaded and executed on a client computer, rather than from a server. Java applets and ActiveX controls are examples of client-side programs.

clip art. The term originates from printed sheets of commonly used images that were printed and then literally clipped out and pasted into ad, magazine, or newspaper layouts. In the broader sense, refers to any image that is inserted into a page design.

clipboard. An area in memory, on the Windows platform for instance, to which data can be copied or cut from one program or location and then pasted into another program or location.

component. A built-in object inserted by FrontPage into a Web page that can be evaluated and executed when a page is saved, published, or browsed. For more information on using components, see the Sunday Morning session, "Putting the Power of Components to Work." See also *WebBot*.

Confirmation Field. A component in FrontPage that can be used to insert the contents of a form field in a form confirmation page. It could be used to echo a viewer's name, e-mail address, and so on, from form fields that the viewer has filled out.

confirmation page. A page that confirms to a viewer that a form has been successfully submitted.

comment. A means of inserting text into the body of an HTML file that will not be displayed in a browser. See also *FrontPage comment*.

D

Database Results Wizard. A wizard in FrontPage for publishing an online database and database query results.

definition list. A list in HTML, often also called a *glossary*, created using the DL (Definition List), DT (Definition Term), and DD (Definition Description) tags. In FrontPage 2000, DT and DD tags are applied using the Defined Term and Definition styles, while the DL tags are automatically inserted for you.

DHTML. See *Dynamic HTML*.

discussion group. An interactive Web site that allows visitors to post discussion articles, reply to previous articles, search articles, or browse discussion threads from a table of contents. In FrontPage, discussion groups must be defined within their own web or subweb.

dithering. A method for smoothing out color and tonal transitions. Dithering helps to eliminate "color banding" that is often evident in lower-resolution images displaying fewer than 256 colors or shades of gray. See also *anti-aliasing*.

domain category. A major grouping of domain names (such as .com, .org, .net, .edu, .mil, and .gov), as well as many national domain categories (.us, .uk, .ca, and so on).

domain name. An alphanumeric alternative to an IP address, registered with the InterNIC (Internet Network Information Center).

download. To transfer files from a server to a client. See also *upload*.

DPI. Dots per inch, used in combination with the number of pixels in an image to determine the size of an image. For instance, an image scanned at 75 DPI will be smaller than the same image scanned at 150 DPI.

Dynamic HTML. Various means of providing dynamic Web content that respond interactively to user actions, such as producing on-the-fly Web pages, starting and stopping animations, and so on. (Microsoft refers to its rendition of this as "Dynamic HTML" (or DHTML), while Netscape refers to its rendition as "dynamic HTML.")

E

end tag. The end of a nonempty HTML element (...</P>, for example). See also *start tag*.

extension. An extension to standard HTML (as defined by the World Wide Web Consortium, or W3C) implemented by a particular browser (as in "Netscape extension" or "Microsoft extension") that may or may not be displayable in other browsers.

F

field validation. Default parameters or limits applied to a form field to help user efficiency and data accuracy.

float. The flow or wrap of text around an object on a Web page. You float an image to the left, for example, and text wraps around the right side of the image.

Folders view. Selected by clicking the Folders icon from the Views pane in FrontPage. Displays the folder structure and contents of the current web.

form. A grouping of data-entry fields, check boxes, radio buttons, and so on, that can be filled out by a visitor to a Web site. Forms created in FrontPage require that the site be published to a server that has the FrontPage server extensions installed.

form field. A data entry field on an HTML form.

frames. An extension to HTML pioneered by Netscape that has since been incorporated into HTML 4.0 that allows multiple HTML documents to be displayed at the same time in separate frame windows within a Web page.

frameset. A Web page that contains the HTML codes (defined within a FRAMESET tag) defining the layout for a framed Web site.

FrontPage comment. In FrontPage, a component that inserts a comment that'll be visible when the page is being edited in FrontPage, but will not be displayed when the page is previewed in a browser (or in FrontPage's Preview view). Regular HTML comments, which are inserted into a Web page using HTML comment tags, are only viewable as part of a page's HTML code.

FrontPage server. A Web server that has the FrontPage Server Extensions installed.

FrontPage Server Extensions. A set of programs and scripts installed on a Web server that provide extended server-side functionality for Web sites created with FrontPage.

FrontPage web. A collection of Web pages under the same root folder created in FrontPage. FrontPage webs can be either disk-based webs (C:\My Webs, for instance) or server-based webs (http://*yourweb/*, for instance). Server-based webs can be located on a Web server or on a personal web server (PWS) installed on a local hard drive.

FTP. File Transfer Protocol, the protocol used for downloading or uploading both ASCII and binary files on the Internet. FTP is the method FrontPage 2000 uses to transfer a FrontPage web to a server that doesn't have the FrontPage server extensions installed. FTP should never be used to transfer a FrontPage web to a FrontPage server. See also *FTP server*.

FTP server. A Web server that doesn't have the FrontPage server extensions installed.

G

GIF. Graphics Interchange Format, a popular Web graphics format developed by CompuServe. Each image can include up to 256 colors, transparency, interlacing, and multiple frames (GIF animation). See also *JPEG*.

GIF animation. A GIF-format image file containing multiple images that cumulatively create an animation. Such an animation is usually only viewable in a Web browser or a GIF animation editor.

global. Applicable to the entire Web site. A theme is applied globally, for example.

H

Heading *n*. A format style in FrontPage that specifies a paragraph as one of six heading levels—Heading 1, Heading 2, and so on. Corresponds to the HTML tags, H1, H2, and so on.

hit counter. As the name implies, a hit counter counts the number of "hits" to a Web page. Each visit to a Web page is a hit.

home page. Usually, a Web page that is automatically displayed when a Web site or Web folder in a Web site is accessed in a Web browser.

hot link. A hypertext link. See also *hyperlink*.

hot spot. An area within an image map that activates a hyperlink when clicked.

hover button. A FrontPage component that creates a button that can display visual effects and play sound effects when the mouse passes over the button. Clicking on the button can activate a hyperlink.

HTML. Hypertext Markup Language, a markup language for preparing documents for display on the World Wide Web. The current standard version of HTML is HTML 4.0 (previous versions were HTML 1.0, HTML 2.0, and HTML 3.2).

HTML attribute. A name-value pair in an HTML tag that defines additional display characteristics for an HTML element. For instance, in the HTML tag, <P align="center">, the HTML attribute *align="center"* specifies that the paragraph should be centered when displayed in a browser.

HTML editor. A software program that edits HTML files. HTML editors cover a wide spectrum, from fairly simple Notepad-like editors, in which HTML codes can either be typed or selected using toolbars, menus, or wizards, to fancy WYSIWYG editors that do most of the coding for you like FrontPage.

HTML element. Everything encompassed within a start and end tag in HTML. Stand-alone tags (such as the HR or IMG tag) are both tags and elements.

HTML tag. A markup code in HTML. There are two types of tags in HTML: container tags and empty tags (or stand-alone tags). Container tags start with a start tag (<H1>, for instance) and end with an end tag (</H1>, for instance). End tags always begin with a "/" (</P>, </B>, and so on). Empty tags are single "stand-alone" tags that don't have end tags (<HR>, for instance).

HTML view. Clicking on the HTML tab in FrontPage switches to HTML view. In HTML view, you can directly view and edit a page's HTML codes.

HTTP. Hypertext Transfer Protocol, the protocol used to exchange Web pages and other documents across the Internet. FrontPage 2000 uses the HTTP protocol (http://) to transfer FrontPage webs to a FrontPage server (a server with the FrontPage server extensions).

hyperlink. FrontPage's term for a hypertext link. Hyperlinks can jump to any other object on the Web (a Web page, a graphic image, a text file, a CGI script, and so on) and also to a location (or *bookmark*) within either the same or another Web page. Also sometimes called a *hot link*.

Hyperlinks view. The Hyperlinks icon in the Views pane is used to turn on the Hyperlinks view. The Hyperlinks view displays a diagram of all pages that are linked to the default home page for a FrontPage web.

hypermedia. A term coined by Ted Nelson, the inventor of hypertext. It generally refers to the interlinking of multiple media (text, images, sound, animation, video).

hypertext. Electronic documents that contain links to other documents, allowing non-sequential viewing of large amounts of information. Users can choose their own path through the material by clicking the link to the topic that interests them. A Web site is a collection of hypertext documents.

I

image hyperlink. Also sometimes just called an *image link*. An inline image inserted inside a hypertext link, usually displayed with a blue border to show that it is an active link. However, if you select an image in FrontPage 2000 and then define a hyperlink for it, FrontPage 2000 automatically turns off the border. To make the border visible, in HTML view, just delete the *border="0"* attribute from the IMG tag, or edit the image properties to do the same thing.

image map. An image displayed in a Web browser with hidden "hot spots" that can be clicked on to link to their designated URLs. Older browsers only supported server-side image maps (image maps executed from a server), whereas newer browsers also support client-side image maps (image maps executed from the desktop, or client).

Include Page. A component in FrontPage that automatically includes one Web page within another Web page. Handy, for instance, for including a signature block page at the bottom of other pages.

inline image. An image (GIF, JPEG, or PNG) that is displayed on a Web page.

interlaced GIF. A GIF-format graphics file that can be gradually displayed in a browser while still being downloaded. On each pass, only some of the lines of the image are displayed, allowing a viewer to see what the image is going to be long before it has been downloaded completely.

Internet. A set of protocols for transmitting and exchanging data among networks.

IP address. An Internet Protocol address. A unique number, such as 185.35.117.0, that is assigned to a server on the Internet.

ISP. An Internet service provider, also often called an *access provider*. A company that provides dial-up access to the Internet.

J

Java. Sun Microsystem's object-oriented programming language, designed to create programs that can be run securely on any platform, making it the ideal programming language for the World Wide Web. Because programs distributed across the Web need to be small (because of bandwidth constraints), Java programs, as well as ActiveX controls, are often called "applets."

JavaScript. A scripting language developed by Netscape and Sun that is loosely based on Java. Useful for adding behaviors to a Web page, such as mouse-over effects, for instance. See also *Jscript* and *VBScript*.

JPEG. Joint Photographic Experts Group. Besides GIF, the most common graphics format for the display of images on the Web. Images can use a palette of up to 16.7 million colors. Unlike GIF images, however, JPEG images cannot be transparent, interlaced, or animated. Often referred to as JPG format images, because the file extension for JPEG images under DOS/ Windows is ".jpg." JPEG images are generally best for images that require more than 256 colors, such as continuous tone photographs or images that make use of gradient fills. GIF images are best for images that have fewer than 256 colors. See also *GIF*.

JScript. A version of JavaScript developed by Microsoft for its Internet Explorer browser. It works with ActiveX controls, unlike JavaScript.

K

keyword. A word used in a search form, such as at AltaVista or Infoseek Guide, for instance, to search for matching Web pages (pages that include the keyword).

L

line break. Forces a new line within an HTML element, without starting a new block element. Inserting line breaks is a common way of creating single-spaced lines in HTML.

link list. A list of hyperlinks, sometimes also called a *hotlist*.

link text. The text displayed in a hyperlink, usually in blue and underlined.

M

mailto link. A hyperlink that opens up a window where an e-mail message can be composed and sent to a specified e-mail address. Introduced originally by Netscape, versions of Internet Explorer earlier than 4.0 do not support mailto links.

marquee. An HTML element supported only by Microsoft Internet Explorer that displays scrolling text in a Web page. It is not included in standard HTML. In FrontPage, marquees can be created using the Marquee component.

META tag. A tag in HTML that is used to include meta-information in the header section of an HTML file. A common usage is to include descriptions and keyword lists that can be used by search indexes to index a Web page.

N

navigation bar. A set of text or button hyperlinks, which link to other pages in a Web site.

Navigation view. Opened by clicking the Navigation icon in the Views pane. Displays the navigational structure of a FrontPage web.

nested list. A list that is indented inside of another list. In nested bulleted lists (unordered lists), the bullet character is automatically changed for the different nested list levels. Different types of lists can be nested inside each other—for instance, you can nest a bulleted list inside of a numbered list, or vice versa.

Numbered List. The style in FrontPage that is used to create a numbered list. See also *ordered list*.

O

object. In Microsoft PhotoDraw, any selectable item inserted in the picture or scratch areas, including text, bitmap or vector graphics, shapes or lines, and so on. A picture can be composed of a single or multiple objects. See also *sprite*.

ordered list. A numbered list created in HTML using the OL (Ordered List) tag. Applied in FrontPage by using the Numbered List style.

P

padding. In a Web page table, the amount of space between the inside border of a cell and the outer edge of the text.

personal web server. A web server you can install on your local computer, allowing you to publish and test out your pages locally first, before publishing them to your remote server. Also called a PWS.

pixel. Short for picture element. Identifies a "point" in a graphic image but also includes bytes that represent its color depth. The number of pixels does not determine the size of an image, but only the resolution of the image. The size of the image (whether printed or displayed) is determined by the *DPI* (dots per inch) combined with its pixel dimensions.

plug-in. A software component that can be installed in a Web browser to enable the display or playing of document and media formats not otherwise supported.

PNG. Portable Network Graphics, the newest standard graphics format for the display of images on the Web. It supports up to 48-bit true color (JPEG supports up to 24-bit true color), as well as transparency and interlacing. Not supported on older browsers.

publish. To transfer a FrontPage web to a server. A FrontPage web can be published to either a *FrontPage server* (with the FrontPage server extensions installed) or an *FTP server* (without the FrontPage server extensions installed).

R

radio button. A form field that allows a visitor to select an option by clicking on the button. The button is filled when selected, but empty when not.

relative URL. Also called a *partial URL*. A relative URL is used to link to an object that resides within the same Web site (or FrontPage web) as the linking page. An example of a relative URL, for instance, would be *<IMG SRC="images/myimage.jpg">*, which would display an inline image that is located in a subfolder, *images*, of the current folder (the folder where the linking page is saved). Other examples of relative URLs would be *<A HREF="../project1/welcome.htm">* (linking to a subfolder within the parent folder of the current folder). See also *absolute URL*.

root web. The root folder of a FrontPage web. See also *subweb*.

S

sans serif. A font style that has flat, plain edges. Arial is an example of a sans serif font.

Scheduled Image. A FrontPage component that allows the display of an image only during a specified time period.

Scheduled Include Page. A FrontPage component that allows the display of an include page only during a specified time period.

Search Form. A FrontPage component that allows a visitor to a Web page to do a full-text search of a Web site.

server. A computer on a network that responds to requests from clients. See also *client*.

shared borders. Regions in a Web page that are shared between pages. A common use for shared borders is to include common navigation bars for pages within a FrontPage web. See also *navigation bar*.

smoothing. See *anti-aliasing*.

sprite. In Image Composer 1.5, an image object with shape and transparency.

start tag. The start of a non-empty HTML element (<P>... for instance). See also *end tag*.

style. Can refer either to a format style applied from the Formatting toolbar (Heading 1 or Numbered List, for instance) or to a format defined as part of a style sheet. See also *cascading style sheet*.

subweb. A FrontPage web that is included within another FrontPage web. FrontPage 2000 allows subwebs within other subwebs. See also *root web*.

T

tab order. The order in which form fields are selected as the user presses the Tab key to move through the form.

table. A means in HTML of displaying data in a tabular format using the TABLE tag. Table rows are defined by the TR (Table Row) tag, whereas table cells are defined by the TD (Table Data) tag.

Table of Contents. A FrontPage component that generates an outline of a FrontPage web, with hypertext links to all pages included in the web.

tag. A code in SGML, HTML, and XML used to define a document element. Tags can either be the start and end tags of a "container" element (such as a paragraph or a heading) or stand-alone tags that define an "empty" element (such as an inline image or a horizontal rule).

target anchor. Called a *bookmark* in FrontPage, a target anchor defines the "landing spot" for a hyperlink. See also *bookmark*.

target frame. The name of a frame in which a linked page will be displayed.

Tasks view. In FrontPage, clicking the Tasks icon in the Views pane displays the task list that has been defined for the current web.

TCP/IP. The Transmission Control Protocol/Internet Protocol, the standard protocol set for transmissions across the Internet.

template. A pre-designed page that can contain page settings, formatting, and page elements. You can create your own page templates so that you can create pages for your web quickly and consistently. In FrontPage, pages saved as templates have a *.tem file extension and will be available under the General tab in the New dialog window.

theme. A unified set of design elements and color schemes that can be applied to multiple Web pages to give them a common look and feel. FrontPage users can apply any of the many themes provided with FrontPage, or they can create their own.

thumbnail. A miniature version of a graphic file. Typically, you click on a thumbnail to see a full-size view of a graphic. Thumbnails save your visitors time because they load into the browser more quickly.

throughput. See *bandwidth*.

Timestamp. A FrontPage component that when included in a page will automatically display the date and time when the page was last edited or updated.

toolbar. A collection of onscreen buttons or icons in a graphical user interface (GUI) that usually provides shortcuts to menu and other program functions.

transition. A special effect, such as Dissolve, Fade to Black, or Vertical Blinds, that can be assigned to take effect when a visitor enters or leaves a page. Transitions are Dynamic HTML (DHTML) effects and will only play in Internet Explorer 4.0+.

U

Unix. A multi-user, multitasking operating system originally developed by AT&T Bell Laboratories. Versions include Linux, Xenix, AIX, and A/UX. The majority of servers on the World Wide Web run Unix, although Windows NT servers are also numerous.

unordered list. A bulleted list created in HTML using the UL (Unordered List) tag. See also *Bulleted List*.

upload. To transfer files from a client to a server. See also *client* or *server*.

URL. Uniform Resource Locator. For instance, *http://www.microsoft.com/ frontpage/* is the URL for Microsoft's FrontPage support pages. See also *Web address*.

V

VBScript. Visual Basic Scripting Edition, Microsoft's scripting language for use on the World Wide Web. It is similar to JavaScript but only runs on Internet Explorer or on browsers that use the Internet Explorer engine (such as Neoplanet, for instance).

Visual J++. Microsoft's implementation of the Java programming language.

W

watermark. A non-scrolling background image, only displayable in Internet Explorer.

WAV. An audio file format common to Windows.

WebBot. Short for *WebBot component*. See also *component*.

Web address. A location on the Web. See also *URL*.

Web browser. A software program that browses (or "surfs") HTML and other files on the Internet. See also *client*.

workpane. In Microsoft PhotoDraw, an expandable vertical pane from which you select the tools, effects, textures, colors, and styles you want to use in creating an image.

WSP. Web Service Provider, also called WPP (Web Presence Provider) or hosting service. The company that you hire to store your Web site so that other users can access it on the Internet.

WYSIWYG. What You See Is What You Get. WYSIWYG HTML editors, such as FrontPage, allow you to edit a page in a display that shows how it will be shown in a Web browser.

X

XML. eXtensible Markup Language. Slated by the w3C (World Wide Web Consortium) as the next-generation markup language for display of documents and data not only on the Web, but in all manner of media. Using XML, a single document can be marked up to be displayed on the Web, read in a Braille reader, printed in a book, or spoken by a speech application. The 5.0 versions of both Internet Explorer and Netscape Navigator should be able to display both HTML and XML documents. In many ways, XML is intended as the strict subset of SGML that HTML was supposed to have become. You can find out more about XML at the World Wide Web Consortium's site at **www.w3.org/XML/**.

INDEX

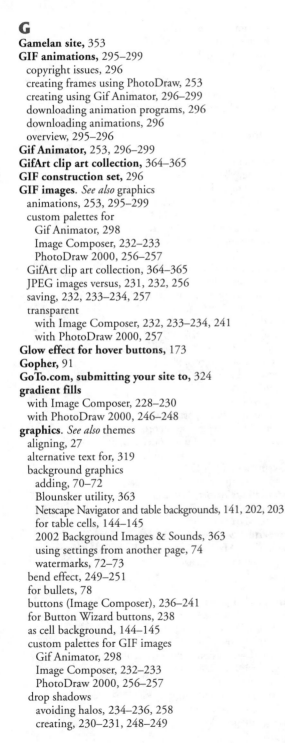

License Agreement/Notice of Limited Warranty

By opening the sealed disk container in this book, you agree to the following terms and conditions. If, upon reading the following license agreement and notice of limited warranty, you cannot agree to the terms and conditions set forth, return the unused book with unopened disk to the place where you purchased it for a refund.

License:

The enclosed software is copyrighted by the copyright holder(s) indicated on the software disk. You are licensed to copy the software onto a single computer for use by a single concurrent user and to a backup disk. You may not reproduce, make copies, or distribute copies or rent or lease the software in whole or in part, except with written permission of the copyright holder(s). You may transfer the enclosed disk only together with this license, and only if you destroy all other copies of the software and the transferee agrees to the terms of the license. You may not decompile, reverse assemble, or reverse engineer the software.

Notice of Limited Warranty:

The enclosed disk is warranted by Prima Publishing to be free of physical defects in materials and workmanship for a period of sixty (60) days from end user's purchase of the book/disk combination. During the sixty-day term of the limited warranty, Prima will provide a replacement disk upon the return of a defective disk.

Limited Liability:

The sole remedy for breach of this limited warranty shall consist entirely of replacement of the defective disk. IN NO EVENT SHALL PRIMA OR THE AUTHORS BE LIABLE FOR ANY other damages, including loss or corruption of data, changes in the functional characteristics of the hardware or operating system, deleterious interaction with other software, or any other special, incidental, or consequential DAMAGES that may arise, even if Prima and/or the author have previously been notified that the possibility of such damages exists.

Disclaimer of Warranties:

Prima and the authors specifically disclaim any and all other warranties, either express or implied, including warranties of merchantability, suitability to a particular task or purpose, or freedom from errors. Some states do not allow for EXCLUSION of implied warranties or limitation of incidental or consequential damages, so these limitations may not apply to you.

Other:

This Agreement is governed by the laws of the State of California without regard to choice of law principles. The United Convention of Contracts for the International Sale of Goods is specifically disclaimed. This Agreement constitutes the entire agreement between you and Prima Publishing regarding use of the software.